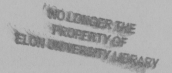

D1349235

~Family~
Installments

Family Installments

Memories of Growing Up Hispanic

EDWARD RIVERA

WILLIAM MORROW AND COMPANY, INC.

New York   1982

Chapters of this book appeared in earlier forms in the following publications:

"Antecedentes" in *New American Review 13,* Simon & Schuster, 1971.

"Caesar and the Bruteses: A Tradegy," in *The Bilingual Review/La Revista Bilingue,* Volume 1, Number 1, January–April 1974.

"Discipline" in *Hispanics in the United States* published by Bilingual Review/Press, Ypsilanti, Michigan, 1980.

"In Black Turf" in *Black Hands on a White Face,* Dodd, Mead, 1971.

"Maromas" under the title "La Situación" in *New York* Magazine, August 7, 1972.

Library of Congress Cataloging in Publication Data

Rivera, Edward.
  Family installments.

  I. Title.
PS3568.I829F3   813'.54   82–2236
ISBN 0–688–01231–0   AACR2

Printed in the United States of America

First Edition

1 2 3 4 5 6 7 8 9 10

BOOK DESIGN BY BERNARD SCHLEIFER

For my mother, my late father, the rest of my family,
  and my friends;
for my former teacher at City College, Irwin Stark;
for Leonard Kriegel of the City College English Department;
for Pauline Woods;
and for T.S.

I wish to thank the Yaddo Corporation, at whose retreat the first section of this book was written in the summer of 1970, and the National Endowment for the Arts for a grant that helped me complete it.

Contents

1: *Antecedentes*

My PATERNAL GRANDFATHER, Xavier F. Alegría, itinerant school-teacher, part-time painter, poetaster, guitar-picker, and Mariolater, jammed a small gun in his mouth and opened fire on his upper jaw. He died slowly, a lousy shot, or the hapless owner of a rusty, second-rate *pistola.* The hole in his palate was pretty big; the bullet lodged somewhere in his brain. He should have died right away, but the All Powerful refused to take him then and there. Instead, He let Abuelo Xavier hold on for weeks, putting him in a coma before finally cutting him loose.

Xavier F. Alegría starved himself dead when my father, Gerán, his third child and second son, was barely five. That was Papi's version, and my mother's. Papi said it had been a common occurrence all over Puerto Rico—all over the world, as a matter of fact. Mami, who claimed she knew little about the world, said sardonically that there had been nothing unusual in Abuelo Xavier's crash-diet death. She said that 1919, the year it happened, had been a good year for meeting the All Merciful, but not an exceptional one. "I could tell you stories, Santos," she told me, "that would make the little hairs on your *fundillo* stand straight out."

In 1919 she had been a little over three years old. Poverty, she said, *la pobreza,* had done a lot of good people in, and some bad ones, too; and she would rattle off the names of people she'd known in Bautabarro, our home village, people whose names and lives, like the names and lives of their parents and grandparents, would disappear when Mami's generation died off. The hilly village of Bautabarro had no chroniclers; illiteracy was high in those days, headstones a luxury. Besides, who would have had time to record all the comings and goings, the births and deaths? Who would have bothered? The people of Bautabarro were peasants, not history-minded, culture-conscious scribes. You died, and a few years later people forgot where you'd been buried. Only the town church recorded the day God had cut you loose, but our town church burned down several times and its records were pretty meager.

Bautabarro was deep in the mountain range called Cordillera Central (the Rockies of Puerto Rico), an area of lush green landscape, a tangle of tropical weeds, smooth and hilly, precipitous and sloped, the monotony of greens relieved only by bald patches of soft red clay called *barro,* which is also the name for mud. The Bauta River, a squiggle on the map, trickles down from somewhere in the Cordillera past Bautabarro and, after coupling with the Toro Negro, flows into the Mar Caribe.

They got Xavier to a hospital somewhere, or to a village clinic, where some local G.P. probably stuffed his mouth with cotton or gauze sopping with anesthesia until a big-town surgeon arrived, took a look at his mouth, probably whispered a few prayers over him, and pronounced him technically dead. God had played a dirty joke on him; dead and alive, a breathing mummy. My grandmother's family took him home. He himself had no relatives in town; the nearest kin lived twenty-five miles away in Ponce, but they had lost track of his existence, and he of theirs. He'd been a loner, something of a snob because his parents, it was said, had been Spaniards, and because he'd received a university education. Besides, he had been too busy teaching and painting and caring for his wife and children to make close friends. They locked him up in a bedroom, though this was unnecessary, since almost no villagers came to see him. A small group of Xavier's pupils came by one day, bringing flowers and poems they had written and illustrated themselves, but his in-laws kept them out of the room. Xavier, they explained, was *"muy grave,"* too ill to receive visitors, and the children left their gifts behind and never saw him alive again.

His in-laws waited on him day and night, kept the flies off his face, lit candles, recited rosaries and other rituals, moaned and belted their breasts, and watched him die. And God for his part let him suffer on and on with that hole in his palate. How long? Not even my aunt Celita, the family gossip, could remember for sure. "A very long time," she would say. "An eternity."

He received spiritual first aid in large doses. Padre Soliván, an Irish missionary from Nueva Jersey, was there every day, bringing prayers, blessed candles, and holy water. Xavier was his Michelangelo, after all, and an educated man. A good father, too, and a missionary when you came down to it. For what else was a traveling schoolteacher in those days of unpaved roads, firetrap schoolhouses, and beggar's wages? Toward the end he got Extreme Unction, that last-ditch sacrament. If you believed in that stuff, and who in those days didn't (Xavier perhaps?), then Xavier was on his way to paradise.

As a schoolteacher Xavier couldn't have earned much, a couple of *dolares* a day, five at most. But that was a good deal more than his neighbors, subsistence farmers, or their peons, made. Besides, he was also a painter—of canvases, not houses. But who needed art in those hills? Who could afford it? He painted portraits, tropical landscapes, birds, still lifes, anything, everything, even church altars. The portraits and landscapes he sold to bourgeois types from Mayagüez or Ponce for next to nothing. He was prolific, the village Velázquez, but very formal. And self-taught. What he didn't or couldn't sell, he gave away to his pupils, neighbors, and admiring strangers. His neat wooden house was full of those portraits and landscapes. As for the religious art, Abuelo had not only designed the altar of the church he, his wife, three sons, and daughter worshiped and confessed their sins in, but decorated it as well: a large mural depicting angels in multicolored flowing gowns, puffed cheeks blowing celestial notes from golden horns and trumpets, pliant fingers plucking harps, and bow-lipped mouths choiring hallelujahs; a score of well-known saints from the comely Virgen María to Santa Bárbara Bendita, patron saint of lightning; and the apostles, all twelve of them; Nuestro Señor Jesucristo, a portrait of Xavier himself, with beard and long black hair thrown in for authenticity, a handsome man; and a touch of evil, too—smirking Judas, that *maricón* traitor, son of the world's great whore, scowling off by himself, clutching soiled silver coins in one hand, the other propping up his pointed chin, two long-nailed, crooked fingers pointing straight down—a symbol of something or other.

The altar and the mural had been commissioned by Padre Soliván. Abuelo had been paid something—not much, but something. He wasn't starving. His children were fed, were possibly plump. They wore starched clothes; the boys got haircuts once a month in the town barbershop, next to the Sundial store, the Thom McAn of Bautabarro, where they replaced their worn-out shoes with the latest styles: patent leather, usually, with brass buckles.

Only a few months before Xavier's death, a "rare disease" (my mother's mysterious phrase) had knocked off his wife, Sara. According to Papi's cloudy recollections, she had been a perfect wife and mother, the kind Puerto Ricans, men and women, like to call "saint," meaning a docile daughter, a submissive wife, and a totally devoted mother. And a saint she died, though a little young to be leaving her husband and four children for a better life. At her funeral Soliván probably pointed out her youth. "She was only thirty-five, my children. *Una muchachita.* We must be ready for God's call from the day we're born. . . ." It's nine to one that he compared her to the Virgin Mary, after whose perfect life she had modeled her own.

After Xavier's death, Sara's parents adopted my father and his two brothers. Papá Santos Malánguez was a poor hillbilly, a *jíbaro desgraciado,* and, said my father, who was his favorite, the kindest man he ever knew. Papá Santos was so good that whenever there wasn't enough food for everyone—and that was often—he used to steal chickens and vegetables from his neighbors. He always paid them back by doing favors, without letting them know the reason. This chicken-thief Robin Hood of Bautabarro was likely to deny himself a pair of badly needed pants or a straw hat (he worked all day in the sun) so that his three grandsons wouldn't have to walk around those hills looking like orphans. Which they did just the same; but the point was that Papá Santos would do anything for those three orphans. He'd been, in short, a saint.

His wife, Josefa, added much misery to Papá Santos's hard-luck life. She was a *loca,* and he had to look after her all the time. One time she tried to burn the house down. Another time she tried to kill Santos with his own machete. She put shit in the food, and sometimes, on a crazy whim, she would shit on the floor instead of using the chamber pot or making a trip to the outhouse. Nightmares haunted her. Seven times a week she woke up the house with her screams; she said her enemies—Papá Santos was one of them—were trying to kill her. Sometimes they tied her to a tree and tried to decapitate her with a machete, but just before the blade cut into her neck, she screamed and woke herself up. Some nights they tried to choke her by shoving human shit down her throat. To calm her down, Papá Santos would give her a concoction of boiled milk with ginger and some wild herb called "good grass," and soothe her with words while she drank it.

The worst thing about her, as far as the boys were concerned, was her violent nature. She might sneak up on one of them and clobber him on the head with the broom or the chamber pot, or empty the chamber pot on their heads. My father blamed his poor eyesight on those regular beatings she gave him. She singled him out for extra torture because he couldn't help talking back to her. One day—he was ten—when he saw a pile of her shit in a corner of the kitchen, he threw up his food and called her a disgusting old *loca*. She came at him with a kitchen knife. He put the table between them. When she started to climb it, determined to get him, holding the knife up for a quick stab, he upended the table and knocked her over. She cut herself with the knife, in the groin, and began screaming: "*Asesino!* He's killing me!" Papi was sure she'd bleed to death. He panicked, ran away, and hid in the hilly woods, living on wild fruit and coffee berries. On the second day, an attack of diarrhea almost killed him.

A posse of village men headed by Papá Santos found him at sunset of the third day. He was on his haunches, trying to move his empty bowels, when they caught up with him. He thought the men had come to hang him, but he was too proud to beg for his life. Instead, he confessed to having murdered Josefa. Accident or no accident, he had killed her, and for that he deserved to be killed in turn. At this point Papá Santos, already weeping, knelt and pulled up Papi's pants. But what difference did it make whether his pants were up or down? They were going to hang him that very day before the sun set. But the posse, all eight of them, were laughing at him.

He broke down, sat on the ground, and wept. Papá Santos took him in his arms and they wept together. The posse of peons stopped laughing. Papá Santos explained to him that Josefa was still very much alive. The wound had been only a scratch. Papá Santos had somehow calmed her down, and had even gotten her to forgive Papi.

Back home they had a big reunion scene. Everybody wept, especially Papi, when Josefa picked up her skirt and displayed her bandaged groin. Her hysteria when she saw her blood flowing— her nightmares come true—had worn off. She had calmed down while sipping a cupful of Papá Santos's "good grass" potion, and even recovered some semblance of sanity. The shock of seeing her blood may have done it. And for almost a week after the incident she behaved like the old Josefa, the sane and sound Josefa whom Papá Santos had eagerly married. God works in strange ways, he and his three adopted sons concluded. Instead of murdering her, as she had insisted, Papi had cured her with a knife wound. A novena was in order. They recited two of them on two successive nights; and for an entire week afterward they recited rosaries and lit votive candles in honor of Josefa's miraculous cure.

But her cure was much too good to last. Her wound had just begun to scab when she relapsed. She got worse, in fact: screamed louder and longer at night, wet the bed and Papá Santos as well, and moved her bowels so often on the floor planks that the three brothers had to take turns cleaning it up; and once she cooked their *sancocho,* a vegetable and meat stew, in the chamber pot. For water she used her own piss. And as for violence, she began attacking the boys with a new passion, Papi especially, because he had tried to assassinate her. Friends of Papá Santos suggested that he have her put away; they were afraid she might attack their own children, or set fire to their firetrap *bohíos.* But he refused to part with her. He was too stuck on nostalgia and pity to abandon her just like that, as if she were some kind of rabid dog. He could still remember the sweet, hefty girl who'd been as good a wife and mother as any in Bautabarro. Also, crazy or not, she was his beloved wife; she was over sixty years old; they'd been married more than forty years. The mother of his poor dead *niños.* True, she'd become mysteriously barren after the birth of her second child, a boy who had died of some *enfermedad* (smallpox probably) at the age of five, but that cut no ice; she was his wife, a part of him, of his life. No, Papá Santos decided, if she goes, I go, and I'm not going anywhere yet. So she stayed, for some four years, crazy and violent to the last. And when she died, suddenly, of a heart failure, he went into mourning. He mourned for the rest of his life, the old-fashioned way: extra prayers at night for the repose of her soul (he figured she must be in purgatory, possibly heaven, but for sure not hell: the insane, like infants, cannot sin); downcast gloomy looks; a self-imposed silence, broken only when speech was absolutely necessary; no more fun, no more stealing, and no music. His old guitar, which he had enjoyed plucking at night after supper, he gave to the three boys, who taught themselves quickly. But they couldn't play it in the house when he was there.

He survived Josefa by four years, and when he died of old age, the three boys and their neighbors buried him somewhere in the hills, alongside his crazy wife. No grave marker. The graves quickly disappeared into the wild vegetation, and even Papi, his favorite, lost sight of their graves.

The three brothers lived in Papá Santos's house for less than a year, planted and picked their own subsistence crops, almost starved when the land, a few acres, overworked and barren to begin with, yielded less and less. The brothers took to blaming each other for its failure. The less it yielded, the more they quarreled, and more than once must have come close to machete blows. Elias, nineteen and the oldest, was also much taller than his brothers and began bossing them. Papi, seventeen, and Mito, sixteen, resented Elias's arrogance. They thought of themselves as equals in their work: no boss, no peons, no unequal distribution of the labor. If anything, Papi thought *he* should be the boss, because he was smarter when it came to farming. But he kept this to himself; Elias and Mito would have laughed in his face.

The quarrels increased and finally Papi and Mito agreed they'd had enough of Elias. They told him off, called him a lazy bastard. Elias threw down his straw hat and challenged them to a fight—fists or machetes, Elias didn't give a damn. Mito backed down. Papi was mad enough to go for his machete, but chose his fists instead. He didn't want his brother's life on his hands. They would have bashed each other in if Mito hadn't stepped in and reminded them of Papá

Santos: what would he think if he saw them fighting? Brothers, for God's sake. The old man would moan in his grave. The shame Mito poured on them was too much; they picked up their straw *pavas* and shook hands, and Mito the peacemaker had his way.

But the next day Elias quit on them. He'd had enough of that dirt farmer's life. He said he was losing his mind in those hills, and his life was wasting away, just like Papá Santos's, or worse. If he stayed, he might even take Xavier's way out. He wanted to get married and settle down somewhere to raise a family. In the big city maybe. San Juan. Papi and Mito told him the big city would kill him faster than the farm. A hillbilly he was and would die one. It was in his blood. For *jíbaros* like them the city was a cemetery. But he insisted he could cope with city life and called them timid *peones.* They were going to rot in that poor excuse for a farm, he warned them; their brains would rot first, then their hearts, then their balls.

He hung his *pava* up on a nail and left for the city. He gave them his share of the farm. Some legacy, Papi said. Useless clay. Less than six months later he and Mito sold the farm for a few pesos to the family whose land adjoined theirs and hired themselves out as peons. They worked for anyone who'd hire them at something like fifty cents a day, average day's wages in those Depression years. But since they weren't always able to get work in the same *finca,* they gradually split up, found new friends and interests, different lodgings, and saw each other less and less.

Papi was almost eighteen now, thin, a little anemic, but not as fragile as he looked. He was quite strong. His light skin was darkened from constant exposure to the burning sun. His face was smooth and sensitive; he had thin lips, hazel eyes, curly brown hair, and a thin nose that my mother was to call Spanish because it did not round off to a pimple-pocked dome like most of the snouts in her family.

He was nineteen when he hired himself out to Gigante Hernández as a full-time field hand. The wages were grubby even for 1933. Gigante was a thrifty *patrón.* He underpaid and overworked his *peones,* who quit on him as soon as they could find better pay. But there were always enough half-starved men looking around for work—any work—to keep Gigante's fields tilled and his strongbox full, if not overflowing. Papi was one of those hard-up *jíbaros.* He looked five years younger than his actual age. An undernourished *niño* like him couldn't compete with the mobs of full-grown men who were willing to work sixteen-hour days all week to feed their large, sickly families. So he was bound to drift toward Gigante's *finca,* and there he stayed for over a year, on and off. When there were no crops to plant or pick, Gigante let all his hands go, empty-handed.

Gigante Hernández was a hard-working, puritanical dirt farmer who found time to produce nine children. "Eight worthless daughters and one half-ass son" was how he used to put it. He could have passed for a Puerto Rican version of the hidalgo of La Mancha. At least in looks. He bore a strong resemblance to those crudely carved imported Quixotes that pass for art in the tourist shops of Old San Juan: wooden, lanky, mournful, the face sunburned and angular, the cheeks collapsed, and the eyes dark and brooding; the bony, lantern jaw extended out of proportion. There was something Taíno Indian about his face, enough to suggest that way back somewhere in the island's hills some ancestor got down off the family tree long enough to knock up an Indian maiden. Or the reverse: that some lickerish warrior from the tribe of Chief Orocovix or Guarionex scampered up the family tree and straddled a fertile virgin of the Hernández tribe. But if anyone had suggested this to Gigante Hernández, he would have reached for his machete and hacked the blasphemer's balls off in a single chop, like sugarcane.

This *puro-macho* old-time patriarch took no shit from either sex, in or out of the family. He was proud, stern, and excessively strict, a boondocks tyrant who'd had the cunning to marry a submissive madonna. From his wicker rocking chair, *El Sillón,* he reared eight compliant daughters and one swaggering son. Hortensio more than any of his sisters, several of whom had the round pale face of their mother, was an A1 reproduction of his old man, except that he was not quite so sullen-looking; and he took after him. Whenever padrefamilias was sweating in the fields or in his paramour's bed after sunset, Hortensio was in the house keeping the girls in line.

Gigante's life must have been as bitter as the cheap, home-grown tobacco he liked to chew and spit out at stinging flies and wasps. The farm he had bought as a young man—recently married

and looking forward to siring five or six boys, and maybe a girl for
the housework—had let him down. The land was too hilly, and too
much of it was nothing but a dense mass of mush that sucked you
in up to the ankles, and during heavy rains poured downhill in red
and yellow streams. What wasn't clay or hills was a jungle of choking undergrowth that grew back as fast as he and Hortensio and his
peones could clear it away with their machetes. Some sixty acres he
owned, but only a fraction of that was farmable. His dreams of
owning a large hacienda someday and directing the labor from his
horse came to *mierda.* God must have had it in for him. Gigante
shat on Him seven times a day.

Even his offspring came out wrong: eight girls and one, just
one, lousy son. Eight useless daughters. No returns on that investment, just hard work to keep them fed, dressed, humble, and
chaste. Hortensio was another losing proposition. He'd rather
shoot craps with the village *peones* than squeeze the clay for whatever it still had. As for keeping an eye on his sisters, half the time
the young lecher had it fixed on someone else's sister. And, as if
God hadn't rubbed Gigante's life enough in shit, Hortensio, as
soon as he turned twenty-one, went and signed up for Uncle Sam's
army. With him gone, Gigante would have to play the master
full-time once again. He cursed himself for having ever sent Hortensio and the eight girls to eight years of worthless school. He
should have kept them all illiterate like himself.

Wifeless, too, he was. Abuela Socorro had died in childbirth,
taking the last of her offspring, a boy, with her. Afraid he'd father
still more girls, he refused to marry his *querida* Maritornes. What
if he died first? Then she would become his legal heir and suck up
a good hunk of his *finca.* Besides, the old Spanish customs of the
countryside condemned remarriage. Not that Gigante couldn't
have remarried and gotten away with it—who of those anemic
neighbors of his would dare condemn him openly? But he liked to
follow the old customs, the face-saving ones especially. So he stuck
fast to the burdens of a *viudo.* Except for celibacy. That would have
been too much for a *puro macho.*

 Gigante's wife had passed away in labor pains. No photographs,
no sketches of her exist. Even if Xavier had offered to paint her
portrait gratis (for Gigante would never have wasted his money on

el arte), she would not have consented. She was a self-effacing woman, and to pose her face for a painter, and then to have that image of herself in the house, even stashed away under the linen— that was vanity, a *pecado mayor.*

My mother said that Socorro had been a saint. A footstool, in other words, Gigante's footstool. But according to Mami, she had been a matchless wife and mother—a kitchen martyr and a bedroom madonna. The kitchen and the bedrooms, cubicles all, were her domain, and her husband was her overlord. He commanded, she obeyed, eyes to the ground. No questions asked and certainly no backtalk. All day she drudged away, fixing meals for the nine and the one (plus the field hands), with help from the older girls. She always ate last, almost never with her husband, who liked to brood by himself while he chewed. She ate standing up, always on the go, piling up starchy stews, rice and beans, codfish, goat and chicken meat on wooden plates, and watchful as a finicky mother hen, double-checking to make sure they'd all had an equal share of food, urging more on them, when there was more. Several times a week she and two or three of the girls loaded dirty laundry on their backs, or set it firmly on their heads, and dragged themselves barefoot to the nearest stream, where they squatted on a rock and scrubbed the wash clean with hard bars of Octagon soap. Socorro pounded away at her husband's underwear. She insisted on doing that herself.

At night, when Gigante was home, she bestowed herself on him, put his seed in private storage, and watched her belly swell right on time year after year. She was pregnant nine months out of twelve for ten years running, and on the tenth year her overworked womb quit on her. I think of her dying with a scream in her gaping mouth, or even a curse on her husband and that all-fours life she'd led. But my mother said she never cursed.

Gigante's neighbors envied him his success in rearing such close-to-perfect daughters almost by himself. What hard workers they all were! What obedience and loyalty! What humility! The Hernández girls were known as *las hermanas humildes,* the humble sisters. And all eight of them, or at least seven, were proud of it, to the point sometimes of committing the sin of *orgullo,* pride. But this the village cleric helped them overcome in the confessional. He reminded them of the Mother of God and of their own mother, a favorite of his, whose humility they could hardly hope to match. "But you can always try, Mija," he would tell each one. And they did; they bent over backward for the Espíritu Santo, that taintless dove who had somehow made María Inmaculada big with child.

Las hermanas humildes: too docile for their own good, a few misguided people thought, too obedient, afraid of displeasing Papá Gigante and their brother Hortensio. They never talked back to Papá Gigante, never even asked him for permission to smoke in his presence (he would have made them eat the cigarettes) or to go out on dates. Gigante regulated everything, right down to sweeping the floor, fetching water from the stream at the bottom of a steep hill, or feeding the pigs and chickens. Anything that emphasized femininity—a blouse or dress that was too colorful or fit too snugly, a new hairdo—was sure to provoke Gigante's displeasure; and displeasure led to chastisement; and God help the *hembra* who tried to defend herself. Gigante would grab her by the hair, yank her head down close to his chest, and let her have it with the flat of his horny right hand.

The head he yanked most was Celita's; she was the one he couldn't break. The only one she bowed her head to, in self-defense, not humility, was Gigante. Nobody messed with him. But behind his back she called him a putrid old pain in the ass, something the other sisters considered blasphemous and cause for getting one's tongue cut off with the machete.

Celita was not an attractive girl; she was short, but rough-hewn and hard-faced like her father. Her sisters wore their dresses above the ankle; Celita wore hers right down to her heels; when she walked, her heavy arms swung stiffly at her sides, as if she were clutching a pail of water in each hand. Her thick black hair was done up in "rats." And her dark and sullen face was stippled with tiny pits, a combination of acne and smallpox scars, like the tiny craters raindrops make on dry dust.

When Papá Gigante wasn't around, Celita liked to sit on his old wicker rocking chair in front of the house and keep an eye on things, the hills especially; she liked to stare at the green, sunny mountains that surrounded the house. Perhaps she daydreamed of *hombres* and of escape from *la finca;* or of the lonely life she would probably have when Gigante died and the others married and left her in that dump with only the wild chickens and pigs, the two

horses and the half-dozen cows, and *la maleza,* the forest that passed
for a farm, and the bugs going at night all at once, and especially
the *coquí,* the little frog whose forlorn, ventriloquial mating call
could be heard all over those hills.

In Celita's outspoken opinion (for which her sisters avoided her
as much as possible) they were "a flock of timid chickens. Papá
Gallo's chickens." When Papa Rooster crowed the wrong way,
displeased with his breakfast eggs or the taste of his bean sauce, his
gallinitas would duck their heads and scatter off to their cubicles.
Eventually Celita was bound to say something or do something that
would make Papá Gallo crow the wrong way. And when that
happened, there was no way she could make herself small enough
and humble enough to escape his right hand.

One of Celita's daily chores was to carry the lunch to the *peones*
in the fields. Gigante had chosen wisely; her husky, peremptory
voice was enough to scare away the most hard-up *jíbaro.* It grated
like a millstone. And like her father, she took no shit from men.

She couldn't help talking back to Gigante whenever he ordered
her to do something she disliked, which was just about anything,
from feeding the pigs and chickens to ironing his underwear. But
of the eight sisters she was the only one he allowed to call him by
his first name and to address him as *tú* instead of the formal, fearful
usted that the others used. This indulgence of Gigante's probably
came from her close resemblance to him and from her toughness
that was not put-on like Hortensio's. In some subconscious way,
Gigante must have seen himself as female in his third daughter. But
this bond did not get Celita any special privileges. She often had
to work harder than the others, almost as if Gigante were grooming
her and not Hortensio to take over.

Gigante kept his daughers isolated. How many times had they
attended a village dance? No more than five or six. And who went
with them? The sons of Bautabarro? God help them if the sisters
so much as stared sideways at those lazy chicken and plantain
thieves. Brother Hortensio had gone with them every time. Hortensio was a machete wielder from the womb, just about; and it was
tough *tetas* for any *jíbaro* who even looked like he was tossing
florecitas at one of the sisters.

Even at dances he wore his *pava,* with its long fringes and pointed peak, at a sharp angle, and dusty baggy pants roped above the ankles with maguey. At his side, dangling from his maguey belt, the ends of which reached down to his *cojones* like a bull's pizzle, was a long, sharp, unsheathed machete. Hortensio, like his father, was all balls—in public at least, and around his eight sisters.

He'd never had to use his machete (which he took with him everywhere, as well as a small switchblade in his back pocket, just in case); every Bautabarro *jíbaro* knew he was the son of Gigante and assumed he was a macho in his own right, and deferred to him. And stayed away from his *hermanas humildes.* Instead of asking one of them for a dance, a *jíbaro* would approach Hortensio first and ask his permission. "Hortensio, may I have the privilege of dancing with Iraida?" or "Hortensio, it would be a great honor for me if you would give me permission to dance with your sister Flavia." And Hortensio, who was destined to become a police sergeant in San Juan and after that the town marshal of Bautabarro, might or might not grant permission. Sometimes, for no clear reason, he would grant the privilege of dancing, not with the sister the *jíbaro* had asked for, but with another one. After a while the sly *jíbaros* learned to request the wrong sister and hope that Hortensio would give them the one they really wanted.

The only men he tolerated talking to his sisters, even on the dance floor, were married, middle-aged *peones* and dried-up grandfathers; but even those had to meet certain qualifications: that he know them personally inside out, that they be responsible fathers, husbands, and hard workers, and that they not hang around too long with his sisters. He was following orders from his father, but the enthusiasm he brought to his task was all his own.

This custom, and others—Catholic and Spanish, with maybe a little Indio thrown in—seven of the sisters never questioned. Every now and then one of them might be tempted by *el diablo* and his legions to live it up, break loose from the strong grip of their father and big brother; but that was a sinful thought, and never got beyond the temptation stage. Everyone took it for granted that they were all *vírgenes,* and that they would remain so until marriage. Dreams they couldn't help having; but even those, the sinful ones at least, they repented of and recited at confession. (Not Celita, though. When *she* went to confession, it was not to confess bad dreams, which she probably enjoyed too much to toss away on an old virgin priest, but to complain about her father's tyranny and her brother's meddling.) The village priest at the time, an elderly Polish one named Klimanskis (Soliván had died a few years before), also from the States, admonished them and gave them extra prayers to say whenever one of the *humilde* sisters, blushing, dropping sweat in the dark confessional, confessed that last night or the one before that—she couldn't be sure, so great was her desire to perish the sin from her mind—she had had a "bad dream."

Such a way of life Lilia had been born into and never once seriously thought to question. Even when Papá Gigante or Hortensio said or did something displeasing to her sense of right and wrong, when some *diablito* somewhere in the back of her head told her she'd just been insulted, or when the blackbird Celita pointed out some injustice she'd been subjected to at the hands of her papá or big brother and tried to convert her to resentment, it was herself Lilia admonished, her own conscience she condemned for it: "Get behind me, Satanás." Because Mamá had taught her again and again, in her saintly fashion, that our earthly life is one trial after another and that "it's not for us to complain, Mija, but to endure. Endure and be humble, Lilia." And endure she did, with humility to spare.

She spent her days sloshing out slops for the pigs, casting dried corn at the chickens, sweeping the dusty threshold, pulling grade-C eggs from beneath the undernourished hens, scooping out the ashes in the firewood stove, replacing the fast-diminishing supply of corn husks, abrasive leaves, and brown-bag paper in the outhouse. Whenever Celita was having her period, or when she couldn't stand the sight of the *peones,* who taunted her for her looks, Lilia exchanged tasks with her. She was happy to do it—she looked forward to breaking her daily routine, which was tedious and lonely, and she found the conversation of the field hands more interesting than the grunts and clucks of the barnyard.

Gerán, the youngest peon, was her favorite. She found him pleasant, delicate though strong, serious but not lacking in humor, and sincere. They were of different stocks. She was a shade or two darker. Her hair, thick and long, was jet-black, like a Borinquen Indian girl's; she had high cheekbones, large limbs, and a strong constitution. She thought nothing of standing on her wide feet all day, from early morning to bedtime, sometimes past midnight.

He was proud-looking and uncommonly courteous. From his weak hazel eyes with the large lids she never got the sex-in-the-brain stares that the other men, eight or nine of them, gave her from the time she arrived with the gunny sack containing their lunch to the time, exactly forty-five minutes later, that she gathered all the forks, spoons, Thermos bottles, and leftovers and walked away with her eyes to the ground, taking quick, barefooted strides.

There, in those steep hills dotted with cows, goats, banana trees, and thatched huts, Lilia and Gerán came to sit together while he ate his lunch of boiled green bananas, salty codfish, raw onion rings—the whole thing drenched in olive oil—and fresh warm milk. He was nineteen; she was a year younger.

He told her about his father Xavier the schoolteacher and painter, and about Papá Santos and Josefa and his two brothers. He told her he had no intention of staying in Bautabarro all his life; he wanted to be more than a peon in rags. He dreamed of having his own *finca* someday, a big one, flatland, not red clay hills and jungle; but for good land he needed a great deal of money. How could he possibly save up when he was just barely keeping his stomach fed on the wages Don Gigante paid him? Unless God worked a miracle on his behalf, he would either remain a hired slave all his life, or—something he'd been giving serious thought to lately—move north to Los Estados. In New York, he had heard from the friends and relatives of those who had gone there, to a place called El Barrio, a man could get a decent job and make enough to put in the bank. Eventually, if you didn't waste your money on luxuries, you could save up enough to return to the island and buy a good *finca*. In New York you could find work that let you live decently. Not like here, in this vale of tears.

He was convinced, as she was, as most Bautabarreños were, that man is put on earth to suffer. But unlike her, he believed that man and woman are entitled to some felicity, that life doesn't have to be *totalmente un martirio*. She, instinctively, knew better. In addition to that, she was too attached to those hills, to her sisters, her brother, Papá Gigante, and to the memory of her mother, to contemplate leaving it just because life there was hard.

She could see his wanting to leave the village, moving to San Juan, Santurce, Ponce, Mayagüez, or any other of the "big" cities and towns on the island where someone with ambition (and he seemed to have a good deal of that) could go into business for himself or find decent work. But Los Estados Unidos de América? No. She knew that other villagers had done what Gerán had in mind. It was nothing new. Those who could read and write sent long letters to their families telling them what a *ciudad magnífica* New York was. They had jobs and they were making, some of them, as much as twenty dollars a week in hotels and factories. That was a lot of money, twenty dollars. Too much. She was suspicious. They were padding their paychecks with lies to impress the *jíbaros* back home. Also, a few had come back after a year or so with different stories of Los Estados. Slums they talked about, rats and *cucarachas,* filth and degradation. And what had offended them most, they said, was that *los americanos* did not respect them, they treated our people with the kind of contempt and disgust a man feels when he sees one of his pigs wallowing in its own excrement.

And even if she was willing to go with Gerán to New York after they got married (she assumed he wanted to marry her; otherwise why tell her all this?), did he think her father was going to bestow his blessing on them and wish them a *vaya con Dios? Con Satanás,* if anything. Papá Gigante had nothing but contempt for those who "abandoned" their families and their country and tried to make themselves into gringos. A man, he thought, should stick it out wherever God places him in life, not run away like a panicked sow pursued by nipping dogs. And as for *las hembras,* their place was with their husbands. She would never have the nerve to tell Papá Gigante she was going to Los Estados with Gerán, married or not.

When word got to Gigante that Lilia had been seen talking to Gerán more than once, he reacted as she'd known he would. He warned her against seeing that useless orphan. But she was in love and persisted. He beat her a couple of times and forbade her to go near Gerán.

The old man and his peon hadn't hit it off; necessity, cheap labor, was the only thing that kept Gigante from throwing Gerán out. The *patrón* had a few other things against him, not the least of which was the strain of solitude, suicide and madness in his family. Since it ran in both sides of the family, the children, all three of them, had to be screwed up. Gigante didn't want any lunatic grandchildren. Bad enough that eight-ninths of his own offspring were useless females.

It wasn't Lilia's well-being that concerned him. Females, *hembras,* as he called them, like *jobos,* a species of wild, fibrous mango that had no market value, were handicaps. Three of them at most were all he needed to keep house, feed the pigs, chickens, and cows, and help out in the fields during the busy season. The other five had been mistakes, cheap kindling, a pestilence on a man's life. Gigante would have willingly swapped them for a couple of fat pregnant sows, or a good milk cow. And now this Lilia had fallen for the first *vagabundo* that had sprinkled a few flowers in her path. But what rankled him most was the prospect of having grandchildren who would almost certainly carry that strain of madness in their blood. Never! he must have told himself during his pensive moments in the rocking chair.

Then there was the rumor among the field hands and other village men that Gerán was a young stud, a skirt-lifting *desgraciado.* This was an unfounded rumor; in fact, it made Gigante laugh to himself that the anemic kid was capable of producing an erection, let alone laying one of those little battleaxes from Bautabarro. Even if it were true, Gigante had no objection to skirt-lifting. Hadn't he done it himself in his youth? In his childhood, for that matter. And still did when the lust came on him. But this was his daughter, now, not Fulano so-and-so's. Let Fulano worry about his own daughters. Gigante was looking out for *his* own.

A man with loose daughters was the victim of vicious rumors and ridicule. Gigante was sure no one in that village would dare mock him to his face, not while he still had that machete arm of his intact. But behind a man's back things were said, evil things usually, that he had no means to prevent. Some men may not be hurt by what their eyes and ears miss, but Gigante was not one of them; he heard things in his sleep—buzzing voices mocking him and his kin. On his rocking chair, while his squinting eyes took in the sun setting, his large, leather-brown ears picked up his neighbors' gossip, the *bochincherías* of idle women and effeminate, henpecked men and horny young *jíbaros.* Already he could hear them: "Gigante's oldest daughter, Lilia, the one with the thin strong legs, is carrying on with young Gerán. He's giving her *las florecitas.* You just wait, in no time at all he'll make her his *querida.*"

His oldest daughter a skinny *peon*'s mistress? If he caught her, from this day on, or even got a hint of a rumor that she was *cortejando* with that suicide's son—*ora pro nobis,* as the town priest might put it, because who was going to stay his strong right hand from violence? And who would condemn him for it? For sure not God. Dios the Father always took the father's side.

Lilia found ways to steal out of the house and meet Gerán. When she took the wash to the stream, he would sneak off from work and join her there. They considered themselves engaged, but who was going to break the bad news to her old man? Gerán was all for it, but she wouldn't let him; she was afraid her father would hack them both to pieces. In that case, Gerán told her, they should elope.

Elope? Only loose girls eloped. Besides, didn't he know Gigante would hunt them down and kill them?

The plan was simple enough, and by no means original. Stealing a girl from her father was common in a village whose marriage customs dated back to the Spanish Catholic conquest. It was a solemn act, matrimony; even childbearing, another blessing, was less important than taking a young bride's "flowers." Not that Bautabarro girls were all that chaste; they were no more chaste nor yielding than other girls in other villages. But, like their counterparts all over the island, they kept up a virgin front. Had to: that was the point, a solid front, a look of vigilant virginity and cautious innocence.

Abducting a nubile girl, then, was a common custom, an old and practical one; for it saved her menfolk's collective face, unburdened her father of an extra gut to feed and her brothers of the strain of protecting her from the local Don Juans for whom seducing unwatched girls was a principle. Still, no honor-conscious father wanted his *hija* stolen from under his snoring nose on a moonless night if he could give her hand away to any respectable, filial, up-and-coming young *jíbaro.* But there weren't many of these young men around; they were the type who quit the village as soon as they could cut themselves off from the family. So those fathers who were tired of turning away unsuitable suitors for their virgin daughters often had to settle for a face-saving abduction.

On a quiet summer night (no moon), Gerán met Lilia near the rock where she scrubbed her father's underwear, and they spent the night, lying close but never touching, beneath an old, dried-up lemon tree. The next morning, while Lilia hid in his rented room, Gerán smeared her underwear with chicken blood and presented Gigante with the "fact" of Lilia's womanhood. He waited until Gigante was undressed and bathing in the stream, so that when he threw his fit and went for his machete, he would have to wade to the shore and scramble up a slope, thick with cattails and thorny weeds, to get to it. By that time, the nimble abductor would have ample time to run for his life—time, if necessary, to race for the nearest bus, with Lilia alongside him, and head for San Juan or Mayagüez.

But Gigante, without being at all conscious of it, sensed that the world was changing, knew that this was only one telltale speck in the great pile to come—women wearing pants and smoking in public, children refusing to be blessed by parents, the loss of those venerable village customs, the end of *his* way. So he just stood there in the stream, naked, the cold morning water lapping at his brown behind, and said nothing, not even a curse for God.

For a wedding present Gigante gave them a part of his worst land, most of it hilly and overgrown with weeds and thorny bushes. The shaky shack Gerán built with the help of his brother Mito and some neighbors was situated on the only level ground to be found in his two-acre wedding present, a convenient two or three up-and-down miles from Gigante's house.

Gerán tried farming it, but that didn't work; somehow the clay wouldn't yield to husbanding, at least not enough to support a family's needs. Only wild things liked to grow on that *finca:* the prickly, starchy pear-shaped chayote; tiny, bitter oranges so inaccessible you were better off buying them six for a cent in the town market; yellow, buckshot-seeded guava; some small, sweet, slimy balls with a tough green skin and a hard white seed called *quenepas;* bananas, plantains, and an incredible abundance of starchy tubers whose Indian names they were seldom to use after they came to the hot-dog, pizza capital of the world.

2: Family Installments

IN A ROUNDABOUT WAY, the Drought of San Evaristo made it possible for my father to raise the plane-ticket money that took him out of our village for good. Evaristo, a Greek pope, had been martyred by Romans during the reign of Trajan, a Spaniard, sometime in the second century. The feast day wasn't worth celebrating, but since it coincided with the day things started drying up in our village, our priest, Hiram Delgado, named the drought in his honor.

It was a strange drought, the first of its kind on our side of the Cordillera. Our village had always received a good deal of rain: floods, tropical storms, hurricanes, five-minute downpours, and so on. Now, out of nowhere, came this "punishment," a calamity in its own way. And since the village of Orocovis, a short walk away, was spared, the people of Bautabarro had good reason to feel singled out. They crowded the church of San Juan the Baptist and asked Padre Delgado for an explanation, and a cure while he was at it. Wasn't that why he was called a *cura*? "Only for the soul," he told them. "So don't look to me for an end to this drought. I wouldn't know how to work a cure of that kind if you put a *daga* to my throat. I don't have the talent for it. However, I do have a convincing explanation."

The explanation convinced some old people, but no one else believed it. Padre Delgado compared the drought to certain Old Testament plagues, like the ten in Exodus, and when no one seemed impressed, he threw in a few remarks on the fall of a sparrow; there was a "providence" behind it, he said. "I'm convinced of it." Good for him.

What sparrow was he talking about, anyway? All the smart sparrows in the village had flown away, and the few that stayed had starved. Served them right. Padre Delgado, sensing dissension, dismissed the people. "Go on home, my children. Take the bitter with the better and stay out of trouble."

"Out of church, he means," one of the younger parishioners was heard to say. Others felt the same way, and from that day on, church attendance began falling off.

My father, who was twenty-one when the drought struck, continued going to Sunday services with my mother, who was pregnant, and with my two-year-old brother. He went mostly out of habit and to hedge his growing suspicion that God had turned His back on our village and its problems.

One day he hung around church after Mass because he had a question to put to the priest, who was known to be a practical man once he came down from the pulpit. What Papi wanted to know was whether he should look for a peon's job outside our village—which would take him away from his wife and son for weeks at a time—or stick it out in Bautabarro and continue to depend on his father-in-law's grudging handouts.

My mother's father had a small shack stocked with provisions that included smoked goat meat. He had seen the drought coming weeks in advance; at least he went around pretending he had, always a couple of steps, or five or six, ahead of his neighbors, who had only themselves to kick for the so-called bad miracles in their lives. My mother went to him for help the day after their last hen, a layer they were thinking of cooking for supper, disappeared. Mami went to look for her and found some blood-stained feathers in a gully. That was all the wild dogs had left of the chicken. She was the closest thing my parents and my brother Tego had to a pet, so there was more to her death than lost food. But Mami couldn't blame that pack of dogs for following their instinct. In their place she would have done the same. So she ended up kicking herself for not thinking ahead. She should have tied that chicken down by one leg in the house.

But chicken or no chicken, she would have had to go to her father for help. Not Papi. If he went, Gigante would have told him to go beg his grub elsewhere. But where elsewhere? Nowhere. Gigante knew it. And when Mami went to his house for the first handout, he went into one of his tirades before telling his son, Hortensio, to stuff some food inside a sack for her and "Ma- lánguez." (That's what he always called Papi, to keep him at a distance.) He told her that her husband was "one of those types," a loser, a man who at the age of twenty-one, no spring chicken, was literally half-blind and more than half nearsighted in other ways, just like his late father, the suicide who couldn't take it when his wife died. But his father at least had held down some kind of job. Not that going around spreading daydreams and disrespect for the facts of life was Papagante's idea of earning a living, but it was something just the same; it brought in the rice and the beans. Whereas this son-of-a-suicide son-in-law of his couldn't even keep his last hen away from a pack of starving mutts.

Mami said nothing in self-defense—she had no choice; she just kept her eyes to the ground and heard him out. Nor did she tell Papi what her father had said about him till the drought lifted, because she was afraid his pride would get in the way and he'd refuse any more help from Gigante. Even worse, he might pay the man a surprise visit and exchange insults, maybe challenge him to a duel ("Choose your machete, Gigante")—and get his head or fingers chopped off, same as Arsenio Pagán, the general-store owner whose thumb and index finger flew off the night Mami's mother died giving birth to a stillborn son.

Just the same, Papi got hold of a rumor that Gigante was putting him down behind his back, calling him every insult he'd ever heard and inventing a couple of his own. And that was why he went to the priest for advice. What Padre Delgado told him, first of all, was that he didn't see how anyone could stomach that horrible-smelling goat meat Gigante had hanging from the ceiling of his provisions shack. "It keeps me awake all night, Gerán," the priest said, "when the wind is blowing in the direction of this church. At times like that I think God must be sending me a message. Maybe punishing me for beating around the bush too much." He went on about how even the wild dogs that had eaten Mami's and Papi's last hen kept their distance from that goat meat; or so he'd heard. This was the kind of evasive strategy Padre Delgado fell back on whenever he felt confused or stumped or otherwise needed to stall. Finally, after

Papi brought him politely back around to the point, the priest told him to do what he had to do, but that in his opinion it was better to continue depending on Gigante. "For the time being, anyway. No matter how long that might be. It's better than leaving your wife and son alone for a week or two at a time. What are they supposed to do while you're away?"

Good question. An even better one was what they were going to do if he had to leave for New York without them and they had to wait years before he could send them their own plane tickets. The priest was too tactful to ask him that; Papi asked it of himself. And the answer, the only honest one, was a blank. He'd come to that one when he had to. Right now the problem was how to stay on one's feet during San Evaristo's "bad miracle."

ꞏ So the handouts from Gigante continued, and so did the resentment and the bad-mouthing behind each other's backs, with Papi determined to pay him back for every donation of tubers and goat meat, and with Gigante convinced that his son-in-law was one of those occasional mistakes every village is cursed with to punish the fathers of certain daughters with bad taste in men. If in fact Malánguez could be called a man. At least one real man had his doubts about that, though he never came out and said so. Gigante wanted the provocation to come from Malánguez, and he might have had it if Mami hadn't insisted on paying those charity visits by herself.

Then, after four months, San Evaristo lifted and the crops came back with the rains. There were floods at first, as if to compensate for the dry spell, and when those let up, everybody began to grow more crops than his piece of land could crowd in. In a short time there was an enormous surplus; the only way to dispose of it was to take it to the public market of Jayuya, a town more than fifteen miles away, with rough terrain all the way. If you didn't have a pack animal or two, or couldn't borrow one (hard to do just then), or had no sons or other family to help you carry it, you were stuck with your produce; it would rot before you and your wife and kids could consume even a small part of it. (If anyone knew the secret of preserving tubers, he kept it to himself.)

Papi's only son so far was barely two; his younger brother Mito was tied up with his own situation (he had recently married and was still working as a peon). Gerán decided to take his chances and lug two big sacks of surplus to Jayuya himself.

"That's not the way to do it," Mami told him.

"What else can I do?" he said.

She said nothing more about it, waited for him to pay his brother and sister-in-law a visit, and then slipped away with her son to her father's house. When she got back, she had a mule with her, on loan from her father for less than two days. "Bring her back, one of you, two mornings from now," her father told her. "I don't trust your husband with anything of mine for longer than that." Very well. He had to say something unkind. Face-saving again, one of his basic needs.

This mule was named Mafofa. Mami's only brother, Hortensio, had named her that, after a girl who had turned him down even though she had a harelip. Mafofa was the oldest of the three mules Papagante owned, and was no longer in shape for heavy work. But this was the best Mami could talk her father into lending her. He wasn't about to risk one of the other two on his son-in-law, not without collateral, which Papi and Mami didn't have.

Mafofa had only one ear left. A roaming pack of dogs had attacked her and chewed off the right one in her sleep. From then on she slept standing up, if she slept at all. It was hard to tell. She could have been either an insomniac or a somnambulist, she was that unaware of anything going on around her. Unless she had everybody fooled, which was unlikely, but you could never tell. Her death looked to be due any day now. She should have been put to pasture long ago—she had earned herself a good long rest— but Gigante didn't believe in retirement for anything on legs, two or four, that worked his land. He had walked over to her with a two-foot piece of rotting rope in his hand, tied it around her neck, and turned her over to Mami. "I want her back in one piece," he told Mami. She promised to do that and walked off with Mafofa before he changed his mind or discharged more insults at her husband.

Papi took one look at the dying animal and told Mami to take her right back. "Before it gets dark. I don't think she'll outlive the daylight."

"You take her back," Mami said, feeling insulted.

"I'm not the one who made this mistake, Lilia. I admit I've made a few, but this one is all yours."

"Too bad. I'll take her to Jayuya myself, then. You stay here and take care of Tego. I'll go do the business in Jayuya."

He went back inside the house for a strong cup of coffee, cursing to himself. By the next morning he had changed his mind. She gave him a hand tying the two sacks onto Mafofa. They didn't have enough rope left over to replace Gigante's rotting leash, so that was what he led her by.

It was a long and a difficult trip over miserable, muddy, narrow, rocky roads that wound up and down, hairpin curves alongside of deep chasms, valleys, gullies, ditches, trenches, and streams that contained more silt and rocks than water: an obstacle course contrived to try anybody's patience, stamina, determination, and optimism. He wasn't the only traveler on that road to Jayuya. Plenty of other competitors were heading for the same marketplace: people of all ages, leading or trailing mules and horses, some of them looking as wasted as Mafofa. Sometimes he saw a whole family, the members moving along in single file; grandparents to grandchildren, everybody was in on it. Most of them were crawling along but still moving faster than Papi and the mule. He didn't have much choice, considering Mafofa's condition.

So it was already past noon when he got to the market, the tail end of the stragglers. The place was packed with buyers and their assistants and all kinds of sellers—hustlers and screamers, fast-talkers, sulkers, and pleaders, some coming on like carnival pitchmen and others so timid that they'd probably head back home with their sacks still full and their pockets still empty. There was even a bleeder in the crowd. He was holding a handkerchief to his nose while his daughter, just a kid, haggled with a buyer for their tubers. More than one man was straddling his partner's shoulders, holding up the best samples of their yams and alligator pears to catch the buyers' eyes. It all looked discouraging, so Papi decided to hold off before diving into what he would come to call the *Jayuya Fracaso* and worse names.

He parked himself and the mule under a shady tamarind tree, untied the two sacks to give her a break, sat back between the sacks, one arm resting on each, and turned himself into a contented spectator. In no time he was sleeping, dreaming of airplane tickets, a dishwasher's job, a well-furnished house, and other luxuries. When he woke up, the marketplace was empty, and his sense of time and place had flown off somewhere, like the drought-struck sparrows of Bautabarro. For a minute or so he couldn't even recall what he was called, whether it was Germán or Hernando, Hernán or Fernando, or maybe Xavier Something, a teacher with a smoking pistol in his mouth and rust dribbling out of his nostrils. No one had bothered to wake him up. "Pack up your sacks, *compai*. Time to go home." Mafofa herself was still asleep, or putting on a good act, not even bothering to flick off the flies and mosquitoes; the muddy ground was tracked with human and animal footprints, littered with squashed fruit and vegetables; the sky resembled dirty dishwater; and the weak sun looked like a poor imitation of the sun he knew, a leftover sun, a discard. He stood up; a stiff neck. He felt his chin: heavy stubble. Mule and horse droppings all over the mud. A mess, a gloomy arena.

If Mami denounced him when he got home, if she called him Juan Bobo the village idiot, and crossed her name off their marriage certificate ("Go take your sacks somewhere else, Malánguez") and told him her father had been right about him from the start, that she had committed a hair-raising sin when she married him, and that under the circumstances she was walking out ("For good. And stay out of my life"), he wouldn't be able to denounce her as a faithless woman. How could he? In her place . . .

He was still whipping himself with despair, close to panic, while tying the sacks back on the mule, when a mustachioed man in a white suit, a buyer, materialized and offered to take the sacks off his hands for fifty cents.

"They're worth at least twice that much," Papi said, on his guard.

The buyer replied that, as a matter of fact, "you might have been able to sell them for as high as two dollars a couple of hours ago, but you fell asleep," and since it was going on three o'clock already, and no other buyers were around to bargain with him, "you're lucky to be getting rid of your *viandas* for twenty-five cents a sack, *compai*."

Papi started to haggle anyway, but the man wouldn't budge; he said time was running out, he had to get back to wherever before the sun set, he was getting hungry, as Papi must be (yes), and he had no time to waste over money. "So the whole thing's settled as far as I'm concerned. Twenty-five cents a sack."

Sold to the thief in white. He had a pocket watch on a chain, and his muddied boots were made of leather. As a bonus he threw in a shortcut back to Bautabarro (he seemed to know his way around), but this route turned out to be another mistake on a day made for them. The road he and the mule were on was a winding single track; by the time they got to an altitude called Los Tres Picachos, overlooking a valley of mud, he was daydreaming again; couldn't help thinking of those plane tickets and the fancy house. And somewhere along his mind's nonstop flight to The North, Mafofa lost her balance, the rotten leash snapped, she rolled over the side, all the way down, no rest stops, and when she got to where she was going she sank in the mud.

He knew this was it for her, but he went for help anyway. After a lot of walking, blaming himself for what had happened, he found a man squatting in front of a hut, cutting the stems off tubers with a short machete. A woman was inside the hut cooking something on the fire-stove; she looked back over her shoulder, casually, as if this was nothing new, while Papi told the man his story. When he was finished the man went inside the hut, past his wife, who told him to be back in time for dinner, and came back out with an old gun, into which he was shoving the second of two bullets.

"My last two bullets," he told Papi.

"What are they for?" Papi asked, as if he hadn't guessed already.

"For just in case, *compadre*. Now let's get going. That sun's on its last leg."

When they got to Mafofa's resting place, all the man could see that resembled a mule was a gray wedge that could have been her only ear. Papi's eyes were too weak for anything that far off. "But maybe it's not even that," said the man. "Maybe it's just a leaf shaking, or a wing. Birds die there all the time." Those escaped sparrows? Whatever it was, the man took aim, fired once and put the gun away. "I never miss, *compai*," he said. "And I have a feeling I'll be needing this last bullet soon."

Papi was too frightened to ask him what he meant by that. "You're a man of compassion, señor."

"It's nothing," the man said. "A hobby of mine."

Papi thanked him and turned down the offer of a cup of coffee with roasted yam back at the man's house. "I have to get home before dark. My wife gets nervous after sunset." The man showed him a better shortcut than the fatal one the buyer had put him on, and Papi got home just as it was time to light the kerosene lamp. He explained the whole thing to Mami, who nodded or shook her head depending on which response was appropriate.

"You're no businessman," she said simply, no sarcasm, when he was finished. Then he went and washed up for dinner. "Fifty cents is better than nothing," she told him.

"Absolutely," he said, even if he wasn't sure about that.

Now the problem was how to explain the mule's death to her father. She volunteered to tell him herself, but Papi would have none of that. First thing next morning, shaved and putting on a look of casual seriousness, he went and told Gigante the whole thing, and was treated to a long, insulting sermon and some sarcastic stares. As a farmer, he was told, he was the brother of uselessness; same thing for his fitness as a father, as a husband, as a son-in-law, as a businessman, as a man (but this only by implication), and as a human being when you came down to it (also by implication).

"In other words, Malánguez," Gigante said, wrapping it up, "whenever things like this happen, they always happen to types like you. And you owe me twenty dollars for that mule."

"What about the price of the rope?" Papi said, the only sarcasm he allowed himself during that meeting, their last.

"I threw in the rope," he was told.

"You certainly did."

Even with the rope thrown in, twenty dollars was a lot of money to owe for a mule who had cheated death by a few weeks. But Gigante was out to make his son-in-law pay for having married his daughter without her father's permission. The trouble with this revenge, though, was that all the money Papi had was the fifty cents. He fished the two quarters out of his pocket and held them out to Gigante. "The first installment, Don Gigante."

Gigante let out a cackle. "You call that money?"

"I'll pay you for Mafofa when I strike it rich, then," Papi said, and put the quarters back in his pocket. Then he turned and left in a hurry before his father-in-law reached for his machete and put it to work on his son-in-law's neck or fingers.

On the way home Papi decided it was past time to follow the example of Bautabarro's sparrows and flee the village for good. Go into business, he told himself. What kind of business? The only kind he knew anything about, of course (if from the customer's side of the counter): a *colmado,* a little general store. Groceries and sundries, he decided, would enable him to make the quickest possible killing and to pull out fast. Others had turned to this solution, he had heard. He himself didn't know anyone who had done it successfully, but he knew the brother-in-law of someone who had, so it wasn't just a rumor or a joke. If it was no lie, as he had heard more than once, that our people had a God-given knack for the grocery business (the small variety, not the heavy-turnover type), then he saw no reason why he, whose ancestors were 100 percent Puerto Ricans, should be an exception. At least he owed it to himself to find out, and his brother was going to help him.

"We owe it to ourselves, Mito," he told his brother, whom he rarely got to see anymore because both of them were caught up in the common situation called *la lucha,* the struggle to break out of the tubers cycle. Planting and reaping, they were wasting their best years in age-old frustrations. Mito himself had been waiting a long time for someone with a business head to come and show him the way out of his own labyrinth.

He had married someone from Morovis, a neighboring village, Agripina Delfina Quiles. Her father, Don Wenceslao Calixto Quiles, a widower in his sixties, had been saving up his meager profits for over forty years. He was a master cabinetmaker, and in his own youth, just before the first war with the Germans broke out, he had been set on taking off and settling down in a place that was to be called El Barrio (there were about a thousand compatriots there already, many of them rolling cigars for Cubans); but then he got married on impulse, which was fine, except that his wife was afraid of the English language and the cold, and kept talking him into putting off the move. Her main objection to leaving just then (a pretext, apparently) was a rumor based on another rumor that German ships had sneaked into the Mar Caribe and were blowing up "our" ships left and right, turning decent human beings into food for the sharks. "Let's wait until the powers of light win the war, Wenceslao," she told him.

So for her sake he had put off the move of his life; and then she had gone and died on him—scarlet fever or TB—and there went his ambition to become, as he put it, the first Puerto Rican master cabinetmaker in the U.S.A., a pioneer. Let someone else have the honor. And for over forty years now he had settled for being the only cabinetmaker in Morovis; they didn't come more skilled. A committed widower, he spent most of his spare time, which was most of his time, raising his daughter Agripina. He had been a friend of Mito's and Papi's father and said he still couldn't understand how a man with an honorable profession and three dependent sons could open fire on his own mouth. "That was not the way to treat a broken heart," Don Quiles said. "His wasn't the only broken heart in these parts. So it must have been more than that."

Papi and Mito didn't want to talk about it, but they wouldn't mind a small loan from the cabinetmaker to get their *colmado* venture off the ground. However much money he had stashed away those forty years was for his daughter, which meant her husband was entitled to a percentage; but she wouldn't be getting any of it until her father passed away, and from the looks of it he might live to be 150: he was still hearty and strong, had never had a cold, and had even skipped most of the childhood diseases. So there was no sense sticking around for that percentage Mito was entitled to. It couldn't amount to much anyway.

"*Colmados* are a dime a dozen around here," he told Mito, "and I don't know of any that ever did their owners any damn good. If you and your brother want to throw your money away, don't come to me for mine. The only purpose of a *colmado* is a hangout for the peons at the end of the day, when every anemic without shoes becomes a philosopher. Life this and life that. A sore throat is turned into a tragedy after one shot of rum. Which is fine with me, but you and your brother are talking about going into business, not the theater. Not with my money, Mito."

So much for that attempt to hustle an outside investor. Mito's own fortune came to fifteen dollars, his savings from breaking his back. Plane-ticket money, he called it. Escape funds. But only about half what he needed to save himself and Agripina. In another five years or so, leaving out a miracle, he might have another fifteen saved up, and he and his wife could take off for El Norte, unless the price of plane tickets went up. So he took his chances and went along with Papi's *colmado* scheme.

"Don't say I didn't try to talk you out of it," Don Quiles told him.

"Thanks," Mito said, "but a man has to take his chances in life."

"You sound like one of those shot-of-rum philosophers."

"I'm practicing."

"To lose every penny you have? And your only pair of shorts."

"It's my pennies and my shorts."

"It's my daughter."

"It's my wife. My life, too. My wife and my life, if you don't mind."

"Your wife is my daughter, and I think she's entitled to an intelligent husband. I hope *you* don't mind."

"Are you trying to insult me, Don Quiles?"

"Yes, sir, since common sense doesn't work with types like you and Hernando, or whatever he's called."

"*Gerán!*"

"That sounds to me like *Germán* misspelled. I thought your father was a schoolteacher. No wonder this village is crawling with illiterates."

"And with stingy old men, Don Quiles."

This could go on all day, and might come to blows and deep resentments, so they dropped it before a tragedy set in. They didn't want to start sounding like Gerán and Gigante.

But Don Quiles couldn't help asking Mito something. "Where are you going to set up this losing venture?"

"Malconsejo's shack," Mito said.

Don Quiles crossed himself and mumbled the names of several saints, the kind that visited fools in their dreams or while they were passing water, etc., and made them see the light. But Mito was immune to superstitions, and left.

Malconsejo the schoolmaster had built his own shack and lived in it before he disappeared without leaving a note. He was a studious bachelor—almost as many books as boards in his shack—and very strict with his students, a perfectionist who forced them to memorize paradigms, important dates, and times tables, like a priest in love with the catechism. He had replaced Xavier Alegría, who had combined learning with a little fun once in a while, before his wife's death ended his commitment to educating the children of peasants.

Papi and Mito had studied under Maestro Malconsejo for a while, which must have been painful in more ways than one: having to recite dates, tables, and grammar lessons, chalking up sums on the board at the command of their late father's replacement. Malconsejo must have known how painful it was for them, too. He was no fool. But that didn't incline him to play favorites. No special treatment in his hand-me-down little schoolhouse with the leaky roof, where everyone was equal except himself. "I'm the master here. I hand down the laws. Infractions will be castigated summarily, with a whip." His vocabulary was out of place, and he made his students memorize a lot of dead, useless words, most of them fit only for Spain. "Great mother of our tongue," he called that country.

"And of our misery," Papi would add years later, as if he were reciting a derogatory version of the Hail Holy Queen, Mother of Mercy. "And we had to take turns bringing him a fresh switch every morning," he would add, biting his lip. "That man left a lot of scars on a lot of legs and backsides."

He vanished for good one day or night, and left all his books behind; Padre Delgado was keeping them in storage for him inside the rectory. "He may show up one of these days—you can never tell. Miracles happen all the time"—as no one had to tell this priest who was good at naming droughts after unknown saints and explaining their hidden meanings. But after five years it looked as if Malconsejo was gone for good. There was even a rumor that he had been done away with by the father and brothers of a student he had disciplined too much. Big mystery. No one looked into it.

Until the Malánguez brothers came along with their business scheme, no one had thought to take over the missing schoolteacher's house, and not just because it was too remote from the main roads and cowpaths of Bautabarro and Orocovis. A better reason was that people had become superstitious about it. They thought Malconsejo's ghost was hanging around the place, or that it might be, so why chance it? And it had become a shelter for runaway chickens and an old rooster who had gone there looking for his escaped hens and decided to stay and share it with his harem and the other squatters. Not a bad arrangement, except that the old *gallo* had become impotent; he crowed all night in cracked tones, as if that were going to bring back his youth. All he did was mess up the other tenants' sleep and litter the place with his droppings.

A lot of the Malánguez brothers' sweat went into cleaning up that shack, patching it and weatherproofing it with a ton of tar that Papi said they couldn't afford; but Mito insisted they had no choice.

They also had to evict a lot of tenants: the rooster and his hens, *coquí* frogs, spiders, scorpions, centipedes, and wild dogs. One of those dogs went for Papi when he told it to please get out and stay out if it didn't mind. Mito had to clobber it with his broom. Papi took the dog's resentment as a bad omen.

"Bad omen, nothing," said Mito. "If that *cruzado* had chewed up your leg, *that's* a bad omen. It's called rabies. A good omen's when I step in and save the situation."

"Maybe so," said Papi, "but still . . ." He was skeptical. He had reason to be, as things turned out.

They called their *colmado* "La Situación Malánguez" and painted that name on a board, in red, and nailed the board over the entrance. They couldn't afford fancy merchandise yet, so they stocked it with commonplace items which they bought from other *colmado* owners on discount: canned lard, powdered milk, brittle dried-out stogies (in an area where almost everyone grew his own tobacco), sugar and molasses, all-day-sucker lollipops, flour, ground corn, cornstarch, fine corn powder mixed with sugar (good for sneezing, but hell on teeth), bars of Ivory and Octagon soap, combs, hairpins, barrettes, two or three flavors of chewing gum, and other things that every *colmado* in the area, and all over the Cordillera, had been stocking with indifferent results since the days of the Spaniards. People either couldn't afford most of these things, even on discount, or they could do without them, except once in a while on impulse or in an emergency, in which case they came asking for credit. They usually went to men like Arsenio Pagán of the eight fingers, established merchants who weren't going anywhere, didn't want to go anywhere, and sold whatever they sold on credit.

So this Malánguez venture should have been named The Misconception, although *Situación* was ambiguous enough to qualify. Whatever you called it, Papi's myopia had caught up with him again, and Mito had sunk his savings into a disaster. A few curious people came to the grand opening. The brothers had spread word that they were giving prizes to anyone who showed up. Those who showed, curious to see what Malconsejo's shack had been turned into, were given sour balls, bonbons, sticks of gum, shoelaces, a couple of stogies that stank up the place and almost caused a fight, hairpins, and a red barrette to a lucky, good-looking young girl who couldn't keep her big brown eyes off the thing. This barrette was worth a dime, but the brothers couldn't resist the kid's pleading stare. One man wanted to buy a tin of shoe polish and a pound of lard on credit, probably testing out the brothers' business policy, or their neighborliness. They stuck to their resolve not to sell anything on credit until they'd broken even. It was bad luck to give credit before then, they explained to this man. "Wait a week or two, Abelardo."

But Abelardo, a self-respecting man and a proud one, took this turndown of his bid for credit as a personal put-down, a slight to his character, an insult to the good name of his ancestors, and an attempt on the brothers' part to humiliate him in front of the other people who'd come to the grand opening. He was outraged, and he let them know in a roundabout way exactly what he thought of them and their *colmado*. "You're going to have bad luck for being so stingy, take my word."

"Who's being stingy?" the brothers asked.

"You are, the both of you. Hard-hearted. *Lecheros.* And this place is nothing but a pile of leftovers, a bunch of junk you got on discount from the other *colmadistas,* and you're trying to pass it off like brand-new goods. But like they say, you can disguise the looks of the codfish, but you can't hide the smell. *Te conozco, bacalao,* etcetera. It's not my idea of a smart business. Let's go, boys." And he left with his two small sons, who were sniffing sweet-corn snuff and sneezing.

Hurt feelings may have been responsible for his cynical remarks, but the brothers had to admit he had a point. What hurt them most was that codfish proverb, even though it wasn't true. They weren't trying to fool anybody with their hand-me-down stock, except themselves—and they didn't know that even, not at the time. So Abelardo had them all wrong on that count, but he went around spreading calumny against them anyway: that the Malánguez brothers were out to defraud the public with their cash-and-carry operation, their shoddy merchandise, their specious prizes, corn snuff that made little boys sneeze blood, and stale, dried-up cigars that made grown men nauseous and dizzy and bellicose. That kind of rumor damaged the brothers' reputation before they got a chance to get their business going. There wasn't much they could do to offset the scandal. It was their word against Abelardo's, and Abelardo had a reputation for honesty and accuracy.

Then there was the man who wanted to know about Malconsejo's ghost. "Where are you boys hiding it?" he asked them. This was too much for Mito.

"In your father's grave!" he screamed at the joker. He was fed up with all this ribbing and bad-mouthing. And if Papi hadn't jumped in and kept him away from the other man, and vice versa, blood would have flowed that day over a little weak joke.

"I think we're losing our sense of humor," he told Mito afterward. "That's always a bad sign."

Mito couldn't agree more. He also mumbled something about having misinvested all his savings. "I lost my fifteen dollars, Gerán. I might as well have used it for outhouse paper, that's how bad it looks."

"Don't be so pessimistic too soon," Papi told him, a weak attempt to keep his brother from going into severe depression.

"Give me a choice," Mito said, "a sign. Some hope, Gerán. Anything."

"One of these days, Mito."

"One of these days Malconsejo's ghost is going to come out of hiding, is what I think." Now it was superstition moving in on them. It looked bad, hopeless. But they stuck it out a little longer, for a total of five-plus weeks. They spent most of their business hours sitting outside the *colmado,* not on chairs (which they didn't own), or on benches (which they didn't have the zeal to construct), but on a couple of rocks (which they had dragged over), and took turns accompanying each other on Mito's guitar. This was partly to cheer each other up, partly to kill time, and partly to attract customers, a harmless public-relations gimmick that didn't pan out. None of the people who happened to be passing by and stopped briefly to look and listen, mostly in amazement, was impressed much by Mito's playing and Papi's singing, or Papi's playing and Mito's singing. They even tried composing their own tunes, but the enthusiasm for originality was missing, and the results were colorless and stale.

One passerby, a le-lo-lai buff, offered the brothers some advice that would have cheered anyone else. He told them he thought they should take their "original act" to "almost-cosmopolitan"

places like Caguas and Cayey and eventually work their way up to
the "sophisticated" cuchifrito parlors of Bayamón and the expand-
ing tourist spots of San Juan. "In my opinion, which has always been
a humble one," this wooden-faced enthusiast said to them, "your
wonderful talents are going to waste around here. Unappreciated
by people who don't know what good music is, and that's a shame.
If I were in the shoes of you two young men"—they were both
barefoot at the time—"I'd move to a place where people would
steal from their own mothers to catch my act. Pack up: that's my
advice."

What they did instead was hang it up. They didn't even have
the brio to tell that well-meaning man of advice what he could do
with himself. They simply locked up La Situación (the rusty lock
itself had cost them more than Papi's two-bit investment); and when
they tried reselling their stock to the merchants they'd bought it
from, it was no go, nobody wanted his merchandise back. "What
for?" one of them asked. "As far as I'm concerned, you two boys
were a miracle God Himself sent me for all the wasted years I've
put into my business. And you know I'm not one to abuse God's
will. So don't come back to me with my own merchandise. . . ."
They walked off before he was finished.

"What we need ourselves," Papi told his brother next day when
Mito paid him and Mami an unexpected visit, "is a small miracle.
I don't ask for a lot."

"That's just what I came to tell you and Lilia about," said Mito.

"There's another drought coming? Don't tell me about it."

"We're finished with the droughts, brother. San Evaristo can go
wipe his *fundillo* as far as we're concerned."

"Then somebody set La Situación on fire. Good for him."

"Even better than that, Gerán. My wife's father's come through
for us. No strings attached."

Papi's immediate reaction was a frown of disappointment.
"Now it's my own brother pulling the legs of people with bad luck.
I took you for a better man, Mito. Do you want to leave my house
voluntarily, or should I ask you first?"

"Take it easy, Gerán," Tío Mito told him, frightened by the
extent of Papi's bitterness. "You know me better than to pull a
man's leg when he's down."

"Well, explain yourself, then."

"Very well. Just don't interrupt."

"Don't say a thing till he's finished," Mami said from the sidelines. "That's a bad habit you've got."

"Explain, then," Papi said.

Tío Mito went on to tell him that his wife Agripina had gone to her father's house that morning to ask for her inheritance immediately because she was fed up with using up her youth in those miserable hills. Don Quiles told her to speak for herself. Very well, then, she had told him; as long as he understood that, then he must realize that she was entitled to whatever means was necessary to move somewhere else and start a new life, she and her husband; and he, Don Quiles, was the only one she knew who had her means, which was coming to her anyway; only she didn't think it was fair of him to make her wait till he was 950, like Noah of the ark, or whoever it was. The exchange between daughter and father had lasted all morning. Among other things, Don Quiles accused Agripina of acting as her husband's emissary, and went on to suspect that her husband had been put up to it by his own brother Germán, or whatever his misspelled name was.

"Did she correct him?" Papi wanted to know, and was told by Mami not to interrupt his brother's fairy tale.

"There's no need to bore you anymore with this," said Mito. "The important thing is that Agripina got the money. It's not much after all, enough perhaps for three plane tickets and a week's expenses, but for us it's like becoming millionaires overnight."

Papi's immediate comment was, "Hmmm."

"You don't believe me, do you?" Mito said.

"I believe in the Last Judgment," Papi said, "and in the Word made flesh. In the Immaculate Conception, for Godsake. But this is asking too much."

"You'll see when I come back with the money," Mito said, and left him and Mami standing there with their mouths open and their eyes to the ground.

It was no lie. In addition to the powerful arguments and the shame his daughter had dumped on him, Don Quiles had gone, or was going, through a religious experience of some kind. He was at that age when God begins to exist again; in a dream he had been told that he would not live to be 950 after all, and that his life's

savings would be staying overground. He did suspect, though, that
somehow Papi was behind it all. Apparently Padre Delgado, a man
who had difficulty keeping secrets, in or out of the confessional, had
told him about that exchange he'd had with Papi during the
drought, and had added some inventions of his own; and Don
Quiles had concluded that Papi and his conniving brother would
pull any stunt—*"cualquier maroma"*—to get out of Bautabarro,
which was only almost true. They had their limits. Cheating an old
man out of his savings was one of them, though that scruple didn't
prevent them from accepting those savings once they were offered,
especially with a single-minded woman like Agripina around to
make sure they didn't hedge or come down with an attack of second
thoughts.

So now they had their "gateaway money," as Papi was to mispronounce it a long time later, the funds for a one-way, shopping-
bag, cardboard-suitcase, late-night flight to The North and just
enough left over for roughly two weeks of room and board in a
single-room occupancy, which at first they mistook for a comedown
hotel overrun with "disrespectful cockroaches," since at that point
they had no way of knowing that the city they had fled to was also
"a haven for vermin," an expression that might have been added
to the famous one at the base of the Statue of Liberty. But they
weren't complaining. Yet. In time they would join the unanimous
legions, the brotherhood and sisterhood of displaced and misplaced
ingrates who had escaped to El Bronx, or El Barrio, or Canarsie,
or the run-down regions of upper Park Avenue, or wherever, and
who had only themselves to blame for their situaton.

3: Chuito
and La Manca

Soon after his parents died, Chuito came to live with us. His father, a distant cousin of Papi's, had died of diabetes, and his mother, a second cousin of her husband's, died giving birth. The unborn baby went with her. Mami and Papi brought wild flowers and sprinkled them on the mound of her grave, which was marked with two crossed sticks.

Chuito was fourteen at the time, anemic, sunburned, under-nourished, and sexually innocent: his parents had been strict Catholics. He grinned a lot, as if keeping something to himself. And when Mami asked him what was so funny, he grinned and said, "Nothing, Mami." She stopped asking him and got used to it.

His older brother, Genaro, was adopted by an uncle and aunt who lived in Barranquitas; they had five children of their own. His two sisters went to live with their godparents, Octavio Cardona, a retired Army cook, and his wife, Calpurnia, a small woman with gold and silver bangles on her arms. These two were also related by blood; they lived in San Juan, next to the old Spanish convent that became the Convento Hotel and not far from the ancient church of San José, where Chuito was confirmed instead of in our village church. Calpurnia insisted that she was descended from a foot soldier who had served under Juan Ponce de León when the Captain-Governor put down the Indian uprising in the battle of Yagüecas, 1511, and she wanted her godchildren to worship in the same church where her soldier-ancestor had married a young woman who had been imported from Spain for that purpose. This woman had joined a convent when her husband died. "So what?" Chuito used to say. "Who cares?"

He came to live with us shortly before Papi left for New York, and he insisted that he was the man of the house now. Papi had told him so. "And you two," he told me and Tego, "have to respect me like your father, even though I'm not."

We did, I maybe more than Tego. In fact, until Papi sent for us, Chuito Cardona Santini was Chuito Malánguez, my father, "Papi." It didn't make any difference to me that every now and then, during holidays, holy days, and on our birthdays, Chuito took Tego and me to the village post office to pick up a brown-paper package addressed to us from that other world my real father had moved to, and that Mami received a weekly letter from him full of love and anxiety for all of us, including Chuito; he said he couldn't wait to get us over there with him. The only hitch was money. But as soon as he saved up enough, he'd send for us one and all, and we'd never have to live *separados* again.

But none of that meant much to me, because packaged gifts and weekly messages of love, and the occasional snapshot of a thin, smiling man in a baggy suit who Mami and Chuito insisted must have looked exactly like me when he'd been my age—none of that was the same as the man himself, the slanted, meticulous calligraphy and the snapshots made flesh. All his assurances of *amor* and *ansiedad* for us were second-rate substitutes, just words. *Palabras* on crinkled airmail paper that Mami had to translate for us into her own simple and direct way of putting things. Even Tego, who was in school and could read newspapers without too much trouble, had difficulty figuring out what he called Papi's *palabras grandes,* over-sized words that wouldn't fit our small-sized brains and hearts. Mami worried that we might forget what she called our *propio padre.* She used to say that any day now, he, the real one, was going to send for us, "all of us"; every letter he wrote to us she read out loud during dinner.

"My dear wife," they usually began, and the rest went usually like this: As he took pen in hand he was full of the *impedimentos, importunidades,* and *tropiezos,* the stumbling blocks, of life, and the *ansiedades* of an absent husband and father.

Mami would translate this into: "He's having a hard time and he misses all of us, poor man." Missed us so much, she said, that he thought only of us day and night, at home (a single room), in a moving machine called El Subway, and in a place of work called La Factoría, where it was supposed to be hotter than hell and Ponce combined.

"Worse than the *infierno,*" Chuito would put in, to give us a better picture.

᠊ And then Mami, after lip-reading to herself: "He says they raised the price of plane tickets again. That's the second time this year, and it's only June. He says he's beginning to think the devil is trying to keep us apart for the rest of our lives. But I don't think he means that." (But then maybe he did.) "It's the anxiety. 'However, dear wife, God will help me obtain the plane-ticket money.' "

"God and his job," Chuito would add; he didn't want us to think Papi was spending all his spare time on his knees in church.

And Mami: "He says a cheese sandwich costs twenty-five cents."

To which Chuito replied that "those sandwiches of cheese are going to keep us here all our lives."

And she: "Shhh! Don't talk nonsense."

"What makes you think it's nonsense, Mami?"

"Don't tell me what nonsense is and isn't, Chuito Cardona." He took that as a cue to make himself scarce, and did.

In closing his letters, Papi always conveyed "an embrace and salutations to Chuito, the man of the house in my absence," of whom he was immensely proud. He also signed himself "Your loving husband, Gerán Malánguez."

He didn't have to tell us what his last name was; maybe he was afraid we'd forget. "It's just an old custom," Mami explained. "It doesn't mean anything." Maybe so, but it didn't help things, either. Too formal, distant.

Chuito changed his name to Malánguez when he came to live with us, and he was careful not to call himself our papá. "I'm only your older brother," he'd remind me and Tego, as if to make sure we weren't letting something as trivial as his late arrival in our lives (or in Tego's and Mami's lives, anyway), with a different surname from ours, get in the way of the closeness we were supposed to feel (and did feel) for him and he for us. We never doubted the affection was mutual.

"But Chuito," Tego or I would object, "*you're* our Papi." I for one meant it. He was the real thing, the flesh-and-blood thing, not a letter-writer from another planet. At night he covered me and Tego with our blankets and talked us to sleep if we had trouble falling off; we took turns riding him piggyback to Arsenio Pagán's *colmado,* where he bought us each a large slice of warmed-over penny bread with thick slabs of sweet butter, and hard sour balls that could last you all afternoon if you tucked them away in your cheek, like a little tumor.

He also took us swimming to Papagante's pond, El Poso, at the bottom of a steep, breakneck hill with an irregular, narrow road that had been tamped solid by bare feet over the years and by the hooves of Papagante's mules and horses.

He taught us the dog paddle, or something clumsy close to it, in El Poso; and he once rescued Tego from drowning when Tego slipped and fell in with all his clothes on. Chuito dived in and brought him back up, coughing water, by his hair. "Don't go swimming with your clothes on, boys," was all he said, grinning. That grin of his was a way he had of fighting off the sadness that sometimes came over him out of the blue.

He also carved tops for me and Tego from the branches of a sweet-lime tree that Papi had planted the day Tego was born (a smaller one, planted the day I was born, was growing alongside it; eventually they would become indistinguishable). He showed us how to hurl our tops so that they'd make a wide, buzzing, rapid arc as soon as they hit the hard-packed red earth in front of our house. The time Tego and I were playing a war game with our tops (a game Chuito taught us), and a stranger with a pockmarked face and a deep gouge in his cheek appeared from nowhere and tried to entice me away with a brand-new nickel, Chuito came charging out of the house with his machete and threatened to cut off the pervert's neck "if I ever see your face again, you animal." The man, terrified by this threat and the machete that was supposed to carry it out, wet his pants, begged Chuito not to hurt him, and ran off through some bushes. We never saw his face again.

And it was Chuito who gave Tego and me our first lectures on sex; not the kind of moral lecture Padre Hiram Delgado would have given us if we had stayed in Bautabarro, but the other kind: juicy stuff, pictorial, dripping with details, about girls, women, and cows, depending on his mood, and about what they had that men, roosters, and bulls didn't; what happened to a girl when she reached a certain age ("Twelve or thirteen, boys, but some develop earlier, like Gigante's oranges. Very mysterious stuff"). When Tego was seven, I five, and Chuito fifteen, he decided to put his lectures to practice and show us how to do "it." But since none of the neighborhood girls he said he'd approached were willing to oblige us ("They're scared of you two, that's why. They think you'll hurt them"), he decided, sadly, that we'd have to take our first lesson on one of Papagante's cows.

"That's how I got started myself," he said, when we objected that cows were for bulls and milk. "And you two señoritos are no better than me." So he forced us to choose between him and the cow and our squeamish objections. Except it wasn't a real choice; he didn't give us one.

Early one Saturday morning, after one of Papagante's seven single daughters had taken his three milk cows out to pasture, Chuito took Tego and me out there (telling Mami we were going to look for birds' eggs), through fields and hills still wet from that night's dew. He fingered out La Manca, the cow with a broken horn; she was the youngest of Papagante's three, and for that reason, said Chuito, the healthiest and the most likely to cooperate with us. First, to show us how it should be done, he backed her up carefully to a shaky wooden pasture fence and mounted her. I got the impression he was hooked on cows, even though (if he was telling the truth) he had no lack of girls for his lust. He said he slept with a different one every night, but I think he was exaggerating, unless he meant a different cow.

In about a minute, he had done his dirty business with La Manca; and then, as if she had given him a high-voltage charge, he sprang back and landed on his feet. "Nothing to it, boys."

Tego, tense, was next. Chuito helped him up onto the fence and instructed him step by step; he was very patient and considerate of Tego's tension. But when Tego tried, nothing happened; he couldn't get it up; he just went green in the face, and instead of getting his first taste of sex, no matter how unequal the coupling, he started crying when La Manca sighed once, mooed twice, and walked forward a few steps for a bite of grass. If Chuito hadn't been holding on to him, he would have fallen backward and broken something. While I stood by, awaiting my turn and shaking with fear, Chuito calmed him down in a compassionate, big-brotherly voice, trying to restore his self-esteem and confidence.

"Happens to most of us the first time, Teguito," he said, patting Tego's shoulder. "Same exact thing happened to me the first time I tried it. But I got her the second time, so don't lose hope." Then he turned to me and said it was my turn. There was some kind of small rivalry going on between me and Tego, and I couldn't bring myself to back down and tell Chuito I wasn't in the mood for this disgusting business. I also didn't want to disappoint this stand-in father of ours. He had taken pains planning our first try at it. And I knew he was proud of me, because I was supposed to have "courage." I didn't want to let him know he had me all wrong, that I had none of his courage or his kind of curiosity, or his taste in sex, for that matter.

"Let's go, Santos," he said. "La Manca hasn't got all day." Then he walked right up to her, as if she were an old acquaintance, and pulled her back to the fence by her tail. She mooed again a couple of times and batted her queen-size eyelashes, but he didn't seem impressed. Then he grabbed me by the waist and lifted me up to the fence. "Grab her tail," he told me, "and do it fast. I think she's still hungry for grass. Cows have two stomachs, you know." What else they had inside them—diseases?—I was afraid to ask.

I did as he said: grabbed her tail after a couple of misses—it was swishing at flies, or at me—lifted it, and tried to do the business fast with my unimpressive member, which, erect from a strong urge to pee all of a sudden, wasn't much bigger than a straight pin, and not much thicker. I didn't think La Manca was looking forward to this. And I just knew my own attempt wasn't going to work out any better than Tego's; for one thing, even though she was only inches away, the distance between us still wasn't close enough for me to bridge the gap with my peanut. And when Chuito, trying to save my pride, and his (he used to say I was his favorite brother, but he had told Tego the same thing behind my back), pushed me forward, I slumped over on La Manca, helpless, smelling her patchy, pungent hide and staring down at scabs and ticks all over her back. Nauseating.

"Do it, dammit!" Chuito yelled, his voice coming out choked and impatient.

And all I could say, trying to keep the mucus inside my nose, was that I couldn't. "I can't, Chuito, I can't."

"Don't tell me you can't!" He sounded unhappy. It looked as if neither of his "sons" was going to do right by him that day. "Just do it, Santos. There's nothing to it. You're my *brother.*" That came out sounding more like a plea than an order.

"I can't . . ." If I couldn't, I couldn't. Lying wouldn't work.

"How can you miss a target like that, Santos?"

I couldn't even see the target. I didn't have eyeballs between my legs. I gave it a good try, though. I got ahold of myself, out of respect for him, as well as some fear, and tried again. All this time La Manca, all patience, jawed away at her mouthful of grass and took no notice of the stingless insect at her haunches. Chuito, desperate now, grabbed ahold of me and began moving me up and down and back and forth on her, as if I were a loose-limbed puppet, and shouting instructions at me; but it didn't work. And after a couple of minutes La Manca lost patience, sighed, jerked her head backward, twitched her ears, and moved her bowels on me. Then she walked off for more grass, as if nothing had happened. I began crying and denouncing Chuito.

At first confused himself, he pulled me down from the fence, and when he got a look at what La Manca had done he collapsed on the grass, rolled around on his back and stomach, and laughed himself into a fit of stomach cramps. So did Tego, imitating him. I sat on the grass crying, and anticipating what Mami was going to do to me when she took a look at my pants. I grabbed a handful of grass and began scrubbing myself, but that only spread the stuff.

"We'll wash it off," Chuito said when he had recovered.

We took a walk to Papagante's *poso* (Chuito sat me on his shoulders and got his neck and hair soiled), where we stripped and washed up. I was to tell Mami I'd slipped when she asked about my wet pants. We dog-paddled and thrashed around in the water for a while, Chuito on his back, squirting water at me and Tego and mooing like a cow with weak vocal cords. Then he took us to Arsenio Pagán's *colmado* for bread and butter and a sour bonbon each.

"We're not finished with her yet, boys," he said on the way home. "We'll get her some other time. She owes it to us."

And we did get her. When I was old enough for the first grade, as if to celebrate my coming of age he mounted me again on La Manca, and this time, as he put it, "it worked." (I disagreed, privately, but then he was the expert on this business.)

"You better give her a rest, Santos," he said in a serious voice. "She looks exhausted." Not to me, she didn't. Then Tego took his turn, and Chuito took his. At least two of us felt as if we'd graduated from grade school that day. Chuito just grinned in his usual way.

Later he justified the "rape" of La Manca on the grounds that Papagante, his employer, was underpaying him. "I'm his slave, in fact," he added. He worked for Mami's father six days a week, or seven, depending on the season. He planted, sowed, plowed the mostly red soil, and took sacks of crops to the Jayuya market on Papagante's two mules. At the age of sixteen, he had hands as hard and coarse as tree bark. Like me and Tego he hated shoes, which he insisted were for horses and butterfly sissies. The calluses on his feet resembled raw, livid leather patches glued to his soles and heels. And his thin face was as well-done as a skin of roast pork.

In the fields he worked up a crush for one of my mother's sisters, Milagros, the third youngest of the seven. She and Tía Celita, the man-hater, took turns delivering lunch to the field hands. But Milagros would have nothing to do with Chuito, even if she liked him, because her father was strict about any of his daughters becoming involved with any of his workers, who were socially below him; most of them were fathers themselves, anyway, and he wouldn't be too pleased if any of them pulled any hanky-panky with his daughters. Same for orphans, whether they were his social inferiors or not. One such son-in-law already was disgrace enough. And if Chuito thought he was going to follow in Papi's footsteps, he had a fatal accident coming to him.

At night in bed, while he dragged on a hand-rolled cigarette made with tobacco he'd stolen from Gigante, Chuito apostrophized Milagros. She was, he said, his dark eyes glazed, the moon. "*La luna,* boys," and not just a partial moon but a full one. (She had a round face, so there was some truth to his description.) Or else, to give the moon a break, he compared her to one of those gold dollars Ponce de León had paid his bills with. Or she was an angel, a dark-haired one with a mouth God Himself must have taken pains to model. Tego and I didn't see it exactly that way, but we didn't want to contradict him in the open, so we kept it to ourselves.

"Someday I'm going to marry her," he told us. "But don't tell this to Mami."

"Santos," he told me one day, "I want you to do me a little favor." Anything he said. "I want you to look up Milagros's skirt for me and tell me what it looks like." No problem.

The next time Mami took me and Tego to her father's house, I took a good look at what Milagros was wearing and brought Chuito back a report. "The skirt is blue, Chuito. And long."

He grinned, disappointed. "That's not what I meant, Santos, for Godsake." And he explained what he meant. How was I going to get away with that? "You just crawl around the floor when she's busy. You're small enough." I'd grown out of crawling, but for his sake I'd do anything. He was the boss, *el jefe.*

And so the next time Mami took us on a visit to her father's house, I got on all fours and crawled around while Milagros and the other sisters were going about their household chores, and while Mami was distracted, I looked up the skirts of a couple of aunts. Not Milagros's, because she hadn't stood still long enough. But Chuito wouldn't know the difference. I hoped he wouldn't.

That night in bed, he listened attentively to my report, which didn't amount to much, and then said, stubbing his cigarette inside a dried-gourd ashtray, "Hmmm. Are you sure that's not Celita you were describing? Milagros is skinnier than that, Santos. Maybe you need eyeglasses already." But I denied it, and he said it made no difference anyway. Then, as if to make sure I hadn't invented my report, he asked me to tell him how many hairs I had counted on her. "Twelve," I said, the first number that came to my head. "That's a lot of hairs, Santos," he said, grinning. "Let's see how many more she's grown next time you visit."

"A lot," I told him after our next visit to Papagante's.

"How many?" he demanded. "I want the number."

"A million." That was one of Tego's favorite numbers.

"That's more like it," Chuito said, looking satisfied, and excited. "That means she's a woman already."

I was bound to get caught by one of the aunts. Chuito should have warned me, but he had become addicted to my twice-a-month reports, which I myself found terribly boring; so did Tego, who'd yawn and fall asleep as soon as I started.

It was Tía Celita who caught me, the toughest of the seven

single sisters and the one who was convinced that men were a mistake, a plague on women; though when I thought back on it years later, I couldn't help suspecting that she'd been wise to my crawling all along and had tolerated—maybe even enjoyed—my dirty little habit, until boredom or her conscience caught up with her.

She was ironing shirts and shorts for her father and brother at the time, and I was on my back between her legs, staring straight up at pitch-blackness. There was nothing to see; she was wearing a thick black skirt, and no light was getting through.

All this time she had been humming the old one about the man who takes his produce to town on a mule, only to find the place deserted. Then she stopped humming in the middle of the man's disappointment, put down her iron, stooped, grabbed ahold of my hair, and yanked me to a standing position. Then she grabbed my ear and gave *it* a great yank. I screamed, she yanked my other ear, I screamed again, she called me a little pig. "Next thing you know," she went on, "you'll be mounting cows like some filthy pigs I know who work for Papá." She must have been a Peeping Tom. "Get out of my house, *cochino!*" What did she mean, *her* house? "Go and play with the pigs!" And she dragged me outdoors, where I was to stay until Mami and Tego and the other aunts came back from the laundry stream. "If I catch you again," Celita warned, "something terrible is going to happen to those two little pebbles between your legs." She left me there, on all fours, close to the pigpen, and went back inside, humming.

That night Chuito swabbed the sore spot on my head and both my earlobes with rancid hog fat. "We men," he said, "have to pay a big price for acting like men." Or like pigs. "You're lucky it wasn't Celita who caught you, Santos. She would have cut off your *bonbones.* Stay away from her." I said I would.

I held a grudge against him for a while. He hadn't even apologized, only said it was too bad I wouldn't be able to bring him back any more reports on Milagros. "At least not for a while." And a couple of days later, when we went to Papagante's coffee grove to pick a bagful of berries for Mami (and some for Chuito's private profit), I began throwing my collection at him.

"Stop wasting berries, Santos. This is serious business. God will get you."

So I switched to pebbles and dried pieces of mud, and pelted him with those. He tolerated the bombardment for a while; then, when his sack was full, he put it down, picked up a piece of dried mud, took aim, and caught the corner of my eye with his first throw. I dropped to my knees, screaming. He ran over, hoisted me on his back, and ran me home full speed ahead. On the way there he couldn't apologize enough, cursing his "bad aim" ("I aimed for your chest, Santos") and begging me not to squeal on him. What did he take me for?

At home he told Mami I'd slipped face down on the mud; I backed him up. The two of them took turns cleaning out my eye with warm water, while I bit my lip and kept the mucus back inside my nose. Tego sat there gravely, looking from me to Chuito to Mami, keeping whatever he suspected to himself. By dinnertime, I had an immense bandage, made out of an old shirt Papi had left behind, over my swollen, throbbing eye. After dinner Chuito slipped out of the house and came back with a handful of candy. A prize for having kept my mouth shut. I didn't need a bribe, but free candy was nothing to sneeze at.

The only other time he apologized to me, and the only time Mami, in agony and something like hysterics, almost threw him out of the house for good, was the day he cut my leg with his machete, behind the knee, close to the tendons. That one was also my fault, in a way. The uncut weeds around our sorry-looking house had grown so high that I could lose myself in them, unseen, for hours. One day I spotted a snake in there, probably just a garter snake, but to us a snake was a serpent: something evil and disgusting and deadly. Chuito disagreed. A snake, he said, was just an overgrown worm, and he cut them into pieces whenever he came across one.

I ran inside the house to tell Mami there was a "serpent" in our weeds. "Stay away from there," she said, blanching. When Chuito got home from Papagante's fields that evening, she told him to go do something about the snake.

"They're harmless, Mami," he said, grinning.

"So you say," she said.

"All right, whatever you say. But it's too dark to go hunting snakes now. In the morning."

"Be careful."

Next morning, before he went to pick crops for Papagante, he sharpened his machete and went after the snake. I followed him with a stick in my hand. Ten minutes later, no snake in sight, only the sound of his machete slashing weeds. Then, about a foot away, he yelled, "There it is!" and the chop intended for the snake (he told me later) caught the back of my leg. This time I passed out. As Tego explained it, Chuito and Mami carried me to Doctor Umpierrez's house about a mile away, but the doctor wasn't in, so they took me to the home of a woman who combined faith healing with practical measures. ("If the spirits don't work, there's always iodine.") She did what she could with a tourniquet and a bandage soaked in some herbal concoction, and chanted special mumbo jumbos against the evil spirit that had possessed my leg. ("The spirit of the serpent must be exorcised.") Until the doctor got home and applied his own kind of magic to my wound: drugs, stitches, and bed rest.

Mami swore she'd never trust Chuito with me again; she said there was something incurably bad in his blood which would get us all into the grave before Papi rescued us with the plane tickets. Then she put me to bed, covered me up, and dared Chuito to come near me. He turned and left the house, looking at the ground, and disappeared for a week. We missed him painfully. Tego said he'd seen him hiding in the woods, or somebody who looked just like him, and that he was living on wild fruit, birds' eggs, coffee beans, "good grass," and serpent meat. Mami told him to go wash out his mouth. "That's all we need in this house now—lies!"

Chuito had probably been hiding out in the home of one of his gambling friends, said Mami. And if he thought she was going to look for him and forgive him, or beg him to come back, he had a lifetime of waiting ahead of him. "He's on his own now," she said. But she got over that mood. Without him our house was a gloomy hangout. It was as if we were saddled with a vow of silence. We lost weight, Mami let the floor go unswept, our dirty laundry piled up, attracting spiders, centipedes, frogs, and maybe a snake or two. So through her sisters, who passed the word to their neighbors, the message got to Chuito that he was forgiven, he could come back, provided he didn't use his machete around the house again. He'd have to find some other way to kill the serpents.

We had an emotional reunion, melodrama to spare. He couldn't apologize enough. The sight of my bandaged leg brought tears to his eyes. The first time I saw him cry, and the last. He swore to be "good" from then on, more responsible, harder working, mature; he even joined us for a five-day fit of bedtime novenas, fighting off sleep with rags he'd soaked in water. Our way of thanking God for sparing my leg.

The day after our last novena, he pocketed the money he'd made on a sackful of Papagante's coffee beans and gambled it away. "That," he said, "plus the girls, boys. They're expensive." I think he'd kicked the cow habit for good.

Less than a month later, when the three evil sons of Felipe Guayaba stuck Tego's head inside a sack filled with wasps and left him close to blind and his face looking like a blighted gourd, Chuito gave chase and clubbed two of them unconscious. The third Guayaba got away, but Chuito swore to the bones of his parents that he was going to get him with the two-by-four we locked our door with at night. Then he went and set their corn patch and outhouse on fire. Mami went to her father and explained the whole thing. She pleaded with him to intercede. Felipe owed Papagante some favor for the use of his best horse as a stud. Papagante reminded him of this and hinted at violence if he and his sons came after Chuito.

"You're lucky only two of your sons got their heads busted, Felipe. And I wouldn't be too pleased if my daughter's house burned down one of these days." Felipe and his sons had been suspected of putting the torch to a couple of houses in revenge for one thing or other.

Then, against Mami's protests, Papagante exiled Chuito to San Juan for a month. "It's for his own good," he told Mami. "I don't trust those Guayabas." So we lost him again—twice in a month. During his absence I went into the sulks and refused to pray at night for the departed souls of people Mami had known and a few she'd only heard of. And Tego protested by scrubbing off the Vaseline Mami swabbed on his itching, bloated gourd.

"I had nothing to do with it," she protested back. "It was your grandfather."

"So go talk to *him*," Tego demanded.

"He doesn't want to hear it," she said. She was right.

I began pissing up my bed in my sleep. She made me tie a rag around my loins. Then the bed-wetting stopped as soon as Chuito got back from San Juan. Strange.

He came back a little changed. It took him a full week to get over the evils of banishment in San Juan. He appeared at our door in big-city pants, a floral-print shirt, and oxblood shoes. He had put on a few pounds, there were pimples on his nose and cheeks, and his skin was much lighter now from all the hours he'd had to spend inside Calpurnia's and Octavio's respectable household. "Dinner served at seven, boys. I had to take a bath before they let me eat. Barbarians. And I had to do my business in a special chamberpot with a waterfall when you pull a chain." He explained the box of water to which the chain was attached. "Disgusting."

Sick of idleness and good manners, he returned to his field work, but instead of coming home at sunset to eat with us, he'd go off somewhere in search of gambling partners and girls and not get back till bedtime, smelling of rotgut and cheap perfume, his face and shirtfront stained with lipstick. Sometimes he didn't get back till the night of the next day. To Mami he didn't talk any more than he had to, and toward me and Tego he acted for a while like an intruder, or an unhappy guest with a private grievance. He even told Tego the wasp incident with the Guayaba brothers had been his own fault. "Because you should have picked up a stone and smashed their heads in."

"But they were bigger than me, Chuito. The three of them."

"So what. You're a man, aren't you?"

"Mami said I'm a little boy."

"Makes no difference. Next time fight your own fights."

"But Papi, I'm not—"

"Don't call me that, Tego." Same thing for me. What had they done to him in San Juan? He wasn't saying.

No more craps games, or tops wars, or talk of cows or Milagros the moon, no free puffs of tobacco behind Mami's back. This went on for a week.

Then he began telling us a few things about his month in San Juan. He said he thought four weeks in the house of snobs like Calpurnia and Octavio, the retired Army cook, were too much for a normal man. It wouldn't have been so bad, he said, if Calpurnia and Octavio had let him go off on his own once in a while so he could go look for girls and get drunk; but they had been strict about where he went and what he did. They had him under house arrest, was what it was. This wasn't the wild countryside, they told him.

In a place like San Juan, only loose people ran around and came home at "indecent" hours. They didn't want their neighbors talking behind their backs and his sisters' backs. He should think of his sisters. He said they were becoming a little too sophisticated for him, like Calpurnia, who wore jingling gold and silver bangles all over her short little arms, one for each wedding anniversary. "She put them on every morning, boys, and didn't take them off till she went to bed at night. Like a cow with thirty-something bells. Ridiculous."

He had to go to church with them every day, all dressed up. His sisters and Calpurnia wore mantillas on their heads and big crucifixes on chains around their necks; Octavio's own medal was a Mother and Child that came down to his "tits" (he was overweight). They gave Chuito his own crucifix on a chain; he had to wear it, no choice. But he tucked it inside his shirt so no one would see it. "I wonder what my sisters' bloomers smell like," he said, really talking to himself. "They'll marry rich men, or become nuns, and forget me. Good."

Octavio the vet made him get his hair cropped short. He dragged him to a barbershop and told the barber ("some son of a whore with a pair of scissors") to give him a soldier's haircut. All he needed now was a rifle and a khaki uniform.

But at the end of that first week back with us, he pulled his San Juan shoes, shirt, and pants out of a cardboard box under his bed and hurled them into the weeds. "Don't you touch them," he warned us. "Let the snakes wear them." Barefoot again, his hair thick with dust, and his face regaining its old sunburn, he relapsed into his old ways. The second week, we renewed our nightly dice games and held onanism contests. He dedicated his own performances to Tía Milagros. He won every contest hands down.

His return from exile coincided with Mami's obsessive assurances that we'd be leaving for New York soon, in a few months. She said Papi almost had the money now. But her estimate turned out to be off by more than half. Our leaving was another nine months off, and it wouldn't be, as she had thought, the kind of pleasant departure we'd all expected. One reason was that her father, her brother, and her sisters began putting second thoughts into her head and got her all confused. Why they did that never made much sense. But it seemed that if a husband was away from his wife and children for a long time she reverted to her family, and the kids went with her (except Chuito, in our case: he wasn't a "real" member). So while Papagante and Hortensio both told Mami that she and her two boys were Gerán's business, they were also trying to destroy her confidence in her husband. One trick they pulled was telling her she had no business going off to The North. She belonged with them, they said, and made many references to ancestors.

Then there were the rumors spread by people who had friends and relatives living in *Nueva* York. These friends and relatives wrote back dismal descriptions of the places where they lived and worked. Apparently the devil himself had moved to *Nueva* York, and was working overtime there. Whenever Mami discussed the subject with Chuito her hands shook and her eyes narrowed. Chuito, who saw himself as her moral support, would cluck his tongue and retort that it was all a bunch of lies and distortions, and that her father and brother were behind it. Maybe yes and maybe no, she said, confused. It was ruining her sleep.

One day, her hands shaking, she summarized a letter Papi had just sent her: The plane tickets would be coming soon, and we had to start getting ready. She looked tired, ready to go in any direction they shoved her, whoever shoved first. She prayed for guidance. Nothing.

Then the tickets arrived. Three of them. A mistake? It had to be. There were four of us. But when she read the letter, it said, "Lilia, I'm sending only three tickets. That's all I can afford now, and I can't wait anymore. Chuito will have to stay behind for a few months, six at the most, until I can get the money, and I'll get it, so help me." He went on, apologizing for and explaining his "necessary decision" for a couple of more pages, writing off his guilt. We couldn't believe it; but that's what she was reading to us. I don't think she believed it, either. She must have reread it three or four times, twice out loud and once or twice to herself.

When she was finished, Chuito nodded and said he understood. "He knows what he's doing," he said. "He's a smart man." Then he excused himself, in a formal voice, and walked out of the house.

He was gone again for three days. We didn't talk about him or his whereabouts. We were used to his unexplained disappearances. As a man without a wife and kids, he was entitled to disappear for a day or two once in a while. If some emergency arose for us, he'd show up the moment it happened, as if his eyes and ears, and nose, were hooked up to our house.

Between the time we received the tickets and the day we left, Mami insisted that he move in with his brother Genaro in Barranquitas as soon as we were gone. "I don't want you to stay by yourself, Chuito," she told him.

He said he'd go join his brother, he promised he would, but he told Tego and me on the side that he wouldn't. His brother's foster parents already had a full house and not much room and board to spare. "Anyway," he said, "I know how to take care of myself. I'm not going anywhere till Papi sends me that ticket. This is my house, and it's going to stay that way until it has to. Keep it to yourselves. I'll get a pen and paper and write you these long letters that'll put you to sleep in no time."

We said they wouldn't. And in a way we were glad he wasn't going to leave the house, would look after it, just in case we had to come back. I said I would, someday.

"We'll see," he said.

"I'm holding Gerán to his promise," Mami told him. Chuito said that wasn't necessary. The man who had saved him from starvation when his mother died was a man of his word. "He's never broken a promise, Mami." She couldn't agree more.

"Chuito will die here," Papagante told Mami. We had visited his house several times after the tickets arrived, and he hadn't let up on the business about Papi and his betrayal of Chuito. He overdid these tirades, and we stopped visiting his house altogether. He didn't complain about *that,* but it must have hurt some.

Chuito took an oxcart with us to San Juan, then a bus to the airport, where we sat and stood around a long time with hundreds of others who must have stuffed everything they owned into suitcases braced with rope and belts, and brown paper bags with cardboard handles. It was as if half the island were leaving on the same airplane, and the other, more melancholy half were there to see them off. Through forced smiles, displaying a couple of bad teeth, Chuito told us he was going to spend a week or two with his sisters in San Juan (we didn't believe it), then a couple more weeks with his brother in Barranquitas. "Then I'll go pick up my things at the

house and move in with Genaro, until Papi sends me the ticket."
We knew that much was a lie. It was for Mami's benefit.

   Just before we boarded the plane, he almost broke down (as we
had), but he had conditioned himself against sentimental displays,
and held up, grinning instead. From a window of the airplane, just
before takeoff, we spotted him standing in the waving crowd: a
little sunburned stick of a man with thick black hair, hitched-up
pants, a white shirt that was half-spilling out of his bent waist, and
a lost look on his face. He was squinting up at the plane, trying to
get a last look at us, but the plane's windows were tinted and tiny,
and he was far off. All he must have seen was the kind of glare that
gives headaches.

   According to his, at first long, letters, he stayed at our house for
a few months, "because the house where my brother lives is filled
up"; then, in what must have been a lie, he said he was moving to
San Juan to live with his sisters "and that little marquesa with the
thirty-something cowbells." Then he didn't write anymore, and we
almost lost track of him for good.

4: First Communion

I SPENT THE FIRST grade of school under Luisa Lugones ("Mees Lugones"), the first-grade teacher of Bautabarro, who never laid a hand on anybody. She might hug one of her thirty-something students for standing out in class, but hit one of her neighbors' children for whatever infraction, never. "That's not what I get paid to do," she used to say. (She earned a couple of dollars a week, maybe less.) She took any complaints against you to your father and mother, or your guardians if you were an orphan, and let them handle the situation, which she explained, in front of you, briefly and honestly. If your parents wanted details, she gave them the details, in a serious but not morbid way and without dramatics or sermons. If they wanted to make a big deal out of it, that was their business, and your misfortune, part of the price you had to pay for disturbing her class. It was a well-run class.

I was doubly lucky, because Papi had taken off for New York years before I started school, so I escaped getting it from him during that year I spent in the first grade. Not that I gave Mees Lugones much reason to complain about me. She chose to do it only once, the time I got into a fight with Antonio Carretas. My adopted brother, Chuito, had instigated it when I told him Antonio had stolen a piece of buttered bread Chuito had bought me that morning for lunch. As usual whenever he could get away from his peon's job, Chuito had waited for me outside the schoolhouse—the same site my father and uncle Mito had tried turning into a general store—and walked home with me.

"You look a little hungry today, Santos," he told me. "Anemic. Tomorrow I'll buy you a two-cents piece of bread. I'll tell Arsenio to smear extra butter on it." He was on good terms with Arsenio Pagán, the eight-fingered grocer.

"I didn't eat that bread you gave me, Chuito," I confessed. "That's why I'm anemic today."

"You lost it? A serpent got to it before you did?"

"Antonio Carretas took it. He stole it."

He threw up his hands. "Jesus Christ! It runs in his family, that little punk. They're all crooks. *Ladrones maricones.* Even the grandfather. He's still stealing chickens when you turn your back on them." And one of the Carretas brothers had stolen a good-looking girl from under Chuito's nose. He couldn't come right out and hit the thief for that kind of theft, but he had it in for him; he was waiting for any excuse to get him. "And you didn't grab that piece of bread back from that little cowshit?" he asked me.

"I couldn't. He ate it all up right away. In one swallow. You should have seen his mouth."

"I'll tell you how I want to see his mouth tomorrow, Santos. Without teeth. All gums. And you're going to be his dentist. Let me see your right fist." I made a tight fist and showed it to him. "Fine," he said. "Maybe it's not as big as Antonio's mouth, but it's big enough to destroy it. No?"

Under the circumstances, yes. I should have kept my mouth shut about that piece of bread. Too late. I'd have to fight Antonio for it, and for Chuito's grievance over that stolen anonymous girl.

He took the rest of that afternoon off to give me "special lessons" on how to destroy Antonio Carretas next morning. We had to do it a good distance from the house, because Mami wanted nothing to do with violence and would have given us no end of hell, and no dinner that night, if she had caught us working out (situps, pushups, side-to-side twists, squats, chinning from branches, jogging up and down hills, swinging the arms windmill fashion to, as he put it, "loosen up your muscles, Santos"), and sparring. He cautioned me against leading with my right—or maybe my left; I couldn't remember which next morning, after a night of uneasy dreams, and too much breakfast "for stamina"—and when I walked up to Antonio Carretas outside the schoolshack, tapped him on the shoulder, and took a good swing at his mouth when he turned around, I missed. Not by much, but with someone like Antonio you didn't have to miss by much to lose the fight. He caught me on the nose right away—if his big mouth was an "easy" target, so was my oversized nose—and drew blood. He hadn't needed a workout or an extra serving of breakfast to put me out of contention. And he took the two-cents piece of extra-buttered bread Chuito had bought me that morning. He ran off with it before Mees Lugones arrived on the scene of my defeat, my second in two days.

She told one of the other students to go pick a handful of medicinal grass for my nose and took me inside the shack, where I had to lie on her two-plank desk, flat on my back and feeling pretty demolished, circled by about twenty-eight fellow students of both sexes, for about thirty minutes. It took the medicinal grass that long to stop the flow of blood from my swollen nose. She and a couple of students had taken turns chewing the grass into compresses, one to a nostril, with frequent changes of compress, before the flow let up and finally stopped.

"I wouldn't go into boxing if I were you, Santos," Chuito was to tell me that night (our beds adjoined). "I think you're the kind that's going to need a friend or a weapon when you get into trouble with the Antonio Carretases of this shitty world." The day before my defeat, he had called it "the greatest world ever invented" and even gave God some credit for it. Now it was a shitty world all of a sudden. He had some confusions to straighten out.

And Mees Lugones, without giving me a sermon on decent behavior and other moralities, took me home after class let out for that day. "By swinging at Antonio first, you put yourself in the wrong, Santos," was all she told me on the walk home, trailed by all my fellow students except Antonio Carretas, who had made himself scarce.

Chuito had been spying on us from behind the bushes all along. He had seen me get it in the nose and failed to show himself all morning; and unknown to any of us, he followed us all the way home and stayed within easy reach, hiding until it was time for him to come back from "work" in my grandfather's fields. Papagante reported his absence to Mami next day, and he had to make up a quick lie to get out of it. I don't think they were taken in by it—he wasn't a good liar; his lips always shook when he wasn't being honest—but there was nothing they could do about it. He was on his own.

So I was the one who ended up paying the price for his unsuccessful revenge on the Carretas brother who had swiped his sweetheart. "I don't think it was all Santos's fault, Doña Lilia," Mees Lugones told Mami (she was older than Mami). "But—well, I don't want to preach, but just take a look at him. His poor nose."

"Poor nose nothing," Mami said. She must have been trying to sound as Papi would have if he had been there to take charge. "If it stays swollen like that, he may keep out of trouble the rest of his life and live longer." Then she thanked Mees Lugones and walked out with her as far as our chicken coop, where four hens were keeping our breakfast eggs warm.

She was applying a damp rag to my nose when Chuito got back from his labors, put on a startled look to disguise his guilt—taking it for granted I wasn't going to rat on him—and said, after shaking his head, "It'll come off by itself, Mami." He was talking about the blood that had caked in my nostrils. "It's *dry* blood. Let him suffer a little." He couldn't hold back a big grin.

"Get out!" she told him. "I'll call you when it's time to eat." But when she stepped out and called him, about an hour later, he was gone off somewhere.

Less than a year after I graduated from Mees Lugones's class, I was enrolled in Saint Misericordia's Academy for Boys and Girls, a parochial school in East Harlem, on the advice of our next-door neighbors, whose daughter and son were in the sixth and seventh grades at "Saint Miseria's," as they called the school. So did I, after a while. It turned out to be a very strict institution. Penalties galore. Maybe that was why our neighbors in apartment 19 had enrolled their kids there: for discipline—*fuetazos,* whiplashings, as the husband called it—and not for a good education and an old-fashioned religious "indoctrination," as our priests and teachers called it. Whatever it was, it was way beyond what my future public-school friends got: next to nothing, except for sports and a way with girls that left us "parochials" in the dust.

Another advantage the "publics" had over us was that their teachers couldn't lay a hand on them. By law. The opposite was true

in Saint Miseria's. The law there seemed to be that if your teacher
didn't let you have it good from time to time, there was something
morally wrong with him or her. It was as if our hands had been
made for the Cat's Paw rubber strap that could leave the imprint
of a winking, smiling cat on your palm, or the twelve-inch metal-
edged ruler (centimeters on one side, inches on the other) that
could draw blood from your knuckles if you acted up once your
mother delivered you into "their" hands at 8:30 A.M. in front of the
church, where you began the day with the Mass.

Just as bad as "corporal punishment"—or worse, because it
made you feel like a rat on the run from hell for a long time
afterward—was the message they gave you about losing your soul
if you persisted in sinning. Meaning you hadn't done your homework by Catholic standards, or had talked out of turn in class; in
fact, almost anything they decided wasn't "right" or—as Sister
Mary McCullough, our principal, used to put it, with her eyebrows
bunched up and her lips pursed—anything that did not "redound
to the greater honor and glory of Holy Mother." "Holy Mother"
was always *Church.* The other mother, the Mother of our Lord, was
usually referred to as "Our Blesséd Mother" or "Blesséd Mary" or
"Holy Virgin." She had lots of nicknames. She was seldom called
simply Mary. That might encourage vulgar liberties, abusive adjec-
tives.

There was something both cold-hearted and generous about
our nuns that gave at least some of us reason to be grateful our
parents had signed us up at Saint Miseria's. Sister Mary Felicia, for
example. Third grade. The nicest thing Sister Felicia did for me was
buy me an unused First Communion outfit in the Marqueta on Park
Avenue when she found out I was a Welfare case. She didn't have
to do that, because Papi somehow always found a way to scrounge
up the funds for whatever we needed. I think he had credit everywhere, though he wasn't one to abuse it. But Sister didn't bother
consulting him or Mami about their resources. Maybe my plain,
Third Avenue clothes and my apologetic look gave her the impression we were in such bad shape at home that Papi couldn't put out
the money for a cheap Communion outfit: a white shirt without a
label inside the collar, a pair of Thom McAn shoes (blisters guaranteed) that expanded like John's Bargain Store sponges as soon as
it rained, and an even-cheaper Howard Clothes suit with a vest and

a big label over the jacket's wallet pocket, so that whenever a man opened up that jacket and reached inside for his wallet, others could see he was moving up in this world. No more Third Avenue cheap stuff for this *elemento*. Unless he had somehow stolen that label and had his wife the seamstress sew it onto the wallet pocket just to impress the kind of people who kept an eye on labels. If Sister Felicia was one of those types, she kept it to herself. All she wanted was for every boy and girl in her class to show up at First Communion ceremonies in a prescribed, presentable outfit: the girls in white, the boys in black, with an oversized red ribbon around the elbow.

"Making your First Communion," Mami told me in private one day when she was in a joking mood, "is almost as important as making your first *caca* all by yourself."

"So why do I have to wear this uniform, then?" I said, confused.

"Because it's a ceremony. The most important of your life so far. Except for Baptism. It's like when you get married for the first time." Meaning what, I didn't know or ask. And what was this about people getting married more than once? Another joke? Sometimes she went over my head and didn't explain the point. Some things I should find out for myself, I guessed. You can't always be depending on your mother to fill you in. She wouldn't even tell me how she felt about Sister Felicia's generosity.

At the time it may have been a nice favor on Sister's part—and on Sister Principal's, because she was the one who dispensed their funds—putting out all that money for a kid on ADC. For one thing, they were Irish, all of them, so why should they give a damn for people like me? But they did sometimes. More confusion on my side. And a long time later, when I thought back on it, I was still confused.

One afternoon, after the last class bell, Sister told me and a couple of other classmates not to leave the room because she wanted to talk to us about something important. Right away I figured she was going to bleed our knuckles with her twelve-incher for something, some sin we had committed unawares. Unawares was no excuse. Happened all the time in St. Miseria's. I started going over all the things I'd said and done that day in public, and then in private, and I couldn't come up with a single sin. Which didn't mean a thing. The nuns knew a lot better than you did what a sin was and wasn't; they had technical training in those things, and they didn't miss a thing. Almost every day somebody got extra homework for daydreaming in class, or the knuckles job for laughing at something serious somebody had said, or for picking his or her nose in public. That's what Marta Cuevas had done the week before I got my outfit. She was good-looking, too. She was short and hefty, she had a good profile, and she sat in the first row, right up there where every move you made was seen by everyone else, especially by Sister, who used to pace back and forth, with an opened book in one hand, and the twelve-inch ruler in the other, from the exit (closed) to the window (opened just a crack for fresh oxygen). And she, Marta, nervous because Sister was going to call on her next, forgot the rule about picking your nose and committed that infraction right under Sister's own nose. She must have thought she was back home or something; in a dark movie, where nobody noticed what you were doing with your hands.

Sister shut her mouth in the middle of a question, placed her book face down on her desk—her hands were shaking—and put a difficult question to Marta: Where had she learned such repulsive manners? Certainly not in school, hinting that in Marta's home personal habits were still primitive. One could just imagine, if one had that kind of stomach, what their table manners must be like, and what kind of "meals" they sat down to, if they bothered to sit at all. They probably all ate standing, or squatting right there on the kitchen floor, like their ancestors the Caribs, cannibalistic Indians from the jungles of South America (we had read about them already during the history hour; they ate their enemies raw). The only fire they knew anything about came from Huracán, their thunder god. She went on to tell us that the Caribs hadn't even discovered friction, that's how primitive they were. It was the Europeans, the Spaniards, who had brought them friction, the True Faith, and other forms of Christian civilization.

"The word friction comes from the Latin *fricare*, children," she said. "And when you rub two dry sticks or stones or bodies of certain things together, if you do it long enough and briskly enough, you produce fire. And fire is necessary for cooking and warmth."

She went on to demonstrate friction by rubbing her index fingers together. Briskly. I had seen a magician do the same thing in a movie, and it had worked. His fingers—all ten of them—went up in flames. I had tried it myself, and it hadn't worked. I knew I was no magician. I'd have to stick to matches. And now Sister Felicia was trying it herself, and it wasn't working, either. No flames. Not even sparks. So she stopped rubbing, looked around at no one, embarrassed for a few seconds, and said, "It doesn't always work, boys and girls. My hands are cold this morning." She began slapping her cold hands, as if to wipe off the failure of her friction magic. "No fire this time," she said, smiling. Then she became serious again. "Now open up your catechisms"—the Baltimore edition—"to page forty-three. Briskly, briskly." I felt letdown and confused. And she never mentioned friction again in class.

But there was another kind of friction going on in our class all the time, and Marta Cuevas, who had no answer to Sister's tough question on her repulsive nose-picking, was demonstrating it. All she could do just then was stare up at Sister—I had a good view of her attractive cannibal profile—with a paralyzed, agonized look.

"Stand up, Marta Cuevas!" Sister commanded—boomed. She could have scared the loincloth off Huracán himself.

Marta stood up as if stone-faced José Bosquez, sitting right behind her, had given her the biggest goose of her life so far—and it wasn't likely she'd be getting another one like it soon—and before Sister asked her to, she put out her hand, the right one (she knew which one was going to get it), and made a tight fist, with her thumb curled outward and wagging away like the classy-looking stump of a fancy dog's former tail. Her fingernails needed trimming, too. This kid descended from pagans had a lot to learn. With her free hand she had to hold the other hand by the wrist, because it kept shaking so much, this hand that got it, that Sister swung and missed the first and third times she took a cut at it with her ruler. Marta didn't scream, thank God. And when it was all over she just sat back down, her jaw clenched as tight as she could make it, and dropped a few tears on her opened book, a reader about a group of boys and girls, Jean and Paul, Monique and Simone, who lived in a place called Timber Town up in French Canada. From time to time Marta sneaked her right hand up to her mouth, unclenched her jaw, and blew on her knuckles. Sister pretended not to notice. She didn't even call on her the rest of the day. So in a way Marta got herself off the hook, because I don't think she had studied too

much the night before. Probably spent her homework hours reading comic books. *The Living Hulk, Wonder Woman, Heart Throb*
—enough to corrupt "an idle brain," as Sister said.

So as far as I could tell, when Sister asked a handful of us to stay
behind after class let out that day, we had violated some rule and
were going to get it, a mass purge, or "purgation," a word the
sisters liked to throw around, the way Father Rooney back in
church liked to throw around Latin things like *Dominus vobiscum*
and *Hoc est* my body and blood, before the Pope said you had to
use English in church and spoiled the whole mystery. "Gave the
whole game away, Gino," I heard one of the ushers say to another
usher in church one Sunday.

But I was wrong about Sister's intentions. "We're going to
purchase your First Communion outfits, boys and girls," Sister
Felicia told us. Now she was smiling. A fine smile, too. They took
good care of their teeth in that order. And all we could do was look
at each other in wonder. First they hit you and make certain embarrassing hints about your family habits and your man-eating ancestors, and then they treat you to a free purchase of clothes. The
whole bunch of us had a lot to learn about these women, and a lot
to be grateful for as well. Not that we had much choice, but
still . . .

Six boys and girls and two nuns. One of the girls was Marta
Cuevas, who wasn't crying anymore or bringing her fingers anywhere near her nose, no sign on her face that she'd been "purgat-
ed" that very morning in front of the public. We split up as soon
as we hit the first Marqueta stall on 110th and Park, where a
pandemonium of merchants sold a mixed bag of merchandise:
tropical products (mostly starchy tubers), religious articles (plastic
and plaster statuettes and badly reproduced prints of wonder-work-
ing saints), "botanical" herbs with healing properties (Mami had a
few back home, but they never healed anything from what I could
tell; they just smelled up the house), voodoo pamphlets and recipes,
evil-looking effigies with stringy hair, and charms for secret rituals
of one kind or another. But that was only a fraction of the merchandise you could buy in those stalls. There was an immense assortment of private wear, too, most of it for women and girls: girdles,
brassieres, skirts, blouses, panties; nylon stockings in every possible
shade; slippers, plain or with bright-colored pompons over the toes;

bathing suits, one-piece outfits for girls of all ages, or for women who could still fit into a girl's size and didn't mind looking like a case of arrested development; teenage girls' "jumpers"; widows' black shawls, chintzy mantillas for that special Spanish look, happily married women's polka-dot neckerchiefs, headkerchiefs of all kinds and colors; and a lot of other stuff, including smoked, boiled, and uncooked pork.

One of the stands we passed was displaying the close-shaved head of a pig with bent ears that had lost their pink—maybe it was embalmed to retard spoilage. It was wearing a sailor's cap on a slant, a pair of smoked glasses, and a red bow tie, and in its mouth the owner had stuck a half-smoked cigar, the long, thin panatela type. On the cap the embalmer had pinned a message in red: "Eat Me, Im' Delishious." Moses would have passed out.

"That man can't spell," said Sister Felicia, and turned her head away. The rest of her train, three boys, followed her timidly, no smiles. I was feeling a little snobbish about that man's lousy spelling. Here was a grown man, probably the father of half a dozen or more, and he didn't know where to put his apostrophe. This was the kind of father who handed down his ignorance to his children, and then they would pass it on to theirs and drive women like Sister Felicia out of their minds. She was looking mad, too, but under control, tolerant, long-suffering. And she was leading us through the mobs of shoppers at a fast clip. A lot of them, mostly mothers and their kids, made way for us when they saw her coming toward them with that long-suffering, angry look on her face. Their own surprised faces would turn serious all of a sudden, and they'd step out of our way and follow us with frightened eyes. Nobody was going to mess with us as long as we stuck close to her, this woman who was going to spend money on us even though the Sisters of Misericordia were always on a tight budget.

They carried all their funds for the day in a little black purse made of leather, or something that looked just like leather, with a silver-looking snap at the top; they kept it inside their plackets, the mysterious innards of their long plain gowns, and they always cast a cautious scan around them whenever they reached inside the placket for the purse. You could never tell who was a thief. One of the boys in my class had sneaked back inside the classroom once during lunch hour and stolen a red-and-white magnet she had confiscated from another student, who had been applying it to the head of the girl sitting in front of him. His excuse, when sister caught him, was that he had been looking for lice in that girl's hair. He found a few, too, he said, but that didn't get him off the hook. And the other one, the one who sneaked upstairs and stole the magnet, was caught by Sister Mary Monitor, as we called whichever nun was guarding the stairs that day. They made him bring in his parents next day for a good dressing-down—all three of them were dressed down—and if the parents hadn't apologized with all their might, their son would have been expelled, exiled to public school, which as we saw it was as close as you could come to perdition before actually dying with all your sins unconfessed. "Let that be a lesson," Sister Felicia had told the rest of us, just in case we had missed the point. We hadn't.

Now she was smiling away as everyone in the Marqueta made way for us. She was a fast walker, almost as if she were running to catch the New York Central, which was rumbling right over our heads: The market stalls were inside the arcade beneath the elevated railroad tracks, and I was always afraid one of those trains, crammed with well-dressed passengers headed for their homes in the country, would come crashing down through the ceiling of those stalls and destroy everyone in the place. A good headline for *El Diario,* worse than the Lisbon earthquake we had read about already.

With that peril rumbling overhead, I couldn't understand why Sister was all smiles all of a sudden, as if she were actually enjoying the sight of all that Marqueta merchandise. "It's all chit, man," one of the two boys I was with said. "Right?"

"That's *your* opinion, Almendras," I said. (During school hours we were all on a last-name basis, and as far as I was concerned, we were still in school just then.)

"So what's wrong with *your* opinion?" Almendras said.

"My mother shops here," I said. "Every Saturday."

"And you come with her, right?"

"Yeah, so what?"

"Nothing."

I knew what he was getting at, but with Sister right there I couldn't start anything. She wasn't speaking to anyone until we got to the stall she wanted.

"I want," she told Don Jorge Mercado, who specialized in ceremonial outfits, "three white shirts for these three boys, three red ties, three red armbands, the First Communion kind, three pairs of white socks, and three tie clasps with a cross, if you have them. If you don't have them with a cross, please tell me who does. We're in a hurry." Just like that. Brisk, no nonsense, always in character.

"Absolutelymente, Sister," said Don Jorge. What kind of answer was that? I thought he was avoiding her question about the three crucifixion clasps. I knew that at least one other merchant had them: Doña Dolores Flores of the Flores Botánica establishment on Park Avenue, a short walk away. Doña Flores, a widow without dependents, sold odds and ends on the side, almost like contraband; but Don Jorge wasn't about to put in a good word for one of his competitors, not even for the benefit of a nun. He had an extended family to feed.

He squatted behind his high counter for a few seconds, disappeared completely, and then reappeared with a big grin and a nine-by-twelve box full of those First Communion tie clasps. It was like looking at a large collection of dead grasshoppers. He sifted through the collection and picked three out in a showy, meticulous way, as if only the very best dried grasshoppers would do for Sister Felicia and her three timid charges. Then, like a master magician, still grinning away, he held them up for her inspection and approval.

She nodded, unsmiling, as if she could expect no better from a swindler of his sort. "We'll take them."

"They all come out of the same mother hopper, Malánguez," Almendras whispered in my ear. "Spooky." I gave him a little kick on the ankle to shut him up. His sarcasm might end up getting us in trouble with Sister.

". . . shirts," she was telling Don Jorge.

"What's your neck size, boys?" Don Jorge asked us.

Almendras and our other companion had no trouble telling him, and he pulled the same vanishing act behind the counter and came up with two identical-looking First Communion shirts and three red ties with a clasp at the back and a ready-made knot.

"Those came out of the same mother too," Almendras whispered to me. This time I ignored him. His type eventually got into trouble with the law and all kinds of authorities, because he couldn't take anything serious seriously.

"And what's your neck size, young man?" Sister asked me. I knew she would. I didn't know my neck size. Mami always took care of that. She had it written down somewhere in the house, along with my shoe size, my waist, the number and kind of vaccinations I'd already had, and when, what other vaccinations I still had coming to me, and other vital statistics and records. And now, because I hadn't bothered to check any of that out, I was about to get into trouble with Sister, and to suffer a humiliation in front of my two classmates and Don Jorge the First Communion magician. And if all those shoppers around us got wind of my ignorance, I'd just have to live with the humiliation. I turned red while she and Don Jorge and the other two charges waited for my answer. This was turning into a test of my intelligence.

"Well, Mr. Malánguezzz?" she hissed, losing patience. She had things to do back at the nunnery.

"I am not sure, Seester," I said, finally.

She couldn't believe it. "Do you mean to tell me, Ssantosss Malánguezzz, that you still don't know your own neck size?" Don Jorge and the other two charges chuckled. The merchant in the next stall was grinning.

"I think it is a fifteen and a half, Seester," I said. That was Papi's neck size. He kept it and other sizes written down in a little memo notebook inside our dining-room closet. I'd peeked into it. I knew his sizes better than mine.

"Fifteen and a half?" Sister said. "That's impossible. I'm almost tempted to suspect you of lying, young man. Just look at your neck." I tried but I couldn't. "You're not a fifteen and a half. You're more like a *five* and a half. Isn't that what you meant?" She was trying to save face for me in front of Don Jorge and the others; so I nodded. Don Jorge was still smiling; so was the other merchant, and Almendras, and the other charge, someone named Macario something. I couldn't remember his last name just then. I didn't want to.

"That is okay, Sister," Don Jorge cut in. "I take care of it no trouble. I know from the experience long the sizes right." He disappeared behind the counter again and came up with a tape measure. It was long and yellow, a huge tapeworm that looked to be coming apart from years of use; so maybe I wasn't the only ignorant customer Don Jorge had ever had. "Here, Sister," he said, "you take the size from the neck of my friend Malánguez over here, and I will pull out for him the shirt. I will bet to you that it is a six, no?"

"I don't gamble, Mr. Mercado," she said, frowning at his familiarity, and took the tape measure from him with a look of disgust.

"Anyway, Sister," he went on, "if Jorge Mercado is wrong, he will give to you a free cruficixion claps. And if you are the one who is all wrong, I don't charge extra."

"It's cruci-fix, Mr. Mercado," she corrected. "And clasp. Claps is a verb, sir. Third person singular."

"That is what I say, Sister," he said, winking at the rest of us. I didn't like people pulling our nuns' legs, and pretended not to understand his prank.

She ringed the tapeworm around my neck and stooped to squint at the answer. For a second there I thought she might decide to choke me with that thing, and just then I couldn't blame her. "It's more than five and a half and less than six," she told Don Jorge, changing her mind about choking me.

"What kind of size that is?" Almendras asked Macario Something. His own neck was fat, too much starch in his diet. Rice and beans for breakfast, lunch, and dinner. He was one of those who went home for lunch and missed out on the peanut butter sandwiches, cold macaroni and cheese, and green apples the rest of us were treated to most of the time.

"I don't split the hairs," Don Jorge was telling Sister. "I will give to you one free cruficixion for the tie."

"As you wish," she told him, unsmiling. But I think she was pleased by his generosity; and he for his part was ensuring himself of more First Communion business from her and the other nuns. A shrewd merchant.

The other items Sister bought us—the red-ribbon armband, the white socks, the belts with the cardboard lining—were no problem. The socks were the nylon stretch-hose type, the armbands, like the knotted ties, were all the same size, and the tape measure took care of our waists. We measured those ourselves.

The complete purchase must have come to over fifteen dollars, a lot of money to be spending on us. She pulled her purse out of her placket and pulled two fives and a ten out of the purse and handed them to Don Jorge, who gave her her change back, while Almendras, Macario, and I looked at each other in amazement: all that money changing hands for our benefit.

"Come back again fast, Seester," Don Jorge said, handing her three boxes, each box neatly tied with blue string.

She thanked him, he thanked her back and said any time, and then she told him she'd see him next day at the same time. "I have six other boys just like these three," she said, making us sound like her sons, and probably thinking of us as sons of a sort.

She handed each of us his gift box. My hands were shaking and I dropped mine, right there on the dirty Marqueta floor, among crushed vegetables and all kinds of garbage. She didn't say anything; nobody did. She just stood over me, looking down at me, while I stooped and quickly picked up the box. I was afraid to look her in the eye, and didn't. The ground was the only place fit for my stare just then. And she didn't say a thing to me, to any of us, on our way to the exit, or out on the street; nor did we say anything to her or to each other—a very solemn exit—until we got to the corner of 107th and Park, where I was going to make a right turn toward my block.

"Get your correct suit size and shoe size from your mother, Santos Malánguez," she told me.

"Yes, Seester," I said. Another surprise coming. I was afraid to ask her why, but I could guess.

"You too, Almendras," she said. "And you, Macario Iglesias." So that was his last name. Macario "Churches," in translation. A future priest, it turned out.

Almendras couldn't control himself. "For why, Sister?"

"You mean *what for,* young man." A stickler for correctness. "Because we're not finished shopping for your outfits. This was only the first stage of our purchase. Next week we shop for suits and shoes." No comment, only looks of additional amazement exchanged by Almendras, Iglesias, and Malánguez.

"Well, Malánguez," she said, "take good care of that outfit. You'll look fine in it, I'm sure. Don't dawdle on the way home." They actually used words like that. Sometimes they even said "tarry." "And don't be tardy for Mass tomorrow morning."

Of course not. When had I ever been? She knew I knew what was good for me. I told her I wouldn't be, and thanked her for Part One of the outfit.

"You're welcome. And don't forget to ask your mother for those *sizes.*" Now she was rubbing it in about my neck again. I said I wouldn't, and made a quick turn toward my block, forgetting to say goodbye to Almendras and Iglesias, who would be walking with her for a couple more blocks. Her bodyguards, though she didn't need any protection. Nobody started trouble with our nuns, at least not before the drug pushers and their customers entered our neighborhood like that great Medieval plague she had told us about during our history period.

I didn't dawdle on the way home, either. I double-timed it there, just in case some thief spotted me; and I ran up the stairs to our fifth-story apartment feeling like a thief myself. Taking gifts from anyone outside our family made me feel dishonest.

"*Pues,*" Mami told me, suspicious, "if she gave you all this, I guess you'll have to keep it." I never doubted that. "Put it away in your bureau." I did, right away. I would have locked it up in there, just in case, if I'd had a lock.

And it was only much later, long after dinner and most of my homework for that night, that I told her and Papi about Stage Two of that First Communion outfit. I broke it to them timidly, almost as if it had been my fault. Maybe it was. I had no idea why, except that I was timid in school (I was timid everywhere, in fact) and that my English, broken and mispronounced, was a disgraceful version of the real thing, the one Sister Felicia and her fellow nuns threw around the way they were throwing their money away on some of us. Shyness and poor English were unmistakable signs of someone who needed to have his outfit bought for him. That was my explanation of Sister's charity. But I kept it to myself.

Papi and Mami kept it to themselves too, for a couple of minutes after I asked Mami for those sizes Sister wanted. "I'm not telling anybody," she said, looking depressed. In a minute she'd be calling down her favorite saints and asking them to explain just what it was she had done to deserve this.

"You have to tell him, Lilia," Papi said, trying to keep his cool.

"*You* tell him, then," she said.

"If I knew his sizes, I would."

"What kind of father are you that you don't know what size shoes your own son wears?"

"I guess I'm irresponsible," he said. I think he was being sarcastic. It was hard to tell; there was no emotion in his voice.

"I guess you are, Gerán." She wasn't going to let up on him too quickly.

"But I'm going to reform my ways. Right now. Santos, take off your right shoe." He gave me a big serious nod. No nonsense.

"Why that one?" I said. I had a hole in my right-foot sock. The big toe of that foot was always twitching and boring holes into whatever socks it got hold of. Mami, who was getting a little tired of patching up those abused socks, had threatened to tie the guilty toe to its neighbor, the "index" toe, as a way of holding it down.

"That's right, why that one?" Mami said, keeping up her aggression.

"All right, take off the left one, then," he said. "One foot is as good as the other in this house."

Mami got up and left to go do something in the bedroom. Whenever she did that abruptly, it was either a sign of defeat or else a temporary withdrawal so she could come up with a new strategy in peace. And I had lost my ally.

I took off my left shoe and handed it to Papi, who had put on his telescopic eyeglasses for a good squint.

"I can't find the size, Santos. Where is it?" I could have saved him the trouble.

"I don't know, Papi. It was there when I looked for it. Yesterday."

"It wasn't there this morning?"

"I didn't look this morning."

"Why not?" I didn't have an answer to that one. Then he sat back, held the suspicious shoe at arm's length, and inflicted a careful inspection on it. "It's not only the odor," he said in Spanish. "Foh. It's also the condition it's in." And then, training his look on me through those gruesome spectacles he couldn't do without, he said. "Is that why you didn't want to show to me the right one?"

"I don't know what you are talking, Papi." I didn't.

"Because the other one is in a more bad condition. That is what

I am talking, my son." English again. We could get confused sometimes.

And I didn't want to tell him about the hole in my sock, about my twitching big toe, and about what Mami had threatened if I didn't cut it out; so I nodded, and he said it figured (in Spanish). "So there's no sense inspecting that one for the size of your foot, is there?" I said no, there wasn't. "Maybe a mouse stole it last night," he said in Spanish. "When you was sleeping." That came out in English. He handed the shoe back to me, and began laughing to himself. There was no malice in it that I could see, but I couldn't help feeling hurt, and instead of laughing with him—if I could have joined in, I would have—I shoved my left foot back inside its abused shoe and, without bothering to lace it, got up and went back to my own room, where I forced myself, a little less than happy, to finish Sister Felicia's homework for that day. While I was memorizing a couple of things that Saint Augustine supposedly had said (this was for Catechism), I could hear him and Mami having a serious exchange in their bedroom. Since my bedroom door was shut (homework was a very private task, secret as well as sacred), I couldn't make out what they were telling each other; but I picked up enough snatches to conclude, undoubtfully, that what they were discussing, in their own privacy, and in such a serious tone of voice, was me and my First Communion outfit. And Sister, too. Her name kept coming up in their dialogue. From their tone, I could tell for certain that they weren't too happy with the charity she had imposed on me—on the three of us—and the unintended insult that came with the package.

"This time *you* tell him," Mami was telling him, her voice a little higher than her normal.

"*Muy bien,*" he said. They never spoke English to each other. It would have been insulting, almost unforgivable, pretentious, in bad taste.

He came into my room, after knocking twice, to tell me that he and Mami, upon careful consideration, had decided against accepting more gifts from Sister Felicia, "or any Sister in that school, Santos, because we have the money, and if we didn't have it, we would find it. I think there was a misunderstanding."

"So why you don't write her a note?" I said. I was ready to rip out a clean sheet from my notebook and hand it to him, along with my combination fountain-pen-retractable-pencil (a recent present from him, bought at Kresge's, first day of classes; he had taken off from work that morning to accompany me because I'd been too nervous to stand up straight, and Mami had come down with a September virus, not for the first time).

"Because she doesn't understand Spanish, and my English is— imperfect."

"So I help you with the spelling."

"Is more than the spelling, Santos," he said, smiling. "Is also the *gramática* and the commas." Something I had trouble with myself. "I will take off from the job tomorrow morning and tell to her."

We went to church together next morning. He was dressed up in his best, which wasn't all that hot: a gray suit that made him look too solemn for my taste, and Mami's, but he insisted it was the right color for formal occasions and confrontations; and what was this private interview with Sister Felicia if not a formal occasion, as well as a confrontation of some kind? So gray suit it was. Gray suit, and tie (gray too, with blue stripes), a freshly laundered white shirt (courtesy of Mami, who mixed her own starch) with button-down collar, so the points wouldn't pop up perversely and embarrass him, as had happened, highly polished black shoes with formal-looking round tips, and matching cotton socks. (He had contempt for flammable nylon. "I don't want my feet catching on fire," he used to say.)

He talked to Sister, in his own timid, formal way, just before Mass got going, and after I went to sit with my class in our designated section (between the eighth and eleventh Stations of the Cross), so I had no way of overhearing their confidential exchange. I hoped he wouldn't say anything that would get me into trouble with Sister, and I hoped his English held up so she wouldn't feel scornful of him, and of me in connection, and get the impression that he himself could use a change of outfit. He did, too, as I saw it; that gray suit was embarrassing me. If Almendras said anything even slightly sarcastic about it, two of us were going to get it good for fighting like public-school savages. But he didn't. He knew his limits, up to a point.

"I'll see you at six," Papi told me right after Mass let out. He had sat through it, in the back, with other adults, on the side that adjoined the nunnery. We were already forming a double line, which meant no talking, so I couldn't ask him whether she had accepted his refusal. But he was smiling, so it must have gone well.

"Your father," Sister told me in class before we sat down to work, "has decided to buy you the rest of the First Communion outfit himself, Malánguez. I guess you knew that." I nodded. If she thought I was responsible for this setback, she didn't say, and I wasn't about to ask her.

"Why your father turn down Sister's outfit, Malánguez?" Almendras asked me after lunch.

"He got a big pay raise," I said. I didn't have to tell him the truth. "Mind your own business."

"So what?"

"So nothing."

"So suit yourself, if you want to talk like that."

"Okay. I suit myself."

Euclides Cruz got the shoes and suit I'd had coming to me.

You couldn't tell the charity cases from those boys and girls whose parents had paid for their outfits, or signed the credit agreement. Some sixty of us boys sat on the right-hand side of the center pews (best seats in the House); girls, more of them than of us, on the left. A traditional arrangement. Everything was prescribed, nothing left to impulse or accident. We boys were in black, with the red arm ribbon and the red tie. Each one of us had a new black missal and a matching rosary; the Sisters had passed them out to us outside the church, as soon as we lined up in double file. And the girls were wearing the same white dress, the same white imitation-lace mantilla, the same white shoes, knee-length stockings, and gloves that came halfway up their arms. They also had white plastic purses on leashes looped around their arms, white missals, and white rosaries, and instead of an arm ribbon they were holding a bouquet of artificial flowers. I thought they looked better than we did. They always did anyway, even when they were wearing hand-me-downs. Clean human beings—that's what they were—always neat. They took pains with themselves. They had better "characters" than the boys. ("Character" was a big word at our school.)

Every boy had a fresh haircut—standing room only at my barber's the day before, and he had a couple of fast-working assistants, too—slicked-back hair, most of it black except for some of the Irish students, whose genes were different; some of them even had freckles that matched their arm ribbons. I was wearing patent-leather shoes. I wasn't the only one. Papi had insisted on that kind. "So they won't lose their shine, Santos." Fine with me.

"Faggots," I had heard someone call us outside on the sidewalk, while we waited for the order to march inside the church. "Girls," someone else had called us. "Mama's boys," "bunch of punks." And other put-downs of that kind. We knew who it was: the public-school barbarians. They were hiding in the crowd of parents, relatives, next-door neighbors, and people who just happened to be passing by and wanted to see what this was all about.

Under orders from Sister Felicia, we had to ignore the barbarians. "Pretend they don't exist, boys," she told us. That wasn't easy. They were always around somewhere, rubbing it in every chance they got because we were their "betters," we were told, and we believed it; and because they envied us and had to get back at us somehow. The Sisters and our parents and other sympathizers tried to shoo them away but didn't get anywhere. From behind parked cars, from across the street (in front of the Good Neighbor Protestant Church), from the overflow mob gathered on the sidewalk and spilling into the gutter, those P.S. Vandals, as Sister called them, were giving it to us good. And as long as the Sisters had us in their charge, as long as we were in a state of something called "grace," and fasting, too—starving for the Host—there was nothing we could do about it. We were a bunch of "twats" in "pretty" outfits, as our enemies called them. Envy. I couldn't wait to get inside the church, and I hoped the priests would get it over with fast so I could beat it back home in a hurry and change into normal human pants and sneakers. This wasn't my idea of the greatest event in my life since Baptism.

Our parents and guardians felt differently, though. They were actually enjoying this painful event. Otherwise why all the smiles? And those cameras. At least one pair of parents had hired a professional photographer to immortalize the whole thing for their son or daughter and for their old age. This pro, Mr. Taupiero, who had his own storefront studio on Madison Avenue, between Rudi's *butchería* and Al Arentsky's *bodega,* specialized in weddings and funerals. He was always coming in and out of churches and funeral parlors with his equipment. He also made home visits for an extra

fee and all the food and drink he could pack in. There was hardly
a bride and groom in the neighborhood who hadn't been "shot"
by him; he displayed his best portraits in his window, retouched out
of recognition, looking embalmed, so that you could be staring at
a member of your own family or at yourself and not know it. This
Mr. Taupiero was a stout, well-dressed man with a perfect mustache
(waxed, I think) and more photographic stuff than a movie set. He
had brought his colossal tripod along, and after struggling for an
open spot to set it up in, had seen it knocked over, with the camera
mounted in place. Now he was almost in tears, cursing the public-
school *"bárbaros* and *bandoleros"* in two languages and threatening to call *la policía* on them if they didn't reimburse him for his
broken camera. Just let him try catching them. He was still cursing
when we marched in twos up the steps.

Another mob scene inside, except less noise and disorder. Every
student's entire family must have been there, and some of those
families were pretty big, from suckling babies to weak grandparents
who had to be held by the hand and elbow and walked patiently
up the high church steps, steered delicately through the mob, and
squeezed carefully into the crowded pews. They had come to see
their grandsons and granddaughters receive the Host for the first
time; nothing would have kept them home. Then there were the
next-door neighbors and friends, the curious snoopers and well-
wishers, and a few hung-over crashers who were sneaking into the
back pews for a free show and a nap. There was nothing the ushers
could do with them.

"It's a free church," one of them told an usher when the usher
told him to go home and sleep it off there.

"It's free for sober Christians, Tom," the usher said.

"Who's not sober?" the wino asked. And the usher just walked
off disgusted.

Way up at the top, over the main entrance, was the Saint Misericordia Church Choir: twenty or more parishioners, about equally
divided between single men and single women, some of them
widows and widowers committed to long-term mourning, maybe
addicted to it. The others were still looking around; they had a
good view of the prospects from their loft way up there. And they
were led by a man who called himself Maestro Padilla (he also
rehearsed our entire school in choir practice every Friday). He was

an organist, too, and (his real vocation, he insisted) a pianist. He was thin and nervous, a fastidious man with a tic in the right shoulder; it would jump up unexpectedly whenever things weren't going his way. He had been trying for years to make it as a concert pianist so he could quit the church-organ circuit. During choir practice he would tell us in a raised voice, while his right shoulder was ticking away, that the only reason he was "stucked" with us in our basement auditorium (no heat, peeling walls, long benches for chairs) was because the concert halls were discriminating against him on account of his "national origins."

"On account of he's cracked, he means," one of the American Christian Brothers had told another ACB one afternoon during practice.

And the other Brother had said, seriously: "Bejesus, will you just listen to the man's playing?"

"What's wrong with it, Mick?" the other Brother had said.

"Arrah, it's not my idea of music, Jerry. I wouldn't pay him to grind me own organ on a street corner. Who does he think he is! Stuck with us in our basement, me foot."

Maestro Padilla, right or wrong, was also outspoken about his wages, which he called indecent. Our pastor, he said, was working him to the bone and paying him nothing for it. As we took our seats in the church pews, he was playing one of the four Puerto Rican national anthems, "La Borinqueña," on the huge organ, blasting the church with it, shaking statues on their pedestals. The pastor had warned him about playing unauthorized secular music there, and about pulling out all the stops except during rehearsals, when Our Lord was locked up in the tabernacle, and the key safe in the sacristan's cabinet. But Padilla couldn't care less about these regulations and threats. He was both an artist and a diehard Puerto Rican patriot, and this organ racket was his way of both proclaiming his loyalty and protesting the wages he received from the "tied-fisted pastor." But Pastor Rooney's budget was so tight that, as he used to say, "all our saints are peeling off of the walls." Not only the painted saints but the statues, too, many of which were missing vital parts. The Christ Child on Saint Christopher's back had lost one of His hands and looked as though He might slip off the saint's back any day now, and another saint, Cecilia, I think, had lost her dulcimer, or harp, or whatever that strange-looking instrument she played was called.

"That's your problem," Maestro Padilla told Father Bardoni one day, when Bardoni, the pastor's right-hand man, tried to reason with him in the matter of wages. "You take care of the peeling saints, Father, I take care of the sacred music, and if I don't get a raise soon, I am going to complain to the Office of the Commonwealth of my country. I have connections with them." His cousin's sister-in-law was a secretary there, he once told Papi. "But keep it to yourself, Don Malánguez."

How could Papi keep it to himself? He told Mami and me right away. "I wish he *would* complain," Mami said. "I wish they'd raise his salary, so we can have some peace in that church."

"I don't think that connection of his is going to do him much good," Papi said. "Even Saint Anthony's better connected than that cousin of nobody."

"What do you mean *even* Saint Anthony?" She was a big fan of Saint Anthony's. Mami and Papi used to sit in one of the pews next to that saint's statue (the bunch of lilies he was holding in one hand needed replastering). That was where they were sitting now, in the back under the balcony, where Padilla's organ was less loud.

They were lost in a mob of well-groomed parents and others who looked as though they'd been put through the same dry-cleaning machine. The two of them had given me a quick kiss on the cheek and a couple of tight hand-squeezes when Sister Mary Principal flounced up to our group in her two-ton uniform and, putting her thumb to one of those metallic hand-crickets that every nun owned, signaled us with hand gestures and eye movements to proceed to our assigned seats. "With all due haste and decorum," she added, as if she needed to. Papi and Mami looked around them, bewildered, when the mob split up and scrambled for the best pews in the House.

I ended up sitting by the aisle, next to a spoiled classmate named Dom Silvestro Grippe, Jr. He was the only one in our class who called himself by three names, plus the Junior, as if his father was someone important. He got the "Dom" from his grandfather, a bricklayer who had come over from somewhere in Europe; and his late father, the original Silvestro, had been into something Grippe called "heavy construction." Dom Silvestro, Jr., was a pretty good example of heavy construction himself. He was so overweight that sometimes, just by looking at him, I'd lose my appetite. In our lunchroom the students called him cruel names, like Dom Grippe Leftovers or the Garbage Machine, and would offer him whatever leftovers they couldn't stomach themselves, preferring to fast till three. Sometimes they collected apple cores, dozens of them, and offered them to him on a platter. He'd throw them back in their faces. For all the heavy doses of religious instruction and discipline we received, we still had a pecking order; and Grippe, with all his weight and compulsive scrounging and scavenging, was our patsy, a martyr to his bottomless stomach.

He was sitting next to me in our packed pew, breathing heavily and staring straight up at the altar festooned with flowers and candles; and from the balcony, right above Mami and Papi and Saint Anthony, his mother was spying him and me out through a pair of heavyweight binoculars, as if this were the opera or the racetrack and we "first-timers" a troupe of overdressed midgets or jockeys. As a one-year widow, she was still dressed in black, head to toe, and the binoculars (also black) were looped around her neck, along with a huge gold medal that looked like a cymbal and flashed like a sunburst when the light caught it.

I don't think the Sisters were crazy about her. She pampered her son, overfed him, made all kinds of excuses for his absences, which were frequent and therefore, in Sister Felicia's opinion, "abusive"; he was always coming down with something, if his mother was telling Sister the truth. "And it can all be blamed on his stomach," I heard Sister tell one of the other nuns one day. "What that boy needs is a gag around his mouth."

"Or a zipper," said the other Sister.

I'd never heard that expression before, and spent a lot of time imagining zippers around Grippe's mouth. None of them fit. It was a capacious mouth, and sad-looking, when you came down to it. After all, he was a half-orphan already, with a mother who would probably go through life wearing those morbid-looking black dresses and dangling those heavyweight binoculars from her three-ring neck. And overfeeding her only son, her only flesh-and-blood possession, it looked like, because I don't think they had any relatives in this country. (Not that Papi and Mami and I had much to brag about on that score.)

But I wished she'd take those binoculars off my immediate area. I was feeling self-conscious enough to begin with, a semi-charity case in an outfit that the barbarians outside had called a "faggot fashion show." I didn't need in addition Mrs. Grippe's close-up inspection, or any comparisons with her dolled-up son, who was already sweating away to the left of me, sucking up all the scarce oxygen in our vicinity and expelling it in the form of what Sister had once labeled halitosis—one of those big words that stuck in my mind. I wrote it down in my spelling notebook as "holytoses." *Tos:* Spanish for cough. I thought she was referring to one of his frequent, "abusive" absences, and spelled it after my own misconception. But why the "holy" before "toses"? Mami and Papi said they hadn't the scarcest idea. They'd never heard of a cough like that; maybe it was some kind of Italian whooping cough, thought Papi. *"Tos ferina,* Santos."

Whatever it was, I didn't want to catch it, but since I was sitting next to the carrier in our assigned First Communion pews, I had no choice but to hold my breath as much as possible and not turn my mouth and nose his way, in the hope that whenever one of those holytoses germs happened to be coming in my direction, I'd be letting out my own breath, or holding it.

Dom Silvestro, Jr., wasn't what my family called a "considerate human being"; he was more like what Sister Felicia had once labeled a "regardless type," talking about another student who had coughed in a girl's face, and to whose parents she had written a special note: "Please buy Francisco a bottle of Father John's Cough Syrup and a jar of Vick's Vapo-Rub. Put two tablespoons of this medicated ointment in a bowl of boiling water and have your son inhale it. (See the jar label for details on this.) It is effective. Otherwise Francisco may cause an epidemic in our class, and there will be many absences. And please teach him not to cough in other students' faces. It is not very polite." It was regardless.

Grippe's mother had received several such notes herself.

"Did Sister Felicha purchase that First Communion outfit for you, Malánguess?" Dom Silvestro asked me, just as I was inhaling. He had turned his mouth right up close to my nose.

I held my breath and kicked his fat foot, and told him, without exhaling, that it was none of his business. "What the hell's it to you, Grippe?"

"Hey, hey," he said, "you can't curse in here. This is the House of God. Now you can't receive, Malánguess."

"What you talking about, Grippe?" I kept my voice down to a whisper, beginning to feel the panic waking up somewhere in the tail of my spine. "Who says I can't receive?"

"I say," he said.

"Why not?"

"Because you just cursed."

"So mind your business."

"If you receive, I'm gonna tell Sister Felicha."

"Yeah? You tell her and I'm gonna get you right after this is over. Me and Almendras. We're gonna jump you outside. Kick your big ass, Grippe."

"Yeah?" he said, swarming my face with germs. "A whole bunch of my father's friends is in here. They're all over the place. And they got a piece in their pockets. With bullets, Malánguess. You and Almendras try anything with me, you ain't gonna receive no more Hosts in your life. You know what I'm talking about?"

Not quite, but I knew better than to mess with more than one Italian at a time, especially grown-up Italians, whose looks were always serious. So I cooled it with Grippe right there.

"Do me a big favor, Dom," I said, pulling out his first name for the first and last time in my life.

"Yeah? What you want now, Malánguess?" He wasn't about to return the familiarity.

"Don't squeal on me and I won't tell Sister you was talking in church."

"You're nobody to talk yourself, Malánguess."

"If I don't receive the Host," I said, "my father and mother's gonna kill me."

"Good," he said, to which I had nothing to add.

I was despising myself for coming on so abjectly, but this menace on my left wasn't giving me anything like a choice. He thought about it, with his face generously turned away from mine, and while his mother kept her binoculars trained on us.

"I'll give you a break this time, Malánguess," he finally told me, turning his germs loose on me again.

I thanked him, and actually felt grateful for a minute or two before going back to despising the "stoolie," as I put it to myself.

A holytoses carrier, too. It figured. And now, through this degener-
ate specimen sitting on my left, they were trying to infect my people
with it, through me. On top of committing the sin of cursing in
church, I was committing the more serious one of self-righteous-
ness. But I let it slide.

During this exchange, Maestro Padilla had been booming his
idea of music down on us: a combination of sacred sounds, the
strictly prescribed stuff, with intermezzos of all four Puerto Rican
national anthems, which I had no doubt was endangering his immortal soul, and possibly the soul of his number one enemy, Pastor
Rooney, who was officiating with two other priests up at the altar
and probably cursing the choirmaster under his breath in between
snatches of Latin. The choir of men and women who had lost their
spouses, or who had still to find them, was doing its best to be heard
above his irreligious blitz. But it was an unequal contest. Their own
instruments were only vocal cords, many of them damaged from
abuses of one sort or another, including, in at least three cases I
knew of, chain-smoking.

And then, like something made for a pedestal, the looming
apparition of Sister Felicia herself, staring down at me and Grippe,
but mostly at me because I was closer to her.

She was standing there at right angles to me, with the metal
cricket in her hand, thumb at the ready. If she squeezed its belly
it would go off, clic-cloc, and attract everybody's attention, hundreds of eyes—possibly a thousand, the House was that packed.

She was huffing down at me, damning me through her nose, and
ignoring Grippe, who had started it; and she was trying to make me
dislike myself. It was working. As if on orders from her, sweat
started working its way into the corners of my eyes and stinging
them. She was close enough for me to smell her breath. A sweet
odor. Pez. Papi used to chew the stuff himself, when he was off the
Tums. I knew she carried a roll of them in her private placket. It
wasn't all money in there.

She bent down in a swoop and said, right into my ear, "Ssantoss
Malánguezzz!" At least four esses and three zees. "I am going to
talk to you tomorrow morning, mark my word. For talking in
church. Do you hear me?" I nodded at Father Rooney and his
partners and the four altar boys who were helping them out. This
was a fancy Mass.

My nodding sprayed some sweat on Grippe's First Communion ribbon, a classy-looking one. His head jerked in my direction, caught itself halfway, and jerked back to starting position; then he wiped his sleeve and ribbon in a snobbish, show-off fashion, so Sister and his mother could both see what a slob I was. His father's associates must have seen it too. But at that point, whatever menace they represented couldn't have been as terrible as Sister, who had the whole Church behind her, right back to Saint Peter and his Rock. Though you could never tell how far Grippe's bodyguards went themselves. Heavy construction must have gone back a long ways.

Some of that same sweat had sprayed Sister's uniform; she either didn't notice or she was ignoring it for the time being. I'd find out first thing tomorrow morning. Right now I was self-consciously swiping a couple of telltale blotches off my missal. "If you ever talk in church again," she said, squinting down at me, "I myself will escort you outside in front of everyone, and—"

The end of her sentence was cut short by the altar boy in charge of the tintinnabulations. As if she had suddenly lost the lower half of her legs, she dropped to her knees—we all did—and bowed her covered head, joined her hands in the prescribed arch, tips of fingers touching chin, just like the rest of us, and kept that pose while Father Rooney up front held the chalice over his head and turned burgundy to blood with the magic of Latin. Then he repeated the razzle-dazzle with the "unlivened" wafers, and the tintinnabulator went into a fit of ring-a-lings, as if the spirit of Saint Vitus had entered him; and the rest of us in the pews, and Sister in the nave, stared down at the ground, having ourselves a good dose of awe and other important emotions. Even Padilla's organ was behaving itself during this mysterious thing called transubstantiation, another one of those big words that somehow seemed to illustrate the thing it was talking about.

Then Father Rooney lowered the cup called a ciborium, and the altar boy with the bells shook them again to inform us that the tasteless wafers had been turned by Padilla's number one enemy into Our Savior's flesh, fit for human consumption. Some of us cannibals back in the pews couldn't wait to get our teeth into Him.

"You're not supposed to chew It," Sister had told us repeatedly. Almendras had wanted to know why not. "Because you're sup-

posed to let It dissolve. If It sticks to your palate, don't stick your
fingers in your mouths. It's a sin to touch It. Just leave It alone."
And other admonitions like that, plus a disappointing description
of It as being tasteless, "so don't stick out your tongues expecting
to taste jam on toast. It is unleavened."

And Almendras the curious had asked her, "What is unlivened,
Sister?"

"You'll find out, Mr. Almendras," she said. "If you behave
yourself and make a clean confession"—meaning by that a sincere
one. No lies and no omissions. Every penny we'd stolen from our
mothers had to come out, whispered in Father Confessor's neutral
ear, in order to qualify ourselves for the Eucharist.

"The Real Presence," she had called it during our First Communion rehearsals, confusing every boy and girl in our classroom.
She also called it "the Eucharistic banquet" (which Almendras later
twisted into "You carry this blanket, man"), the "mystical body,"
the "sacrament of charity," the "central sacrament," the "source of
grace," the "gift of His body," the "abiding presence," the "consecrated species," and the "sacramental dispensation." She told us,
"His body broken and torn is why the priest breaks the bread into
pieces," and other explanations and strange new Catholic words
that had everyone in class confused. Our "spiritual vocabulary," as
she sometimes called these new words, was catching up with our
"profane" one, which I took to mean our dirty one.

She never got around to explaining the difference between a
"real" presence and a fake one. We had to take her word for all
sorts of things, so this mysterious presence was nothing new. "You
have to take some things on faith," was one of her common injunc-
tions.

We had to take a lot of things on faith, except for doubting types
like Almendras, who wouldn't take his own mother's word for
anything. "My mother, I don't think she know too good what she
is always talking," he once told me. "Keep this secret to yourself,
Malánguez." He didn't have to worry. It had something to do with
his unvarying lunch of rice and beans, and why his mother wouldn't
pack it up in a container for him, like some other mothers, so he
could eat with the rest of us in our lunchroom.

He was sitting three pews behind mine, and when I snapped my
head over my shoulder to see what he was up to, I was pinched hard

just above the crook of my elbow, a tender spot without any muscle
to speak of. It was Sister again; she had sneaked up to my right arm,
which was dangling over the armrest, and brought me to painful
attention in no time. I held back the scream I was entitled to, and
fixed my eyes on the well-shaved neck in front of me.

"I'll talk to you in class tomorrow morning, Malánguezzz," she
whispered. Right into my ear. Those three zees again: a bad omen.
"Take-home punish lessons" coming up. A "castigation," it was
called . . . something about my barbaric behavior in church . . . no
defense from Papi and Mami, who also took some things on faith,
so there was nothing to discuss. "Just do what she says, Santos. And
don't do it again, whatever it was you did."

From that pinch on, the rest of the Mass was a letdown. Things
blurred: lights, flowers, linen altar cloth, priests' bright vestments,
peeling murals and flaking statues of everybody's favorite saints,
some of them dubious; and the entire community of faithfuls and
hangers-on packed into those mahogany pews with scrollwork
armrests. Sounds turned to stew. There was Father Rooney's falset-
to Latin with a little sinus condition thrown in ("Hoc est my locos-
pocus, my viva voce, my pro et con . . ."), and Padilla's profane
artillery shelling the place. Then the Sisters' crickets jumped in.
About a dozen of them went off at the same time: clic-cloc-clic-cloc.
An attack of grasshoppers, the signal for us to get off our knees and
go get It, the "mystical body," the "unlivened Host" Almendras
had been talking about.

With Dom Grippe breathing toses behind me ("Get up, Malánguess—this is it, man. Even though you cursed in church"), and
his mother's binoculars trained on me, just in case I was thinking
of pulling any "Portorican" stunts on her son, I got to my feet and
faced the girl across the aisle—who was biting her lip, either out
of nervousness or in expectation—and waited for the next clic-cloc
of Sister's grasshopper. Every pew was a platoon of ten, and if you
were one of the unluckies who had landed the aisle position, you
were automatically the leader of nine others; no backing out. I'd
never led anything in my life and I didn't like this, except for being
ahead of Grippe, who was probably disliking me for my "luck."

The trouble was that you had to look good in front of all those
"foreigners"; otherwise they'd start buzzing to each other about
"that little P.R. over there who can't even walk a straight line to

the abiding presence. He must have got grogged first thing he gets up this morning . . . can of six-pack in a little brown bag . . . keeps Rheingold and Schaefer in business . . . a sin to receive in that state . . . eighty-proof mouthwash . . . I hear they even wash their hair in it. . . ." And my father and mother, sitting back there next to Saint Anthony and his lilies, would feel horrible about themselves, and about their son, the cause of it all.

So I watched my step; and when Sister let go with her cricket and gave me the nod (along with a menacing squint), I stepped out of my pew on tiptoes, looking (I hoped) like a self-important honors student going up to collect his big golden pin or plaque for straight A's and no absences.

I made it up to the Communion railing without tripping over myself. It was a long slow walk, halting half-steps all the way, as if we'd sprained our ankles to qualify for the You-carry-this-blanket. I hit a bump when I got to where the central aisle of the nave ran into another aisle called the "crossing" (all these symbols of what this House was all about didn't help out my nerves). This happened a few feet from the railing, but it wasn't all my fault; I knew a loose floorboard when I stepped on one, even if it was hidden by a Catholic rug with symbolic designs all over it. A couple of other first-time receivers ahead of me had also stepped on it and had given a start as if the rug had teeth in it. It was like a trap set there to catch daydreamers, or anyone who'd cursed before receiving, or held back a couple of "grievous" sins at Confession, cold-feet types who'd go through life lying to Fathers Confessor about how many pennies they'd really stolen from their mothers, while the poor woman was tied up in the kitchen, tending the pot of this and that with hacked codfish and oregano, unaware that she had given birth to a crook who was depleting the family's tight budget and stealing confiscated magnets from Sister's desk during lunch period: giving our people a bad name.

But I was doing it again, daydreaming. I had stopped when I got to the first line of pews at the crossing and waited there, inches from the trap, trying to make myself as stiff as possible so I wouldn't pee in my pants (we had rehearsed all this: "I don't want anyone passing water in his or her pants, whichever applies," Sister had told us during run-throughs), waiting for Sister to give me the go-ahead for the Host. You couldn't just walk up to the railing and kneel there with the others; you had to wait until you were told. Sister had been very strict about that for weeks. "Remember," she had told us, "you're not going up to a cafeteria for a frankfurter. Our church is not a luncheonette and the Host is not a hot dog. So just watch your *deportment.*" (I wrote that new one down in my spelling notebook first chance I got, but I misspelled it as "department," and misused it for a long time.)

While I was waiting there, turning to stone, or salt, or liquid, someone grabbed my arm, the same spot where Sister had pinched it. It was still sore. "Don't move." It was her voice again, down low. It sounded like something out of a cowboy movie I'd seen with Papi. "Okay, Malánguezzz, don't move. This is a chodown."

She was only getting me ready for the walk to the railing. She held me there in a tight grip for about ten seconds, and as soon as one of the kneeling receivers, looking no better than before, had made a stiff about-face and started solemnly back to his pew with the Host in his mouth, Sister pointed a finger at the opening and told me to go get It, before one of Sister Haughney's girls beat me to It. Then she let go my arm, and it was as if she had pressed a button or released a spring I didn't know I had: I took off for that railing like a hungry dog tearing ass for a bowl of chow. But there was a lot of "chow" for everyone. Father Rooney's ciborium was stacked, and there was plenty more Host back in the tabernacle. One of the assisting priests, Father Mooney, had already replaced Father Rooney's empty ciborium with a fresh ciborium, and was standing by in front of the altar, waiting for another nod from the railing.

"Walk, Ssantoss Malánguezzz, don't run!" Sister hizzed behind me. Too late. I was already kneeling at the railing, hands joined under my chin. She'd get me tomorrow morning. Maybe in the auditorium. Special assembly for the execution. Organ music and chorus.

And then Father Rooney and his other assistant were on top of me with the ciborium. The assistant stuck a golden plate with a handle under my chin—a paten, it was called, a metallic bib just in case. Father Rooney was holding the Host between thumb and index and wagging It in front of my mouth, which suddenly wouldn't open. Lockjaw from fright. My punishment for cursing in church.

"Open your mouth, young man," Father Rooney suggested. We hadn't rehearsed this part.

I used both hands to do it: one hand under my nose, the other pushing down on my chin. But then my tongue wouldn't come out for the presence. The spit in my mouth had thickened and turned to glue, and my tongue was stuck to my palate.

"Stick out your tongue," the priest with the paten said.

I stuck two fingers in my mouth and unstuck my tongue.

"What's he doing, Matt?" Father Rooney asked his assistant.

"You got me, Mark. What are you doing, kid?"

"I am sorry, Father," I said. "The tongue got stuck to the—"

"Shh! You're not supposed to talk in here during Mass," the pastor said. He wasn't looking too happy.

"I am sorry, Father," I said automatically, trying to get the spit going again.

"Out with the tongue, son," Father Matt repeated. "Or leave the railing."

I closed my eyes and did as he said. Then Father Rooney delivered his Latin lines: *"Corpus Domini nostri Jesu Christi custodiat animam tuam*, etcetera. Amen." Father Matt had his paten under my chin—cold metal—and I felt a familiar warm dribble working its way down my thigh, spoiling my fresh pair of First Communion shorts. The whole place was looking on, except possibly Papi and Mami, who must have been staring down at their hands in embarrassment. Then the worst of all possible things happened: the Host broke in half on my nose. I still had my eyes shut, so I didn't see just how Father Rooney managed to do it but I could figure it out. I must have made him nervous, and instead of slapping It down on the tip of my tongue, he caught the tip of my nose, and the presence broke in two. One half stayed in Father Rooney's fingers, and the other floated past my tongue, bounced off the railing, missing Father Matt's paten altogether, and came to a stop on the symbol-crowded rug on their side of the railing, between Father Matt's shoes, which were barely visible under his alb, as Sister Felicia had called that fancy undergarment.

Both priests gasped at the same time and crossed themselves. Everyone in church, except for the sleeping winos in the back, must have done the same thing. Padilla's organ began playing *"En mi viejo San Juan,"* a golden oldie, probably to distract everyone from

the horrible accident I'd just caused at the railing. And my bladder
was having itself a time with my new shorts. Father Matt stooped
quickly, with his paten held tight to his heart, and started looking
for the half-Host. I remembered what Sister had said about "His
body broken in pieces" is why something-something, and felt horrible. The people who had nailed Him to the Cross couldn't have felt
worse afterwards than I did just then.

Father Matt was still down on his knees looking for It. He was
getting warm. I could have told him, but I was afraid to open my
mouth. He was saying something under his breath, and Father
Rooney, all out of patience, said, "Just pick It up, Matt. We'll be
here all day at this rate."

"Sorry, Mark," said Father Matt. "Here It is." He used his
paten as a dust pan to scoop It up, nudging It with his index finger.
It broke again during this delicate recovery, but that didn't matter.
You could split It up into a couple of hundred pieces, and It was
still one. That was part of the mystery behind It. The "accidents"
were one thing, Sister had told us; the "essence" was something
else. You couldn't violate *that*. She had told us about an egg named
Humpty Dumpty to illustrate the difference between a "material"
object, in this case a talking egg, and the mysterious "indivisible
Host." Just the same I was having my doubts. One piece was in
Father Rooney's chalice (he had slipped it back inside when no one
was looking), and the other half was down there, getting scooped
up by Father Matt; and I was having trouble understanding how
both pieces were one and the same. Sister Felicia would tell me all
about it first thing tomorrow morning, in front of everyone. I
wanted to go back home. I wanted no part of this business; I was
unfit, unworthy, un-everything, but I was frozen there on my knees,
terrified.

Father Matt finally got back to his feet, the paten with the two
extra pieces held against his chest, and the thumb and index finger
of his other hand pinning Them down to prevent another accident.
Then Father Rooney held out his ciborium, which looked like a
fancy trophy to me—it had jewels in the middle and was made of
gold, or something that resembled gold—and Father Matt nudged
the two pieces into it. I thought Father Rooney was going to slap
a fresh sample on my tongue, but he had nothing like that in mind.
I didn't even get the three broken pieces. I had my tongue out

again, but all I got was a piece of advice. "Go back to your pew, kid," he told me. "You're not ready to receive."

And Father Matt said, "Grow up, son. You're seven already." I was eight, already one year behind, and no end in sight. And then he turned to Father Rooney and said, in a whisper, "This whole neighborhood's going to the—"

But Father Rooney cut him short: "Not here, Matt. Later, in the rectory."

"You're the boss, Mark." And off they went to plant an intact presence on Grippe's tongue. The worst disgrace in my life to date; and once you started in with the disgraces, it was hard to stop. Some types couldn't do a thing right. They talked in church when they should have been praying in silence, they cursed before receiving, they didn't know their own neck size, or the size of their feet, and they conned their parents into paying for half their First Communion outfits, just to insult Sister. And now this. In public, too. Hundreds had seen it. Maybe a thousand. And my own parents sitting in the back, next to Saint Anthony and his lilies, pretending they didn't know who I was. At least I thought they were pretending. I wanted them to.

Sister Felicia helped me up to my feet and turned me around toward the pews. She walked back there with me, slowly, because my knees seemed to have run out of the oil that makes knees work and my shoes felt like something poured from cement. Heavy construction. She led me back to my pew by the arm she'd pinched, and as she was sitting me down she put her mouth to my ear and said, "Ssantoss Malánguezzz, you are a disgrace to our school," bearing down on "disgrace." "You are not fit for First Communion, and maybe never will be. We have a lot to discuss tomorrow morning."

I nodded; but did she think I was going to show up at school next morning? Even as I sat there in my wet shorts, my mind was out in Central Park playing hooky next day. They were going to get me anyway, day after next, no way out of it; but in the meantime I thought I was entitled to a day of rest and I was going to take it. Maybe they'd send me to P.S. Genghis Khan, where I'd have no trouble blending in with the "barbarians," which might not be a bad idea.

Papi and Mami didn't bring it up on the way home—we left in

a hurry—or in the house, where they insisted I sit down to eat after I changed out of my outfit, washed the pee off my thighs, and changed into normal clothes and sneakers.

Menu: Fricasseed chicken (boneless), saffron rice, a hot loaf of unconsecrated garlic bread, a bottle of grape juice (full strength), and Humpty Dumpty egg custard. Not exactly my first post-Communion meal, but no reason to throw it out, either. Mami reminded me that in the world at large a lot of people were going hungry right now. I knew she'd say that.

"You was nervous, Santos," Papi said in English while we were living it up in the dining room. I'd been expecting that one too. But he wasn't going to preach at me. "Next time," he added in Spanish, "no more accidents, okay?"

"Okay, Papi." But didn't he know it wasn't up to me?

5: Discipline

THE AMERICAN CHRISTIAN BROTHERS of Saint Misericordia Parochial had more rules of conduct than we could keep track of. Sooner or later every student got his hands slammed with the strap, a foot-long piece of Cat's Paw rubber made for shoe soles. Anyone could buy himself a strip in any shoe repair shop, but only the ACBs had thought to use it on our "paws," as Brother Lomasney sometimes called our hands.

"Put out your paw, Chief," Brother would command when he caught you breaking one of the rules. You stepped right up to him with your hand already shaking and offered it to him. He pulled the Cat's Paw out of his cassock and let you have it from two to twelve times, depending on what it was you had done. On the way back to your seat you were scanned by twenty-five or thirty pairs of "periscopes" (Brother's synonym for eyes). Some of those periscopes were sympathetic, others were glad it was someone else who got it this time, and others kept whatever they felt to themselves. A few were even bored by the whole thing, that's how commonplace it was.

Below the wrist you were dead for a while, swollen, as pink as a fresh slab of Govt. Inspected ham. After a while a tingling sensation started, and you knew you'd survived. Any student who couldn't take it and made a "spectacle" of himself was sent down to the Principal's office.

Brother Principal wasn't partial to anyone who "fiddled with the rules" and then broke down when Brother Whoever gave him the business with his strap. Any boy sent down to his office was given a punish lesson along with that night's homework ("I must not fiddle with the rules of our school," or "I must take my punishment like a Soldier for Christ")—silly reminders, but it took time to write them down. You had to turn the list in to Brother Principal next morning, on your way to class. He went over it with you, as if he were analyzing a poem or a legal contract, and if he said it was sloppy, you had to do it over again that night, plus your regular homework, plus an extra punish lesson on the subject of sloppiness versus neatness.

Some students found themselves trapped for weeks with a backlog of homework and punish lessons and the horrible feeling that this bad dream was going to last till graduation, if they could hold out that long without cracking up—this had happened once at least—unless they got kicked out, or signed out by their parents before they turned in their piled-up punish lessons.

Sometimes, when Brother was in a good mood, or if he told a clean Roman Catholic joke (like the one about the priest in Panama who mistook a head louse on the lens of his binoculars for a camel walking on the line of the Equator), you could laugh out loud in class. It was always smart to laugh when Brother came out with one of his jokes, even if it wasn't all that funny; it put you on his good side. And if you laughed often enough at his sense of humor, he might take a special liking to you and spare the strap a little.

But don't let him catch you laughing at another student's joke. If he did, you had to share the joke with the whole class. "What's so funny, Chief?" Brother Lomasney, seventh grade, would ask. He had a powerful neck and shoulders and a regulation crewcut. He had spent four years in the Navy before joining the ACBs, and liked to use sailors' jargon in class. His students were "lubbers," the floor was the "deck," the john was the "head," windows were "portholes"; "aft" and "abaft" were the back of the classroom and "fore" was the front. One of the wiseguys in class called it the "forefront." Just let Brother hear him.

"What are you laughing at, Chief?"

The usual reply to this was, "Nothing, Brother." Unless you could think fast. If you couldn't, Brother reached inside his pocket for the strap. He had named it Audrey, after a hurricane that hit the city one year.

"Well, come on, tell us the joke so we can all laugh. Let's not be parsimonious with our humor." He had a big vocabulary.

And you had no choice. If the joke you repeated wasn't funny, you could get as many six shots on each hand; if it was half-funny, you got three or four; and if it cracked up the class, you might get away with a written punish lesson, or you'd be asked to stay after class for an hour of study. This was called "Jug," a popular period.

And if you were one of those incurables who horsed around too much, you might get expelled from Saint Misericordia's. One of my classmates, Pericles Contreras, disappeared one day, the day after Brother Lomasney gave it to him for laughing on the sly. Pericles was about thirteen, the oldest student in the class. His father, a boxer, had been shot by a double-crossed prostitute. At least so he told me; he wasn't always honest. When he came to Saint Misericordia's, Brother Principal left him back a full year because he had what was called a "language-interference problem," meaning he couldn't speak a word of English. But he was a fast learner, and at the end of his first year in New York he was doing better than half the class. Just the same, Brother Principal held him back; maybe he forgot about him.

I used to help him out with his grammar and spelling after class, and he paid me back by lending me his battered collection of French postcards. Those "collector's items," as he called them in Spanish, were my introduction to the eye-popping varieties of sexual intercourse. "Jesus," I used to say, "people have a hell of an imagination, the filthy animals."

"They even do it in bed, Santos," Pericles would add.

"I can believe it."

He must have had his own introduction to this "animal stuff" as soon as he outgrew diapers. In his wallet he carried a stack of girls' snapshots, thin ones, middling ones, and fat ones; he wasn't choosy about weight. But most of them looked older than he was; one of them must have been twice his age. It wasn't his mother, he said, and it wasn't one of his aunts. "It was somebody special. They was all my girl friends one time or the other, Santos. Before I move to New York. They must be crying like the cocrodiles back in

Jayuya. They miss me so much." He said that with a grin, so it was hard to tell if he was putting me on.

When he described his "affairs" with them in detail, it sounded like a commentary on his postcard collection. After a while I got the feeling he was a first-class bull artist. Those "girls" of his must have been members of his own family, or next-door neighbors who didn't know what stories he'd be spreading about them among his New York pals.

During lunch period, when we boys were allowed to talk to the girls, with a couple of nuns and Brothers looking on to make sure we didn't give our school a bad name, Pericles used to stay out of sight. Considering all the bragging he did about his Jayuya sex life, he was coming off as pretty shy. Usually, while some of the older students were talking to the girls behind parked cars or against the pillars at the entrance to our school, Pericles was playing Chinese handball against the post office wall. He didn't have trouble finding partners and rivals. Most of us were shy around the girls, thanks to our school's policy of separating us from them during the school day.

One afternoon, Piscatorio Rosa, a tough, well-built son of Gypsies (so he said), decided to join our handball game without waiting for winners. He belonged to a gang of vandals that called themselves the Red Wings, meaning what we didn't dare ask him. All of East Harlem east of Third Avenue was their "turf" before we Puerto Ricans "swarmed in and plagued the whole place," as I heard one of the ACBs tell another ACB one day. "They got all of Fifth Avenue already," he went on. "Now they're moving east to the river." "You think they'll jump in, Jerry?" the other ACB asked him. "Let's wait and see, Tom."

Piscatorio had carved his name wherever he could: on desks, on the walls of our halls and toilet, on car fenders and hoods, on the sides of trailer trucks, post office vans, garbage trucks and U-Hauls, on stoops, on the sidewalk, and on the street itself (he was almost hit by an oil truck once while putting his switchblade to work on the tar top; he cursed the driver back in "gypsy" and returned to his carving); everywhere was his turf. Even the top of a cop car. "Piscatorio was here." Sometimes, instead of just his first name, he wrote "Gypsi" or "Gipsy" (a lousy speller), or "Piscatorio the Gipsi," with a French-curve swirl under name and title. He got the strap almost every day for breaking some rule he'd never heard of, like the one about not poking one's fingers into another student's ribs or stomach. And he never flinched or pulled his hand back when Brother Lomasney's Audrey came down on it. He had calluses the size of garlic cloves on both hands, which helped. On the way back to his seat, he made it a point to smile; but if anybody else smiled, Piscatorio would get him after class. Sometimes he got help from his friends in the Wings. Not that he needed it.

When I had been "killed" out of my handball box and went to take my place at the end of the line, Piscatorio was standing there, leaning forward, hands on knees, ready for action.

"You ain't playing this one, Piscatorio," I said, faking self-confidence. "Wait for winners."

He told me what to do with myself, if I knew how ("I'll teach you, Malánguez"), and jabbed two fingers in my stomach—playfully, but it upset my digestion. I'd just finished eating macaroni with mozzarella and a McIntosh with lukewarm milk.

Pericles, who was in the server's box, shoved the rubber ball inside his pocket and sized Piscatorio up for a few seconds, giving him a hint; but the Gypsy wouldn't take it.

So Pericles told him. "You ain't playing in this one, Piscatoro," mispronouncing his name on purpose.

"Just shut up and serve, Prickeles," Piscatorio came back, rubbing his hands. Two could mispronounce. "I'll take your postcards and sell them to Brother Losmoney."

"Get outa the box, man," Pericles repeated. "You ain't playing over my dead body." This was the wrong time to fix up his bad English, so I said nothing.

"Any way you want it," Piscatorio said. He straightened up and stuck out his chest. Then he poked Pericles in the stomach.

Pericles stepped aside and swiped him with a left to the nose; then he moved in for a bolo punch (his father must have been a fan of Kid Gavilán). But Brother Eufemio Sánchez, a Spaniard known as Brother Toro, stepped in and grabbed Pericles by the neck as if Pericles were a plucked chicken. Piscatorio's nose was bleeding when Brother Toro took them in to Brother Principal's office for their medicine. Piscatorio got first aid and was sent home for the afternoon; Pericles got ten or more shots on each hand and was suspended for the rest of the week with a warning: If he laid his hands on another student again, out he went. Saint Misericordia's was no place for thugs.

The Monday after that I asked him about the punishment. He sucked his teeth and rubbed his hands. "It don't make no difference, Santos. They don't want to listen to my side of it. Come on, I play you a furious game of Chinese."

After that, Piscatorio and the other class Wings kept away from him; but they gave it to him behind his back with graffiti: "Contreras is a crip," a "lousy spikc," his "ass was on a slign," signed, the RED WIGNS," with about six exclamation points after "wigns." Contreras found the graffiti funny. "They can't even spell their own name, Santos. *Idiotas.*"

One day during religious instruction, Piscatorio, who sat behind Pericles, slipped him a piece of paper doubled in half. Pericles took one look at it and pinched his nose to keep from going into a fit. His other hand passed me the paper. It showed two balloon creatures copulating like a pair of dogs and under them an inscription in caps: "THOU SHALT NOT COMITT ADULTREY." I stashed it under my desk and took a side glance at Pericles. "He misspelled it, that jerk," I whispered. Pericles nodded. "That's why is so funny, you esnob."

"What's so funny, Contreras?" Brother Lomasney called out from the forefront.

Pericles sat up straight. "Oh, is nothing, Brother," he said, serious all of a sudden. Too late.

Brother stared at him for a few seconds, slapping his leg with the religious text. "Well, come on, tell the whole crew. Let's everyone on board have ourselves a good hysterics."

By this time I had slid halfway down my seat, making myself scarce for what was coming. If Pericles didn't come up with a funny, clean joke, he was going home with a pair of "killed" hands. And if he told Brother the truth (which would get me hanged as well), we'd never see him in school again. I'd get thrown out too. Obscenity was no joke in our school.

"Well," Pericles started, "it was just something I remember, Brother." That wasn't even a good try, and he knew it. His thumb was tapping the writing surface of his desk, like a metronome.

Brother Lomasney had heard this excuse before; he was bored by it. It was what he sometimes called "a low-IQ lie." He slapped

the text down on his desk and reached into his cassock for Audrey.
Then he started a slow walk down the aisle without once taking his
eyes off Pericles, who was staring at his tapping thumb. Brother's
walk was a sailor's roll, neck forward and hands swinging at his
sides, always ready for action. He looked like the survivor of many
sea storms and torpedoes. Maybe he'd harpooned a few whales in
his time. Pericles sometimes called him "Brother Captain."

He was standing in front of Pericles's desk and staring down at
him. From my seat, still slouched, I could see Brother's jaw grind-
ing away and bubbles of saliva forming in the corners of his mouth,
flecks of sea foam.

"Okay, Chief," he said to Pericles, "let's hear the joke."

"Hear *what*, Brother?"

"Don't give me the ignorance bit, Contreras."

"I told you, Brother, is nothing."

"Well, here's something for nothing!" And with one hand
Brother grabbed Pericles by the collar of his leather jacket and
lifted him to a standing position. Pericles looked as though he'd lost
his neck. Then Brother's other hand raised Audrey high for the kill.
I shut my eyes and waited for the sound.

"Get your dirty, filthy hands off of me, you aminal!" Pericles
screamed.

Aminal? Where had he learned to pronounce like that? I looked
again.

Brother's first and only chop, from the shoulder, caught Pericles
on the cheek. Then he slammed him back into his seat. Pericles
clutched his cheek and sucked a glob of mucus back inside his nose.
The rest of us sat slumped, looking from Brother to Pericles to
Piscatorio, who was impersonating an angel; and who could blame
him? If we said a thing, we'd all get it, and nobody was about to
take a chance on getting his own cheek chopped up for somebody
else's felony.

"All right," Brother ordered, "the rest of you lubbers step
outside and wait there. Quietly. I don't want to hear any horsing
around." Who was in any mood to horse around just then?

So we walked out and waited; nobody said a word. Piscatorio
took a walk to the john, a sudden urge. He had a Magic Marker
in his hand.

When Brother came out, his face needed a transfusion and his strap hand was trembling a little. "Bolger," he told one of the students, "go get Brother Principal on the double." Then he stepped back inside the classroom.

Brother Principal came up two steps at a time and rushed inside the classroom. About five minutes later Brother Lomasney stepped out and let us go for the day. "Go home, boys. Class dismissed. Don't hang around the streets before three." We went quietly. No looking back.

Pericles didn't show up next day. His seat was the only unoccupied one. We couldn't help staring at it, like a pothole in the middle of Third Avenue. Brother didn't call out his name during roll call. That morning's lessons were more boring than usual, and strained; our answers to Brother's questions were like the kind of thing you heard in courtroom movies. Everyone sat up stiff, while Brother, as if nothing had happened the day before, paced back and forth in front of his desk, or behind it, and put expected questions to us without looking up from his book. Sometimes he called on the same student twice in a row, and sometimes he stared out the "porthole" nearest his desk or asked something he'd already asked, or he might stammer and then stop to get ahold of himself.

At three o'clock, just before dismissing us, he said, "It was an accident, boys. I aimed at Contreras's hand, not his face. He moved his head."

"I think he lost his cool, was what it was," one of the students said to another student down on the street.

"What else?" said the other student, and got no reply.

At lunch next afternoon one of the students whose classroom was next to Brother Principal's office told some of us that Pericles's mother had come in with him that morning, for a conference with the Principal. She raised her voice, which was a bad move, and then made things worse by threatening to call the cops, which got her nowhere. She didn't know the ropes. A couple of times she talked back to Brother Principal in a mix of Spanish and English and got him all confused; and finally, fed up with her hysterics, he told her that under the circumstances she should sign her son out of our school and sign him up in a place where the teachers couldn't touch you. There was a catch to that "advantage," though, he reminded her: no strap, no learning; no learning, no nothing, as she'd soon find out, when her son started coming home with lousy report cards and turned into a behavior problem. Up to her.

About a month later I saw Pericles on Madison Avenue. I was on the way to school from Flower Fifth Avenue Hospital. I'd just delivered a sample of my stool to a doctor there because they suspected I was a carrier of tropical worms. That would explain my anemia. It was a little after one, a time when only hooky players and suspended cases walked the streets and swelled the playgrounds.

Pericles was shooting a furious game of basketball in a housing-project playground with a couple of buddies. It was a warm spring day and they had taken off their shirts. Pericles had rolled a handkerchief around his head to keep the sweat off his eyes. I stopped behind the hurricane fence to look on for a minute. I wanted to say hello, but his friends didn't look too friendly, so I just stared, ready to run if they started something.

One of them, who had been waiting on the sidelines for winners, walked over to me. He had something to ask me. "What's your trouble, stud?"

I took my hands off the fence, in case he decided to grab ahold of my fingers and squeeze. "Nothing," I said. He gave me an unbelieving grin.

The others stopped playing and looked on. Pericles was sizing me up; he looked serious. There was still some trace of Audrey's mark on his cheek, unless it was all in my head. I waved at him automatically, but he wasn't having any of that. He turned and walked back toward the backboard. It was a mean walk. It went with the rolled-up hankie.

One of his friends aimed a glob of mucus at my feet and missed by an inch or less. It was time to go. Another one started growling, and then they were all growling, barking, howling. ASPCA cases, I thought, and walked back to school on the double.

6: Caesar and the Bruteses: A Tradegy

IN THE EIGHTH GRADE, Brother Cassian O'Leary, nicknamed by his students "Bro'Leary," gave us what he himself called "a pretty tough" Christmas assignment. "But," he added, "youse guys are gonna have to start getting in shape for the Diocesans. I don't want anybody in my class failing them." The Diocesans were annual city-wide exams that all parochial school students had to take willy-nilly. They were our equivalent of the public school Regents, and, as Bro'Leary reminded us five times a week, they got tougher every year. "If you blubbers want to graduate from Misericordia, you're gonna have to pass those Diocesans." He made the whole thing sound like a choice between salvation and hell. "And the readiness says all."

But it wasn't only the Diocesans he was preparing us for; it was also, he said, the "stiff and crucial entrance examinations to five or six parochial high schools." For seven stiff and crucial years I had heard it said, over and over, by nuns, Brothers, priests, fellow students, and even parents, that the worst fate a Catholic-school student could suffer was to "land," "fall into," "end up in," a public school. Public schools, to the Sisters of Misericordia and the American Christian Brothers, were "pagan places" and "heathen temples," the closest thing to Purgatory in all of East Harlem—a "limbo" itself—where we lived, studied, prayed morning and night, and played stickball after classes closed for the day.

Bro'Leary, like Brother Lomasney, was a former sailor who had turned in his bellbottoms and stiff Navy cap for a black cassock and starched white collar. He may have been trying to catch up on his reading of the great books that year. The other ACBs, most of them younger than he, were well ahead of him in their command of the "immortal thinkers and poets" (a term I first heard in his class); and this must have given him a lot of gas pains (he belched a lot in class) and kept him up later than normal at night. I used to picture him drying up his brain reading under his blanket with a penlight or candle while his better-educated colleagues snored in peace and held dreamy dialogues with the smarter angels and the Founding Fathers of Holy Mother Church. That fantasy of mine grew out of a weird habit he had: In class, almost daily, he would drop the names of strange people that none of his students knew anything about. In the middle of subjects like math and geography, names like Homer, Virgil, Dante, Saints Thomas and Augustine, Cervantes, and Shakespeare poured out of him like the names of dearly departed during the Canon of the Mass. One day, when no one could come up with the right answer to an involved long-division problem, he said that the number we wanted was the same as the number of circles in "Dandy's *Inferno.*" My Spanish helped me out with the meaning of "inferno," but like the other students, except maybe Rafael Díez, the class genius, I had no idea who this "Dandy" was, and I couldn't give a damn; same for his father, mother, and circles.

"It's nine, blubbers!" Bro'Leary barked, baring large canines connected by webs of saliva. "And you better start doing some real serious reading instead of those 'Living-Hulk' type comics youse waste your fathers' and mothers' money on. Wise up, or you won't even make it into Miserere Nobis—youse hear?" Miserere Nobis was a last-choice high school, the closest thing to public school in the archdiocese. It had high standards of tuition and low standards of admission, and it didn't even have a gym or swimming pool.

We knew—because Bro'Leary had told us repeatedly—that he had served in a battleship during World War II and that he was a decorated hero. He had rescued a shipmate from sharks during an aerial attack. And we were convinced, though he didn't tell us, that he had been shell-shocked, which probably explained why he'd joined the ACBs so late in life. He was in his thirties when he started teaching; he had the bags of middle age under his watery blue eyes, and his crewcut was overrun with gray quills. Gray hairs, said Papi, who knew, were a sign of bad nerves and early old age.

So most of us in Bro'Leary's class didn't take his foaming fits too seriously, except when he went for his strap, a piece of shoemaker's sole rubber, and ordered the entire class, even the obviously innocent, to line up—"all of youse!"—for a shot on each hand when class was dismissed for the day.

"He is crazy, man," my friend Virgilio Silva would say to me after class. "If he touch me one more time with that focken strap, I'm gonna call the cops."

"I'll kick his big ass," I swore.

But we didn't mean that. We didn't want to hurt him. He may have been a little shell-shocked, but we respected him, though we couldn't tell why: maybe because we thought he liked us, whereas the others, Brothers and nuns, often acted as if they were educating savages for the good of their souls, and only for that. We were also afraid of Bro'Leary. He looked like a TV wrestler who'd been defeated by the Holy Spirit: over six feet tall and weighing a ton, he had thick-as-banister wrists with enough hair on each to make wigs for two life-size dolls. And he was Irish. So were the cops Virgilio was always secretly threatening to call on him. Whenever a Puerto Rican or other Latin student got into a fight with an Irish or Italian student, the Irish sided with the Irish, the Italians with the Italians, and the Latins with the Latins. The same was true when an Irish student fought an Italian. The law was that you always sided with Your Own Kind; if you didn't, you lost your membership in that unofficial club and were subject to assassination in one form or another. Even our adults belonged to that club; even cops. Blood came first, even, we were sure, for Bro'Leary, who seemed to have no favorites in class—except for high-grade brains like Díez, whose parents were Puerto Rican, and Ant'ny Saccaffidi, who was from Sicily.

And there was going to be some blood lost, warned Bro'Leary, if we didn't study good and hard over the Christmas vacation. "This ain't gonna be no vacation, Santos," Virgilio told me. "It's gonna be chit, with all that focken homework." Aside from the usual double load of holy-day homework, Bro'Leary assigned us a "close reading" of a play (our first) by someone he must have been reading under his blanket: William Shakespeare's *Julius Caesar;* "a tradegy," Bro'Leary called it.

"What the hell's that, Ant'ny?" I asked Saccaffidi, our class's number two genius.

"It's a Roman empruh, Malánguez," he answered smugly, as if it was something I should have learned back in the second grade.

"It's an Italian love story," Virgilio said.

"A tradegy, from the word *goat,*" Bro'Leary explained, "is the death of a great man who either flips or slips up somewheres. Except Our Lord, because he never made any slips. Any questions on that?"

Most of us didn't see any need to raise our hands. Why should we? If he had told us the planet Venus was composed of five parts blood and five parts broken hearts, why should we dispute him? He was the teacher. But then Pasquale Sudano, who was trying to oust Saccaffidi from the number two genius position, raised his hand, with the worried look on his face of someone who's going to shit all over his seat if he's not given immediate permission to run to the john:

"Brother, if the President of the United States slips on a banana peel and breaks his ass, is that a tradegy?"

Bro'Leary gave him a deadpan look of disapproval. "Breaks his what, Sudano?"

"I mean his neck, Brother. Sorry."

"Let's watch our language in this class. Repeat the question for the class, Sudano. Loud and clear."

Sudano repeated it at the top of his voice.

"No, that's not a tradegy, Sudano. A tradegy has to have a fatal flaw. A banana peel's not a fatal flaw. That's just a tough break. Happens all the time. To err is immortal, and so on."

But Sudano persisted. "Suppose His Holiness the Pope slips on a banana?"

"That's not a tradegy either, for Pete's sake! I just told you: It's gotta have a *fatal* flaw attached! Christ God allm—"

But Sudano, too ambitious to know when to let up, wasn't finished. "Not even if the Pope ends up on a wheelchair, Brother? Ain't that a fatal flaw?"

Bro'Leary shut one eye and cocked his head at Sudano. "Don't use bad grammar in my class, kid. That's for public school." Then he swiveled his head in Díez's direction. "Maybe Rafe can field that one. Rafe? Go on, son."

Díez stood up stiffly, like a Cub Scout at attention. "It can't be a tragedy, Brother, because death is worse than paralysis. And death is fin—"

"It's not always fin—, Rafe, but I guess it is most of the time. Whom are we to say? Anyway, your answer's essentially sound, very perspective. Take your seat, Rafe. Boys, a tradegy-type play always ends up with the death of the main character. The protanogist, as the Greeks used to call him or her."

Sudano wasn't convinced. "But, Brother—" The pest.

"Shut up, Sudano! I've had enough of your disruptionary tactics for one day. Whatsa matter with youse guys today? You're acting like a bunch of fat blue whales. A school of purposes. Either youse got too much spermacity in your heads to understand what I'm driving at, or youse haven't been listening. Huh?"

I think most of us had, but he was getting too deep for us with his tradegy stuff, making it sound like the algebra and science that awaited us in high school.

"So that's the homework for Christmas, boys. And youse guys better get *Julius Caesar* under your belts. I'm gonna quiz youse on it when we get back."

"Under your ass," Virgilio grumbled in the seat behind mine. I nodded.

If we didn't take his assignment seriously, Bro'Leary warned us, *he* would, and we'd be paying for it, mark his word. He raised his forearm and showed us the palm of his hand to assure us he wasn't kidding. Then he reaffirmed his vow: "Youse hear me? *Mark my word.*"

A chorus went up: "Yes, Brother." Virgilio, who thought an "oath" was always a curse, added *"maricón"* to "Brother," and jabbed a finger under my shoulder blade to show me he wasn't a sheep who took Bro'Leary's threats to heart.

Bro'Leary was always threatening us, a habit he may have picked up from his Chief in the Navy. But unlike the other fifteen ACBs in Saint Misery's, as we called the school, he didn't always live up to his threats, especially big threats. His tour on a wartime battleship, and the war itself, may have softened him into sparing the strap at times when his colleagues would have doubled the shots to our outstretched hands. But whenever he thought we were taking advantage of him, of his "lean-yentzee" (his word), he might go into a fit of rage during which his mouth would foam at the corners; he'd chastise us with sharp deep-sea words and sprayed spit. One morning Virgilio, bored with geography, was entertaining himself by blowing air through his vibrating lips. Bro'Leary walked up behind him and asked, "Are you a sea cow or something, son?"

Virgilio, mistaking the question for an insult to his mother, swore to me later that he was going to castrate Bro'Leary. "Nobody say that about my mother, man."

It took me a long time to explain to him that Bro'Leary hadn't meant anything by it. "He was just kidding, Virgilio."

"He don't know how to kidding, Santos. He called my mother a cow. He is out to get me, so I will get him first."

Misunderstandings like that sometimes led us to think that Bro'-Leary had it in for us, but his punishment rarely lived up to our fears. He might give us a "mandatory" shot on each hand, sometimes in front of the class but usually outside in the empty corridor; and that kind of punishment might ruin the rest of the day for him, leave him depressed and low-voiced. Otherwise he only gave us the foam-and-threats treatment and doubled our homework. Or he might keep us after school to write out some routine punish lesson: silly things like "I mustn't whistle like a purpose in class" or "Cheating on exams is the same as lying and stealing." By next day he'd forgotten the offense and would joke with us, or he might join some of us in a game or two of Chinese handball in front of the post office. He played a fierce game. In the Navy, he told us, he had played "four-hand wallball with a hard black ball, boys." We could see that.

During one of our lunchtime games, after slamming a low drive against the wall, he slipped, and in trying to regain his balance knocked down a postman with his load of letters. While the rest of us players were down on our knees picking up dozens of scattered letters and postcards and stuffing them back inside the victim's mail pouch, Bro'Leary was picking up the dazed postman and chanting a litany of apologies. He was also sweating and pink-faced; his hands were shaking, as if he were already confessing the "sin" to a shocked priest that coming Saturday. A short distance away our two principals, Bro'Moriarty and Sister Mary Scholastica, were looking on stone-faced: this O'Leary bore careful vigilance. Everybody was looking on, in fact: smiling, giggling, shaking their heads, or blushing for him. The postman mumbled something about "priests" acting like kids, and walked off, still dizzy, to deliver his load. Bro'Leary, his face all red, left the game and disappeared inside the school building. Back in class that afternoon he mumbled so much that we thought he'd flipped for good.

But next day he was snarling away, and during lunch hour he stood on the sidelines, his back to a parked car, and watched our handball game with a look of contrition and longing on his aging face. Two cars down, Brother Moriarty was keeping an eye on him. So were some of Sister Mary Scholastica's nuns; they didn't approve of their colleagues, male or female, joining in their students' horseplay. We might lose respect for them, and if that came to pass, why, they might as well declare St. Misery's another public school, sell it at a loss to the Board of Education, and go educate other Catholic boys and girls in a more civilized section of the city.

All Bro'Leary's homework assignments were handed down to us in the form of threats because, taking seriously the doctrine that original sin had doomed us all to mendacity, malice, and deception, it would be both stupid and naïve of him simply to write our assignments on the chalkboard and expect us to take *that* seriously. Only types like Díez and Saccaffidi took mere words seriously; the rest of us needed reinforcements: threats, snarls, and summonses sent home requesting our parents in blunt language to come in next day for a chat on our "progress and deportment." He was a self-conscious, nervous man who blushed easily, and his conferences with our parents were usually more painful and embarrassing than productive. That was why he didn't send many notes home; he'd rather deal with us directly: "Ciaco, if I catch you smearing your dirty snots on somebody's back again, I'm gonna take your head off and throw it out the window!"

The one to avoid was Moriarty: the head-man, the testicles, the hangman and pontiff of Saint Misericordia's R.C. School. If he summoned your parents, forget it: he had a mean strap and a wrist

to go with it. Bro'Leary promised to send "each and every one" of
us "lubbers" down to Moriarty's office if we didn't pass the tough
Julius Caesar quiz he was going to hit us with the day we got back
from Christmas.

Somebody—one of his fellow ACBs—should have wised him
up and told him that even Saint Misery's eighth-graders, lots of us
with second-language problems, endless home and street distractions, and a deep addiction to two-fisted comic books, weren't likely
to know or give a damn about what an ancient English fag in tight
pants and balloon bloomers was talking about in his tedious Roman
"tradegy." We weren't used to reading about men who wore
dresses called togas, and braided leaves on their heads to hide their
baldness. They dressed like fags and they talked like fags:

I would not, Cassius; yet I love him well.

I have not from your eyes that gentleness
And show of love
. . . your friend that loves you.

That you do love me, I am nothing jealous . . .

Caesar doth bear me hard-on; but he loves Brutus . . .

O Cicero!

O Cassius.

Cassius first did *wet* me against Caesar . . .

Give me your hands all over, one by one.

To prick us to redress?

But what of Cicero? Shall we *sound* him? . . .
O let us have him . . . all be buried in his *gravy.*

. . . for he loves . . . unicorns . . . , bears with glasses, elephants
   with holes,
Lions with toils, and men with flatterers. . . .
He says he does . . .

Caius Ligarius doth bear Caesar hard-on,
Who *rated* him for speaking well of Pompey.

Now, good Metellus . . . Send him hither, and I'll *fashion* him.

Romans, countrymen, and lovers . . .

As Caesar loved me, I weep for him.

I slew my best lover for the good of Rome.

Brutus, as you know, was Caesar's angel:
Judge, O ye gods, how Caesar Lov'd him.

. . . their names are prick'd.

Prick him down, Antony.

. . . and let no man come to our tent till we have done our
conference.

Let me tell you, Cassius, you . . . have an itching palm,
To sell and mart your orifices for gold / To underservers.

I an itching palm!

You love me not.

. . . Must I stand and crouch under your testicles? By the
gods . . .

He doth bestride the world like a *culoso.*

My heart is in the coughing there with Caesar. (So was
something else, if you read behind the lines.)

Yea, beg a pubic hair of him for memory . . .

'Tis good you know not that you are his hairs . . .

Before the ass of both our armies here . . .
Let us not *wrangle* . . .

Then in my tent, Cassius, *enlarge* your griefs,
And I will give you *audience.*

For Cassius is a weary of the world . . . / all his parts
observed . . .
That they *pass* . . . me as the idle *wind,* / Which I respect not.

. . . thou lov'dst Caesar better / Than . . . Cassius.

Give me your hand.

And my heart too.

O Brutus!

I cannot drink too much of Brutus' love.

. . . you'll bear me a *bang* for that . . .

FIRST PLEBEIAN: Pricklickers is what they was, Virgilio.

SECOND PLEBEIAN: Toilsuckers for sure, man.

FIRST PLEBEIAN: Elephants' holes. Lions with toils. What's a toil, anyhow? Some kind of private part?

SECOND PLEBEIAN: Maybe it mean a towel. They mispoil it, Santos.

FIRST PLEBEIAN: Lions with towels around their tails? Haven't you ever been to the zoo? Jesus Christ! You're worst than Bro'Leary. (Or me.)

SECOND PLEBEIAN: Don't take Our Lord in vainity, Santos.

FIRST PLEBEIAN: I'll take *you* in vainity, Virgilius Vobi*scum*.

SECOND PLEBEIAN: What you did call me, you suckerson?

FIRST PLEBEIAN: You heard me. I'll enlarge your griefs, Virgil. Into your tent I'll . . .

He got all tensed up. His round, pale face was a blood-red sun all of a sudden. And it wasn't setting, either.

"I am burnéd off, Santos Malánguez."

As soon as he used my full name, I knew I wasn't his friend.

"Don't take my name in vainity, man. Take it back!"

He was ready to belt me one, to give my face a sermon with his stunted fists. He could be mean when his vainity was injured. Very touchy when it came to his good name. So I cooled it, took it back, and turned the topic back to Caesar and his bunch of Bruteses.

"A bunch of Romans motherflies," Virgilio said, his face turning back to its normal anemia. "Oh, man, am I a weary of this focken wordl!"

"*World,* Virgilio. People don't talk like that. They never did. I should know."

"No, you don't. You lie. You wasn't there to take it all down. You are not a chorthand secretary, my man."

"So maybe they did, Silver. Whom are we to say?"

"Unless they use to used bad English," he said, thinking it over. "But I am not absolutelymente positive of it. This wordl is the weardiest focken—"

"It's *used* to *use,* Virgilio. And *ab-so-lute-ly. Mente*'s a Spanish *ly.*" (Bro'Leary had called it "an adverb's tail," or toil.) "Don't you know that yet?"

"Okay, teacher. I got you. Roger." (Jerk.) "Anyhow you put it, that is how come the Holy Roman Umpire got all washed up by that other throatcuts with the blonds hair."

Bro'Leary had told us all "the true facts" behind ancient gang wars, one of his favorite digressions, especially when he was bored, or when he saw the class snoozing through one of his normal, dry lessons. Some of those gang wars he used to tell us about, like the Romans versus the "Hunniballs," had sounded to me—to all of us, except maybe Díez—like one big bad rumble after another between blonds and brunets, "German thugs and Carthegensian mur-murdons against Latin mercynarians." And now that we knew the dark-haired Latins had been brunette "in-cog-*knee*-toes in disguise, boys," we were sorry the Hunniball hooligans and their elephants had lost what Virgilio called their "holeses" to Caesar and his "spear-shaking motherflies." We were also glad the "blond knaves, cockrodiles, and plain-and-simple caitiffs, boys," had triumphed, German Huns or not.

"Of course," Brother said, "this was all part of Our Lord's inscrutable scheme. See Saint Augustine. If any great mind I've read up on knew what he was talking about, it was him. You can vouch my word for it." He held up his hand, palm facing us: his way of swearing without sinning.

"He meant *he*," I whispered to Virgilio. "Not *him*. He said *him*."

"Who?" he whispered back.

"*Him*, youf—. Saint Augustine. Eh?"

"Shhh!" he said, shaking his head. "Tell it to me all later."

"Forget it."

The ignorance in that class was sometimes inscrutable. Díez the genius must have felt he'd been damned to an idiots' *purgatorio,* or to one of Dandy's lowest circles.

"I don't pick up what kind of chit Bro'Leary's coming off with, Santos," Virgilio said.

"Maybe he just wants us to read up all about the fall of Rome."

"I think he is some kind of faggot too. That is absolute-lily what it is. I am convincéd."

"Him one? I think you got him wrong. He don't act like one. He was in the Navy, in the World War Two. He told me he keeps

the medals they gave him under lock and key up in their sacristy
or something."

"That don't cut no ice with me. Nope. I think he is lying with
the medals. In any way, lots of Ward Worl heroes is a bunch of
faggotones. And the Navy don't mean chit too. I got a cousin or
something that was in the Sixt Flit."

"The Fixed Slit, you mean," I said sarcastically. Asking for that
sermon in the face again.

"Whatever I mean, Santos, my cousin he say the faggots is
crawling like maggots all over the hatchets."

"I can believe it. You never could tell." You could never tell
about those ACBs, either. They all lived together in the same house
up in Harlem. They always traveled in pairs or more, in "tripli-
cates" and quartettes. I had even seen them in sextettes, that's how
solid they were with each other. Maybe they held hands on the cold
Number 7 bus, for balance and warmth. And we seldom saw them
talking to the Sisters or girls of Saint Misericordia, or to our mothers. They preferred to discuss our progress and deportment with
our fathers, for some reason. A big hint, I thought.

A couple of days before Christmas, I locked myself up in the
cold last room of the house, our family eating room, and Papi's
study, and opened up *The Tragedy of Julius Caesar.* "Gayest
Orange Julius Caesar," I mangled his name in my notebook, already getting off on what Bro'Leary would have called a bad foot.
The book, full of misprints ("It's a slightly corrupted text, boys,"
Brother had warned us. Slightly corrupted nothing. Colossally corrupted, he meant.)—the text was brand-new, which meant Bro'Leary must have put in a special order for thirty-one copies, one for
himself. A first for Saint Misery's, and probably a last first, too, a
perfect waste of poor-parish money. It was a bright-green copy (our
school's color, that and gold, some Irish symbol, I figured), with the
school's name stamped (by Bro'Leary himself) in bold green caps
at the top of the title page. On another page there was an ink
drawing of "Wm. Shakespeare, Bard of Avon," which I mutilated
into "Bar of Soap." He was wearing tight-fitting pantaloons—Eliza-
bethan pantyhose—and striped pantalettes, and reading a book,
waiting for somebody to come along and goose him.

The school name was also stamped inside the back cover; and

I even discovered it at the top of page 22. Twenty-two was the number of our school building. Several times Bro'Leary had told us: "Boys, the best way to find your books if somebody steals them is to put your name where the thief won't think to find it." He had ordered us to print our full names on a page that matched our birthdays, or the number of the building one lived in, whichever came closest to the center of the book. "A demonic device," I thought I'd heard him call it.

Number 22 also happened to be the day of the month Saint Misericordia, our patron saint, had been martyred for refusing to surrender her teenage virginity to a platoon of Roman legionnaires. Angered by what Bro'Leary had described as her "standfast stance on chastity," the horny foot soldiers had banged her unconscious with their tortoise-shell shields, torn off her "vestal vestments," gang-banged her, and then finished her off with their six-foot spears. All that mess would have been in vain for Miss Misericordia if she hadn't regained consciousness when the last of the foot soldiers was giving it to her, and renounced her parents' paganism. Brother Kotrba in the fifth grade had said, "She expired with Our Lord's name on her lips, boys." Moral: it's never too late to embrace the True Faith; it's never too late to repent; it's never too late to lose your chastity.

"But they weren't done with her yet, boys," Bro'Leary told us three years later. "After Trajan's thugs martyred the poor dame, they tied her to a Roman stallion and dragged her all over the Seven Hills and filthy streets of Rome, the way movie Indians dragged cowboys around in Yuma and Dodge City. Only at least the Indians had the decency to not strip the unfortunate cowboys naked when they pulled their stunt."

But the Roman lechers had done it merely to intimidate and seduce young Christian beauties. And for that—their cruel pagan lechery—God had destroyed their vast, evil empire. He had let the blond *alemánes* from the north inside the great gates of Rome, and they had sacked, looted, burned, pillaged, raped, and plundered the place. Not the Christians: the Christians, being nonviolent and unarmed, and "Catholic," couldn't possibly shed blood themselves. Then, as everyone knew, the bad-and-bold blondies had converted to the True Faith, and everything had ended happily for Christianity. "It was all part of a great, secret scheme, boys. Read St. Augustine." No hurry.

Julius Caesar, I decided, was also part of a great big scheme Bro'Leary, whose wits were slipping, had dreamed up for us between sheets and mattress: He wanted to fail the entire class. For some secret reason he didn't want us to graduate that June. Maybe he *was* queer and didn't want to lose us, his thirty "boys," to the "outside world" or some other planet where he couldn't play First Mate with us. I came to that conclusion halfway through the opening scene of Act I, and I slammed the book shut, for good, I thought, on page 22, where Brutus the butterfly tells his simple-minded "gentle" wife not to kneel, and she says:

I should not need, if you were gentle, Brutus. . . .

There was a spelling error there: "need" should have been "kneel," and the rest of it was antique crap. "Kneel not, gentle Portia," my foot! If I ever saw Mami kneeling for a favor from Papi—she'd never do that, but just suppose—I'd denounce them both in straight language, right on the spot, and walk out of the house. The boathouse in the black and Puerto Rican section of Central Park was better than a house where that kind of shit took place. And that wasn't all. There was also the big faggot talk and the big Roman vocabulary: words like *Lupercal, appertain, suburbs, harlot, plebeians, betimes, carrion, cautelous, cognizance, countenance, Erebus,* and a quarter-million others just as bad. The only English dictionary in our house was my brother Tego's "technical" one, and he didn't like me "playing" with it; he kept it locked up in a cardboard closet Papi had bought him for his graduation from Saint Misericordia's. But a dictionary could only mess up even more my Christmas vacation. Without having to calculate (I wasn't much good at that either), I concluded that it would take me a full year, from Christmas to Christmas, to look up all those Old World words that nobody in my neighborhood had any use for. Besides, what good was a dictionary for things like "But, as it were, in sort of limitation, to keep up with you at meals"? Aside from correcting the grammatical mistake (as it *was,* or *is,* not *were!* I thought), there was nothing I could do with this—no sense to the nonsense.

If this was good English, it was going against the "straightforward English'' Bro'Leary and the other ACBs and nuns had been encouraging, ordering us to use for years. I could also forget about "mastering" my adopted language, what Papi, with good intentions, had been telling me and Tego to do for our own good, our "futures." But had he ever tried reading this syrupy garbage? I preferred to stick to the blunt, no-shit English I traded with my friends on the block, and to my shrinking Spanish, which Saint Misery's was helping me lose fast for good.

Back in my bedroom, furious with the *Caesar* assignment, and the crackpot who'd assigned it, I hurled the bald-headed, pagan Romans against the wall and watched them topple spread-eagled behind the bed. They were going to spend the rest of my Christmas vacation there, too, gathering dust motes, feeding roaches, and sucking up dank and biting vapors till putrefaction set in. I wasn't going to read another line, screw the coming quiz and Bro'Leary's threats and fits of foam.

A couple of days later, though, Mami was sweeping under the bed and found the green "Bar of Soap." She held it under my nose.

"What's this, Santos?"

"A green book."

"It's yours, isn't it?"

It couldn't have been Tego's; he was attending Chelsea Vocational High School and learning a useful trade, not wasting his time on fat Romans in drag. I nodded, though, to keep her calm. "I don't know how it got there, Mami."

"*Pues,* and who do you think is going to pay for it if it gets lost or broken?"

"Papi. I forgot."

I tried to walk around her; the subject wasn't worth going into, especially since she had rescued Caesar and his hoods from the limbo I'd dispatched them to, and saved Papi a dollar and change. She accused me of being disrespectful to books; she didn't care whose books they were, mine, the school's, or the street-corner shoeshine man's. Books, she said, turning eloquent, were so important for so many things that—

"That what, Mami?"

"You know what. I don't have to tell you."

"But I don't know, Mami."

"Don't play dumb with me, *malagradecido.*"

I didn't know. I knew some books, like Tego's radio-TV manual, were good for jobs, money, and girls, but this green book she had rescued from dust and roaches who could use a nibble now and then—what good was this Bird of Soap except as an excuse for poet-crazy lunatics like Bro'Leary to lord it over us with quizzes, grade averages, and threats? If they didn't tell me, why should I take their word for it?

"When," she asked me, "do you think you'll start doing your Christmas homework?"

"I still have time. There's four days left."

"That's nothing, *bobo.* Start now."

She and Papi had a conspiracy to keep me and Tego off the "dangerous" streets. Tego and I thought the streets were more like playgrounds where you learned all kinds of useful things, from sports to sex. You could get hurt down there now and then, but that was true of all playgrounds and gyms. In our church, one of the neighborhood's all-around athletes had slipped one Sunday and sprained his ankle on his way to receiving the Eucharist. When The Almighty had it in for you, He didn't care where you were hiding; He'd get your ankle indoors or out.

But Mami and Papi disagreed, and our homework, homework, homework, was their trump pretext. They had solid-ranks backing from the ACBs, Sisters of Misery, and Holy Mother Church—all the way back to the New Testament, where, in my confused head, Mary had taken her only begotten Kid to task for farting around with a bunch of bearded old men in their smelly clubhouse. He should have been home learning a useful trade with his flesh-and-blood old man, Joe the Carpenter. Instead He had come on like a wise-ass punk, telling her He was doing His other Old Man's work. For embarrassing her in public, she should have snatched a whip and laid it on His calves and ankles. But He might sic the Holy Ghost on her. That was some fix she was in. Fanatics like her Son would have read *Julius Caesar* front and back once a day for two weeks in preparation for the Big Post-Christmas Quiz.

While I was off stabbing the New Testament, she was busy telling me that she knew the powers of Saint Misery's always gave out extra homework for the holy days (especially Christmas), that she was sure this one was no exception, and that four days of steady

studying would just about suffice for me to squeeze in all the work
I had to do for *el* Brother. *"Inmediatamente, oyes?"*

I heard her all right, but I didn't heed. I shut the bedroom door,
put *Caesar* to sleep inside Tego's tiny desk, and dropped onto the
bed for a long snooze. Then it was Tego's turn to start in on me.
He came inside the room, shook me awake, and said, "Get your
ass off of my side of the bed, Santos."

I put my head where my outstretched feet had been and said,
"That's bad English," as a way of retaliating.

"What's bad English?"

"Off of."

He ignored me and picked up the green book. "What's this
shit?"

"My homework. Wanna read it?"

"That's what I came in here for, Santos."

"No, it's not. You came in here to make me miserable."

"Who's this Shakes Pear?"

"A faggot. He wrote strategies."

He flipped through the book, blinked, shut it, and threw it at
my feet. "Mami told me to come in here and make sure you was
studying."

"I been studying. Four hours."

"Well, you ain't studying now. She said to wake you up."

"So mind your business."

"It is my business. I'm your brother. And just watch yourself."

"Why don't *you* study?"

"I studied already. Two days ago."

"Yeah, down on the stoop. Stud poker."

"Watch your mouth, Santos."

"Wash yours." I liked to practice puns on him.

"You got a bunch of lousy grades last time. Remember what
Papi said." Papi had threatened me with a month's worth of house
arrest if I didn't start acting like a true scholar, instead of like
someone who was going to spend his life opening doors and walking dogs for rich slobs.

"It's my ass, Tego. Whatchu worried about?"

"I tole you. I'm your brother."

"You don't act like it." The real reason, I was sure, was that he
had it in for me because I'd attacked one of his friends with a

broken bottle two weeks back. His one-eyed friend had snatched a basketball away from me and one of my friends so he could play with his own boys. I had succeeded only in slashing the back of his leather jacket with the bottle, when Tego came along and pounced on me. It had taken him a while to convince his buddy that I was crazy and didn't know what the hell I was doing. He used that line whenever I got into trouble and he felt forced to defend me. But he had it in for me for making his life hard, "for giving me the nightmares, Santos."

"Listen, Santos, don't do like me, man. I made a big mistake not working harder when I was in Saint Miseria's. I wouldn't be in the dump I'm in now."

He had failed the entrance exams to five Catholic high schools, and Papi hadn't talked to him for a week.

"What the hell's wrong with that dump?"

"It sucks. I ain't learning a goddam thing. TV-radio's not a real trade, anyway."

"I'll trade places with you."

"Bowlshit."

"Go somewheres else, then."

He couldn't go somewhere else. He was out of their districts. And no parochial school would touch him; he was outside their pale, damned, deported.

"And I still can't put a radio together," he went on. "All I do is get my hands dirty with crap."

"So maybe you're stupid."

"Yeah, Santos, me and you got some things in common. Just remember what Mami said to tell you."

"I'm too stupid to remember, you slob!" I yelled, jumping to my feet. He slammed the door instead of me.

I could do without that kind of pressure; there was something mean and phony in it. Secretly I wanted to enter a vocational high school after Saint Misery's signed me out, but I was afraid to come out and confess it to anyone, except Virgilio. It was bad enough that Tego had failed to "make it" to a priests-and-brothers school. Two failures in a row in our family could lead to a Malánguez tragedy: Papi might leave us, vanish out of our lives with his shamed head drooping like a sunflower on a trampled stem. Mami might take an old idle threat seriously for once and fly back to Puerto Rico, leaving me and Tego, who could take care of himself by himself, back in New York. All that because one overambitious teacher had shot his arrow over his students' heads and assigned us Caesar's assassination for Christmas. Some Christmas. Some teacher.

So once again I sat down to *Don Julio César and the Mariposas,* as I nicknamed them the second time around. This time I read as slowly as if the tyrant himself had ordered me to under pain of swallowing fire or a twelve-ounce can of Papi's rat poison. My knowledge of Spanish helped me out with a lot of Spanish-sounding words, but most of what I read was like Cicero's "Greek" to Casca; and like "Don Cascabel," I didn't see anything to smile about. I also made a half-assed attempt to commit a few of the big speeches to memory—"key speeches," Bro'Leary had called them, and he had written down the "key acts," "key scenes," and "key lines" on the board, which meant we'd have no excuse for not getting them right on his colossal quiz. I memorized a few lines of Brutus's and Antony's funeral speeches, then forgot them quickly, all but the first line of Antony's big ears speech. Maybe it was because I kept thinking that people who talked like that didn't even know how to screw.

Then I got tired of the "honourable man" gibberish and went back to bed. I'd done as much as I could with nothing. And I pitied myself to sleep. I was the kind of student my seventh-grade brother, looking for a witty put-down label, had called a member of the "Limbo Gang," the middle state. Not even "middle"; "middle" was Purgatory, a temporary burn. Limbo was nothing, and I adjusted my ambitions to nothing, *nada, mierda,* the lavatory. "The best thing about that state," my seventh-grade teacher went on, patting his cinctured paunch, "is that most people belong to it. So at least it's not a lonely situation; it's just dull is all." Bro'Leary had never discussed his philosophy of the middle state—oratory unnerved him—but since he was one of them, even if he was an oddball, I assumed he shared those feelings about people like me. They were all in on it: honorable, venerable, chaste men and women.

The day after the Christmas break Bro'Leary hit us with a test that he must have spent two weeks hatching under his blanket:

Part I (30 pts.): Identify fifteen (15) of the ff.characters in one or two sentences (and keep it simple!):

1. M. Aemilius Lepidus (hint: triumph-man)
2. Popilius Lena and Soothsayer (counts as one)
3. Trebonius
4. Caius Ligarius
5. Metellus Cimber
6. Flavius and Marullus (counts as one)
7. Cinna the senator
   (Hint for the last four: their own mothers wouldn't trust them)
8. The other Cinna (hint: mistaken identity can be fatal)
9. Artemidorus (hint: "The mighty gods defend thee! Thy lover . . .")
10. Lucilius
11. Titinius
12. Messala
13. Volumnius
    (Hint for the last four: Tell me who your friends are, and I'll tell you who you are.)
14. Varro, Clitus, Claudious, Straito, Luscious, Dardaneous (counts as one. Hint: Brutus was full of them.)
15. Pindarious (hint: Cassius was poorer than Brutus)
16. Caliphurnia (hint: every great man has a great dame behind him)
17. Portia (hint: "Knell not, gentle Portia.")

    Nota Bene: Try not to get these mixed up. I know they all sound alike, but that's no excuse.)

Part II—short essay (70 pts.). Answer nine (9) fully: (and try to keep it down to one or two paragraphs, you haven't got all day for this):

18. Why does Cassious want Brutus to pluck Casca's sleeve?
    How is *pluck* used here? For example, would Brutus *pluck* a chicken the same way?
19. Why does Caesar only want fat types around him? (Is he on a diet?)
20. Why does Caesar tell Caliphurnia to block off Antony "when he doth run his course"? What course? Ex.: a full-course meal? a race track? an English course?
21. Why does Caesar say *"Et tu, Brutes"*? Are they a bunch of fatheads, or what? (Note: this was explained in a footnote on p. 46, but don't open your books up during the exam. It's too late.)

22. a. Why does Mark Anthony say to the Plaeibians that all he
wants to do up there is bury Caesar? Does he really
mean it, or is he just playing a trick on their
ignorance?

b. Why does he keep calling Brutus and the other thugs
honorable men? Be careful with this, it's tricky.

23. Explain the terms of Caesar's will. For ex., how much does
he leave to the Playbeans? Is this generous or cheap,
considering all he must have owned. (Remember: in
those days when you won a battle, you ransacked and
looted the enemy's towns and villages and kept
everything for yourself. It was Christianity
that changed all this barbarism.)

24. Name at least five (5) examples of Pagan superstition in the
play, and explain what makes them Pagan. (Note:
don't say it was because these characters weren't
Christians. I *know* that.)

25. Father Stanislaus O'MacMahon, a very renowned and
respected Jesuit scholar, once wrote that this play
we're dealing with illustrates the unquestionable fact
that ". . in Pagan times, especially among the Romans
who collitis with Christianity, friendships—and there
were very few exceptions—were as slimy and
slippery as a school of eels in the River
Liffey, . ." and that this is a very crucial
difference between the Pagan Romans
and the Christian Catholics. If you agree
with this statement, take a stand pro-
and-con and explain your position.
But you haven't got all morning.

26. Could this tragedy have taken place in a Catholic country?
E.G., Ireland? Italy? Porto Rico? Poland? Why not?

27. If for the sake of argument the play *had* been possible in a
Catholic country like the ones above (but you can pick
your own country if you like), how would Mother
Church have reacted to Caesar's murder?

28. If Brutus and Cassious had been Catholics, would they have
been buried in consecrated ground with full (or partial)
rites? How about Brutus' wife and Caesar?

29. This and the next one are for extra credit, but don't rush
the other questions just to get to these two. Is there
anything strange about a) the clock going off when

Brutus and his fellow hoodlums are plotting to knife
Caesar in the back? b) about Cassius and his hired
killers coming to Bruteses' house in the middle
of the night with "their *hats pluck'd* about
their ears / And half their faces buried in
their *cloaks* . ."? (II,i,191 and II,i,73–74:
keep your books *closed* at all times)
(Hint: my italics.) (Note how the
word *pluck'd* is used this time.
Could these be feather hats he's
talking about? *Who?* if you
remember.)

30.   This is another clock question. Compare the striking of the
clock in (II,i,191) with the crowing of the cock in a very
famous scene that takes place in the New Testament.
(Mt. 26:57–58, 69–75; Mk. 14:53–54, 66–72;
Lk. 22:31–34; Jn. 18:12–18, 25–27)

31.   What do the two scenes and their chief protanogists
have in common? Is the second one a *tragedy?*
(We talked about this in class.)

Final Note: Don't rush this. Double-check all answers. Points will be
taken off for bad grammar, bad spelling, and bad punctuation, also for
slopy handwritting. You have 2 1/2 hours. Good luck.)

Before letting us start, he warned us about looking around
during the quiz, and about making funny noises which could be
"secret answer signals." Same for gestures of hands, face, and feet.
Even the throat: "Don't start a fit of coughing or blowing your
noses. This room is well-heated. If you have a cold or hoarse throat,
go sit in the stern." About ten guys got up at this point and shuffled
off to the back seats, faking a fit of coughs. He let them. "But seat
two sits apart. I don't want any fishy business back there." Then he
read every question out loud to us, correcting what he called a
couple of "typos" as he went along, and then finally asking if we
had any questions before he looked at his watch and brought his
right hand down as a starting signal. Sudano raised his fat hand, but
Bro'Leary didn't let him open his mouth. "Just sit still, Sudano. I'll
handle your question in private." The rest of us were too nervous
and confused to come up with intelligent questions.

In the seat behind me, Virgilio began acting up. "This is the worstest *mamotreto* I ever seen in my whole life, man! This focken four-hand wallball bastard is crazy! I can't do this shit! Take a look at Number twenty-three, Santos. What the hell is this shit? What's a 'Playbean,' man? Some kinda jelly bean? Eh? Tell me, man!"

I shook my head quickly while Bro'Leary was bent over Suda-no's desk, shaking his own head and shutting his eyes for patience.

"Don't shake your head, man, just tell me! Fuck that Four-Hands."

"It's the mob," I whispered, cupping my mouth and twisting my face in his direction.

"The what?"

"The people, you dumb fuck!"

"It don't look like no people to me, Santos. It says 'playbeans'; you blind?"

"He misspelled it," I hissed, just as Bro'Leary's head shot up like a mammoth porcupine sensing danger.

"Who's talking?"

A startled pause, then:

First Student: "Not me, Brother."

Second Student: "Me neither, Brother."

Third Student: "Me too, Brother."

Fourth Student: "I didn't say a thing, Brother."

Fifth Student: "Me neither, Brother."

Me: "Me two, Brother."

Virgilio: "Me three, Brother."

Bro'Leary: "All right, shut up and start writing or I'll tear up your papers, all-a youse!"

But Virgilio wasn't done with his whining. A minute later, while I was still trying to make out the hint for M. Aemilius Lepi-dus, he began fuming comments at the back of my neck: "Mother hopper! Did you look at Number twenty-five already? What's that, a mountain cleef or something? Who's that Father O'Mojón? What the hell's an 'ells in the River Leafy'?" I jerked my head once to shut him up, but he was out of control. "I'm gonna quit this school before this fock kills me, mother hopper. Who's Number One, Santos? Some kind of leopard? Emilio the Leopard. Some focken faggot. They're all faggots. Brother Four-Hands is the biggest *mari-cón* in this city. Right?"

I ignored him. There was no time to listen to his whining. If I got caught looking as if I was listening to him, Bro'Leary would stomp up to us and tear up our papers. He'd ball them up and play foul-shots with the wastebasket. He'd done just that to cheaters' papers on other tests. I didn't like this test any more than Virgilio, but I didn't want to fail it either. It was bad enough that there was still another semester left us at Saint Misery's.

Virgilio finally cooled off. I figured that, like me, he hadn't finished the play, if he even got beyond the Bird of Soap's portrait. So I wasn't surprised that his pencil wasn't making the labored scratching sounds I was used to hearing whenever Bro'Leary set us to scribbling. In spite of his whining that the work was too hard for someone like him who'd only been in the city two years, he was a hard worker and had inched his way up to the Limbo state. In math he was my better, and helped me out with that part of the homework in exchange for my help with his English grammar and hopeless English spelling. English was his big weakness, and like Papi, and me for that matter, he took it as a tenet that nothing else was any good—no subject, no vocation, no romance, no marriage, and no future—if your English was inferior or even deficient.

I think Bro'Leary believed that too: he was always fishing for the right words (and the more he fished, the more meager his catches), the right grammar and punctuation, the correct pronunciation. And, though as a rule he avoided embarrassing his students in public, he wouldn't hesitate to correct their English errors openly. Some flaws, he felt, should be pointed out and squashed in the open. And of those, English errors were second only to religious ones. It was for our own good, he said. We didn't always doubt it, but liking all this finicky English finesse was something else.

Virgilio started snoring behind me, so loudly that I thought it was coming out of my ears. I woke him up with a cough, which drew Bro'Leary's attention and an apology from my eyes. Virgilio started, and gave off a grunt that distracted others around us. They were probably looking for distractions; maybe Bro'Leary was, too.

"Whatsa matter, Silver?" he asked.

Virgilio began an answer: "Nothing, Bro—"

And Bro'Leary cut him off: "Don't talk in class."

Virgilio let out a fat sigh and began tapping the back of my desk with his pencil. I stretched my leg behind me and kicked his foot. He told me to go fuck myself, and I thought, I'll get you later for that, you lame. A minute later he was snoring again, and this time I let him. Hell with him. In no time Bro'Leary was breathing down on him.

"Whatsa matter, Silver? Staying up late on your vacation?"

"Yeah, Brother," Virgilio began, without any conviction, "I had to take my little brother to the 'mergency clinic last night. I was up till four amen."

"Since when do you have a little brother?" Bro'Leary asked. They knew all about our family backgrounds in that school.

"He's an adopted brother, Brother. His father and mother died in a fire."

"Let me see your paper."

Virgilio handed it to him silently. Brother handled it for a few seconds; he seemed to be turning it back and forth from Side A to Side B, and was breathing hot and hotter on it, and on my head. "There's nothing here," he said finally.

"I know, Brother. My mind is in a very big blank this morning."

"Your mind's always in a big blank, Silver. You think you're gonna get out of this school with a Zero in all your papers?"

"I want to be excuséd, Brother. I think I am not too preparéd."

A long pause full of heavy breathing from the two antagonists. And in no time everyone in that stuffy classroom was expelling heavy breath and sucking in what little oxygen remained. Virgilio had some qualities I envied, although I never told him as much, and tried not to show it; open admiration for someone your own age, especially a friend, was a flaw and could earn you a punk's reputation. His lack of finesse was one of the traits I liked. He didn't like the *Caesar* exam, and he was saying as much to the toughest man in that school—outside of Principal Moriarty, Old Testicles himself.

At that moment nobody else in the class even had the nerve to ask permission for a quick trip to the john. Virgilio was asking to be excused from the entire quiz, which the look on his face just then must have been describing as pure crap, or as a trap Bro'Leary had set to turn us all into little fags. And Bro'Leary must have understood his feelings just then, because all he said was, "Go ahead, then, Silver. Leave the room. Give me your paper. I'll see you at one." Virgilio picked himself up, swiped my shoulder, and marched out. Nobody looked up from *Julius Caesar.* Bro'Leary lumbered back to his desk and sat there silently throughout the rest of the quiz, except to let us know every fifteen minutes how much time we had left. Whenever I looked up momentarily from my paper, I spotted him staring at his hairy wrists and big knuckles, as if he'd never really noticed them before. When our time was up, he collected our quizzes in low whispers. Before letting us go he wished us one and all a good hot lunch.

I wasn't surprised to find Virgilio's cafeteria spot empty that afternoon. I knew he'd go around foraging for empty soda and beer bottles in backyards and alleys and exchanging them for movie and lunch money. He could take care of himself, but I was afraid he might take Brother's *Caesar* threats seriously and disappear from Saint Misery's. The other students spent the lunch hour grumbling about Bro'Leary's "lunatic quiz" and swearing to their mothers, their God, and their interred loved ones that they'd flunked it, "and fuckit." I didn't like discussing my failures, so I stuffed my mouth with baked beans and bread, and refused to join the diatribes.

Virgilio didn't come back that afternoon, and Bro'Leary didn't mention his absence or the *Caesar* test. He stuck strictly to religion and the other afternoon topics.

Virgilio showed up at Mass next morning, grinning, and five minutes late. (Bro'Leary didn't write his name down in his church-attendance pad.) In our class's last pew, where we always sat, he told me during the *Introibo ad altare* that he had spent his hooky afternoon in the Third Avenue Eagle, a three-feature flick frequented by truants, that he had sat through two "boss" flicks—*Key Largo* and "Alan Ladd"—and slept through the third, "some chit with Fred Stair and that dame he chove around the balls room."

During the *Introit* he wanted to know how come I hadn't walked out with him in the middle of the test. I didn't answer that one; it was none of his business.

"The Big Hulk."

"Who?"

"Four-Hands."

"He ain't that bad. He gets carried away is all."

"He always fucking up."

"He ain't the only one, Virgilio. You didn't even read the play."

"I could not figure it."

In class an hour later Bro'Leary, in a sour, lip-biting mood, read out the test results. Virgilio got his expected Zero, no comment; I received a 50, twenty points short of a D; Sudano scored a 58, Saccaffidi a 64, and Díez the genius a 69, one point short of D. Bro'Leary, lumbering back and forth between his desk and the closed classroom door, chewed us out for fifteen minutes.

"I gave youse guys two weeks to bone up on that test, so don't come crying to me when you fail the Diocesans. Overall, thisn't the most brilliant class I ever taught, but even so"—foam began bubbling from his mouth—"this is a total disgrace even for a bunch of fatheads. What were youse guys doing for the holy days—wasting your mothers' money in that cheap movie house out on Third Avenue?" Most of us went to the Star on Lexington, where the price was cheaper and you didn't have to double up, two to a seat, on crowded afternoons. "Youse don't have to graduate from this school, you know. This ain't—this isn't public school, where they have to move you up to the next grade. Unnerstand?"

His spit sprayed every student in the first row. Their arms kept shooting up to their faces, as if expecting him to lay them out with chops and uppercuts. It looked as if that was what he had in mind, too: he kept going into a crouch, hands clenched at chest level, quilled head bobbing, and his barely visible feet shuffling in a clumsy flat-footed dance.

He asked us (and we'd better not answer) how in the name of Saint John Bosco ("Apostle of Youth") we expected to do well on, "let alone pass, the real tough entrances to choice schools like Bishop Tully, and Power Memorial and Carnal Hays. Not even a place like Lily of the Valley High's gonna admit a bunch of fathead delinquents like youse, not with those type grades youse got. What you guys think's gonna happen when they hit you with Latin and logger rhythms?" (Pause: heads drooping in disgrace.) "Whatsa matter with youse, anyway? You wanna end up selling those shaved-ice snowballs off the streets like your fath—you guys wanna disgrace me or something? After the way I sacrifice my spare time working up some real good litrachur and other useful stuff into your heads! Youse know where you're gonna end up?" (Pause.) "Huh? Huh? In *public school.* The buncha youse. That's a promise. And don't come blaming Brother O'Leary." He was close to purple now, close to tears. He should have stayed in the Navy. We kept our eyes fixed on our desks, our hands holding up our heavy heads; every now and then a chorus of coughs broke out.

Before releasing us for lunch, he had two more warnings to foam out: that if our disgrace repeated itself, he was going to write a note to all our parents asking them to come in so he could chew them out for being too easy on us. "And second, I'm gonna hit you blubbers with another tough classic book very soon, just as soon as I get it ordered." "Homer's Old Essay," I thought I heard him call it. "If youse think Shakespeare's tough, wait'll you get a load of this Greek genius, Homer. You're gonna get three quizzes on him, and I dare youse to fail them. Now get out! Go stuff your bellies with hot food."

He waved us off to our hot lunches, reminding us, as we were dragging our feet toward the door, that at one o'clock he was going to quiz us orally on our religion homework. We knew that; it was what he put us through every afternoon.

Down in the green cafeteria, Virgilio told me he was definitely going to a "plumbing school" when he graduated from Saint Misery's. He said he'd rather not go to *any* school than ruin the rest of his school life reading lames like Julius Caesar and Homer the Greek. And that kind of shit, he assured me, was just what we were going to suffer with in "the other high schools that set you up for the lame college." His father and uncle were both plumbers' assistants, which meant he'd be tracking their footsteps, not breaking out on his own and moving beyond papá and tío; but that didn't faze him now. Besides, he swore, he was going to become a real, "good-money" plumber, not a toilet engineer's assistant. "The plommers, they get good *pega,*" he said. "Five bucks an hour. And they don't have to estudy this Chekspier chit."

He wanted to know what I was going to do with myself, where I was going. "I don't know," I said, sulking. "Maybe I'll go to Chelsea Vocational. That's where my brother goes." If I told him the truth, he'd probably call me a "lame punk," which was what I felt like just then.

"You know what I hate with the holy days, Santos?"

"What?"

"They always fock you up."

"Ain't that the truth. And we still got Easter too."

"Let's go steal some chocolate kisses in the Fives and Tens."

Kresge's was out of kisses that afternoon, so we settled for balloons with sand inside them. We snatched about five each. And what we ended up doing with them was, for once, my bright idea: "Let's fill 'em up with water and bomb Bro'Leary with 'em."

"You getting smart, Santos."

Next day we skipped the baked-beans lunch (we skulked out of the cafeteria before a clock alarm went off signaling the official end of chow time), and filled our ten balloons from a leaky hydrant on the corner of Second Avenue. In a plastic shopping bag I'd brought along, we carried our water-and-sand bombs to the roof of a tenement connected to the school building. Then, lying stomachs down on the parapet, we waited for the lunch mob to emerge. Principal Moriarty posted himself at the boys' entrance; Principal Scholastica paced back and forth in front of the girls' entrance, keeping an eye on her underlings, who, along with Moriarty's Brothers, patrolled the sidewalk from Morris' Toys and Stationery to the far end of the Hell Gate Post Office. Bro'Leary, who wasn't sympathetic to patrol duty, parked himself on a car fender and craned his wrestler's neck to kibitz the noontime handball game.

At my signal, we let go the water bombs. The school crowd split and scattered like ants in a downpour. Bro'Leary, confused at first, swiveled his crewcut head in every direction, like a periscope scanning an enemy destroyer. We hurled the other balloons at him and the two principals, who ducked inside the building. But he stood his ground under enemy attack. One balloon splattered inches from his feet; another hit the top of the car he was leaning on and sprayed his face, neck, and chest; a third caught him between the shoulder blades as he turned to retreat. He didn't run or duck or double-time it like the others; he walked off slowly, soaked from head to foot, looking over his shoulder before vanishing inside the school.

At one o'clock he came to class looking as though he'd given in to a childhood impulse and jumped into a shower with his cassock on. His shoes squeaked, but his face and head at least were dry. Usually he sat down at his desk before beginning the first afternoon lesson; this time he stayed on his feet and marched, hands behind his back, from the room door to the window opposite it. Nobody said a thing, not even Virgilio, who usually used words like "bear" and "elerfount" to describe Bro'Leary's back-and-forth rolling gait. I stared at his wet uniform and figured that was nothing for a man who had dived into the Pacific to save a shipmate from sharks, who had spent years floating around in typhoons and tidal waves all over the world's oceans, and who was probably indifferent to umbrellas, galoshes, and raincoats, which he was probably too poor to own anyway. He looked less angry than shaken, shocked by the suspicion that someone, or a group of hooligans, was out to get him, or like those Doomsday Protestants who get baptized in polluted Orchard Beach and come up looking stunned and nauseated after the third dunking. His silent-moving lips seemed to be searching for something to say, but nothing came out. He had to say something on the balloon bombardment, though; he knew we expected him to. At that moment every other Brother and nun in the school must have been disgorging monologues on the souls of heathens and hoodlums who did such immoral things, and maybe pumping their students for clues to the scoundrels' identities.

"I don't know who dropped those things on us," Bro'Leary said finally, in a low voice, "but whoever did is most likely the kind of saps that end up taking drugs and selling numbers. Yeah, that kind." Then, after a long pause during which he eyed me and Virgilio a little too long, I thought, he said, "If any thugs from this school did it, they should transfer out to public school. We don't want their kind here. . . . Anyway, I don't think any boys from this school would pull something like that—do youse?"

We all agreed: "No, Brother!"

"I thought so. This ain't—is not—that kind of reform school. It must have been a bunch of brutes from public school did it." And that was all he said on the balloon incident: no Shakespeare. I didn't think he'd meant a word of it, either.

So we turned our minds and mouths to religion: a long, lifeless discussion of the *Nobis Quoque Peccatoribus* part of the Mass. At five minutes to three, he told us he was going to cross our *Julius Caesar* grades "off of" his grade book. "We're not ready for that stuff yet. Wait till high school."

We weren't ready for "Homer's Old Essay" either, it looked like, because it never arrived. He said Principal Moriarty had canceled the order: too expensive for a school like Saint Misery's.

"*We* canceled the order, Santos," Virgilio told me on the way home. "Me and you."

"Moriarty canceled it."
"Bull. The balloons."

We got a new teacher the following semester, red-faced, heavy-set Brother Fish, fresh from Brooklyn. He told us Bro'Leary had been transferred to a high school on the Hudson. "He said he likes it there," said Fish. "He goes fishing every weekend. He said he misses this place, but moving around is part of the Order's rules. You never know where they're going to send you next. Happens all the time, boys."

Maybe, but none of us had ever heard of a brother getting transferred before the end of the school year.

Virgilio: "Maybe they sended him to the crazy house, Santos."

Me: "Nah. They send 'em to monasteries or something when they flip."

Virgilio: "You think he really flip?"

Me: "Him? Nah. He wasn't all that crazy."

Virgilio: "He was better than this big Fish. Fish smell like the Communion bread. Too clean for my taste, Santos."

Me: "Ten times better than Fish. Maybe he went back to the Navy."

Virgilio: "You never can know, but he look to me too old for the ocean. Maybe they lock him up."

Me: "Shut up, man. Jesus!"

Maybe they *had* put him away. Except for Fish, none of the Brothers ever mentioned his whereabouts. And none of us took Fish's word for it. Nobody we knew had ever heard of that high school up the Hudson. Not even, I suspected, Cassian O'Leary, A.C.B.

7: In Black Turf

THE DAY BEFORE, I had made up my mind to cut Sunday Mass for the fourth straight week. In parochial school, the Christian Brothers gave you no choice about religious matters. But I was out of their clutches now, and there was no punishment to worry about if I got to Mass late, or if I didn't get there at all. Giving up the Holy Ghost and the rest of the religious business was a serious decision, the most serious I'd made to date. I was beginning to feel like a real grown-up. But because it was a critical decision, I couldn't bring myself to make it all at once; growing up, I knew, was a slow process, and I was in no hurry to become a full-grown man before my time. I decided to spend Sunday morning strolling with my buddy Panna in the wilds of Central Park.

At 9:45, fifteen minutes before the young people's Mass began, I came down and found Panna sitting on the steps of my stoop. His real name was Teodoro, but to his friends he was Panna because he called everyone he liked "Partner." He'd picked up the word from cowboy movies. He was small, undernourished, and about as black a Puerto Rican as I'd ever known. I don't think he had a drop of white blood in him. Half his ancestors must have been shipped to the Caribbean from Africa, and the other half, the Indian side of his family tree, must have been waiting for them on the island long before Ponce de León got there. He had an immense head topped with an abundance of thick, unwashed, kinky hair, and tiny, rotting teeth. People sometimes took him for an American black,

but he was as Puerto Rican as I was. Maybe more so, because at least
he didn't try to deny his origins by getting rid of his East Harlem
accent.

My own accent was closer, though not really close, to the speech
of American disc jockeys and TV-radio detergent pushers. This was
a result of having spent eight submissive years under the influence
of the hard-driving Christian Brothers, who subscribed as faithfully
to the myth of the American melting pot as they did to their vows
of poverty, chastity, and obedience. Nobody had ever taken me for
someone whose veins might contain Negro or Arab or Caribbean
Indian blood. I was too light-skinned for that. On various occasions
I had been mistaken for a Jew, an Italian, a Greek, even a Hungari-
an; and each time I had come away feeling secretly proud of myself
for having disguised my Spik accent, and with it my lineage. I could
almost feel myself melting smoothly and evenly into the great Pot.

The north end of Central Park was right across from our block.
We went there to scout around for girls who might be willing to
join us in the bushes. This was a favorite fantasy of ours. It gave our
excursions in the park a specific purpose, and it satisfied one part
of a favorite daydream of mine: saving a nice-looking girl from
rape. She could be a Puerto Rican dusky, or an American blonde,
it didn't matter, as long as she was equipped with big, plump boobs
and a nice round rump.

The time would be early evening, just as the sun was about to
drop between the tall tenements of Central Park West; the place,
a clump of bushes near the baseball diamonds. I would arrive on
the scene just as the pervert, a big, muscular black man with a
shaved head, was tearing off her pink polka-dot panties with one
hand and unzipping his fly with the other. With a baseball bat or
a sawed-off broomstick I just happened to be carrying, I would
splinter the lecher's skull. By risking my life for the poor girl's
chastity, I'd be putting her in my debt. To remind her of this would
be crude; but she'd know it, and she would want to repay me in
kind. At this juncture I would stoop to pick up her panties, and
when I offered them to her, she would take my hand and lead me
into the bushes for a satisfactory settlement. Afterward, holding
hands, we would walk off toward Loui's Luncheonette on the
corner of 108th and Fifth. After a thick malted (two straws, one

glass), she'd leave me her name, address, and phone number, and an open invitation to come and see her whenever I had time.

What usually happened, whenever a girl saw Panna and me approaching her with a look of undisguised lust in our eyes, was that she would clutch her purse to her chest, turn abruptly, and scamper off for the nearest exit. Copping a girl's drawers in that park was even more difficult than stealing a squirrel's hoard of nuts, but we liked to pretend it was easy.

The only people in the park at ten on a Sunday morning were mounted cops on their big, brown, huge-assed horses, perverts like ourselves, and members of the Puerto Rican Baseball League. At the baseball diamonds we watched one inning that lasted over a half hour (the beer-bellied pitchers couldn't get the ball over the plate, which wouldn't have mattered much, since catcher and batters were too sleepy to see the ball; and the fielders, undernourished and weighted down with heavy, loose-fitting uniforms, couldn't catch up with flyballs and groundballs), and when we decided that Puerto Rican baseball had no future as a national pastime, we headed north toward the black people's section of Central Park.

Across the bicycle path, on a grassy area where Puerto Rican families picnicked on sunny weekends, we looked for empty beer and soda bottles. If we found enough empties, we could get them "changed" at Miguel's *bodega* on Madison and head for the movies or Loui's Lunceonette. All we found was a bag of dried chicken bones crawling with ants, and a used condom. Panna picked up the condom with a crooked stick and came at me, swishing it like a secondhand sword inches from my face. I tore off down the sloped picnic grounds and stumbled to a halt in front of a marshy stream that divided "our" section of the park from the black people's section.

Like a scrawny, scraggly blackbird, Panna stumbled after me and jabbed playfully at my chest with his stick and condom.

I stooped and picked up a wet, scummy stone. "Don't touch me with that thing, mother-fo!" I warned him, taking a full windup.

Thrown off guard by my unexpected counterattack, he halted. He was a few inches smaller than me and about half as strong. His head, with its thick tangle of kinky hair, was attached to his thin neck like a bowling ball to a skinny long finger; it swayed uneasily from side to side on its precarious stem. His round, coarse face, dotted here and there with pimples, looked about five years older than his actual age. He was fourteen, my age, but already half his teeth were hopelessly rotting. No amount of dental work could save them. One had been knocked out in a fight with his older brother. I don't think he'd ever seen a dentist. Maybe that was why girls took off when they saw us coming.

"All right," he said, thrusting his head forward and closing in on me with quick little hops, like a starling advancing on a worm. "Drop the rock or I'll plug you with my fuckin' scumbag."

Stabbed helpless with laughter, I lurched backward. He opened his mouth wide and grinned at me, the evil guy stalking his helpless victim. The sight of his putrid teeth, with the black, blank gap in the middle, disarmed me completely. I slipped on the slimy grass, dropped the rock, and tried to fall forward. But I splashed into the stream, flat on my ass.

Panna hurled himself to the ground in convulsions.

"See what the fuck you did?" I screamed, already worrying about what Mami would say when she saw what I'd done to my best pair of pants. Panna was too busy laughing to hear me.

"You black fuck!" I snapped. "You think it's funny?"

He suddenly became silent. He hurled the stick into the stream while I got to my feet. I was completely soaked from the waist down. Green slime dripped from my Sunday pants and clung to my recently polished shoes.

"Don't call me that shit, Santos."

I stood up and slapped at my pants. "You asked for it, shit. Look what the hell you did."

"Just don't call me that," he said, biting his big lower lip. "I don't like nobody calling me a black fuck, understand?"

"Just watch it next time," I said, half sorry I had insulted him.

He bent his head a little and stared at my throat, as if readying himself for a savage fight. "You better say you're sorry, Santos."

I was sure I could take him if he wanted a fight, but the thought of fighting him was as repulsive to me as the condom he had just threatened to stick in my face. He was my "panna."

"All right, forget it, okay?" I had to raise my voice so he wouldn't think I was backing down.

He raised his dark eyes to my face. "So say you're sorry."

"All right, shit. I'm sorry. You satisfied?"

He jerked his shoulders and started to walk off alongside the shallow stream, kicking at the grass with his sneakers.

I followed him.

"Hey, man," I said, "you heard me say I'm sorry, right?"

"Yeah, I heard you." He was staring at the ground.

I walked in front of him and faced him. He stopped abruptly, tilted his large head, and scowled. His hands were clenched tight at his sides.

"I don't wanna fight witchu, Panna."

"So whatchu want, then?"

"Say you're sorry."

"For what?"

I slapped my pants. "You made me fall in the filthy water."

He stepped to the side and shrugged his shoulders. If we got into a fight, the only thing I'd have to guard against was his head. He could crack my jaw with one butt of that bowling ball.

He raised his voice: "I didn't touch you, Santos."

"You stuck that scumbag in my face."

He shook his head and smirked slow-motion. "I don't wanna argue, Santos."

"So say it and I'll call it evens."

He hesitated, squinting at the stream. An apology was a confession of weakness, but so was not asking for one when you felt insulted. So I kept him on the hook. Let him learn better than to humiliate his own friend.

"Okay, muh man," he said. It came out weak. "So I'm sorry you got wet. Next time watch your balance—otherwise, tough shit."

That was all. Take it or leave it. I pretended to be fully satisfied.

"Forget it, Panna. That stream was out to get me."

We continued walking, quietly, keeping the distance between us a little wider than usual. I was afraid he'd hold a lifetime grudge against me for the insult. What I couldn't understand was that he and his older brother, who was a little lighter than he was, were always calling each other names like "nigger" and "spook" whenever they got into an argument, and never thought anything about it. With them it was a game.

What the hell was he being so sensitive about all of a sudden? We spoke the same language, lived in the same block, and shared the same friends. Maybe he'd had another fight with his brother earlier that morning and was taking it out on me. I should have kicked his ass when he poked the condom in my face.

The stream dipped and disappeared under a rise of large, jagged rocks which formed a natural bridge to the "black" part of the park. People got killed there, I'd heard, women raped. It was a hilly area where the vegetation grew thicker than anywhere else in the park and was, for that reason, darker. People from our side of the park, from our neighborhood, stayed away from that section. It was strictly for blacks. I seldom ventured there, never on my own.

When we got to within a few feet of the stone bridge, Panna broke into a quick run and leaped onto a rock.

"Where you going?" I asked.

"Thataway, partnuh." He pointed to the other side of the stream.

I was pleased at his rapid change of mood. "Whatchu going there for?"

"Whatchu mean what I'm going there for? Ain't you coming?"

I stared at a dragonfly hovering over the little stream below the rocks. "What for, man?"

He dropped his hands and shrugged. "I don't know. Maybe we can find some empties."

I grinned. "Or some broad."

He grinned back. "Or some scumbags."

The dragonfly was swooping and circling less than an inch over the water, searching for insects.

"Whatsa matter, Santos, you scared?"

"Whatchu mean, scared?" I leaped up on the rock next to him. "So let's go."

I let him lead the way.

On the other side of the stream, we had to climb a steep hill on all fours; the ground was damp and loose, even though it hadn't rained in over a week. Every time I grabbed a small plant for support, it came up by the roots and I would slide back a foot or more. I was wearing my Sunday shoes, leather-soled and tight-fitting. Panna was wearing sneakers and had less trouble climbing. As long as he didn't tilt his huge head backward, he was all right.

When I got to the top, minutes after he did, he was staring at an old fortress a short way off to our left.

"Hey, Santos, you know"—he was shielding his eyes with one

hand and pointing with the other—"old George Washington fought in there." He sounded like any one of the Brothers of Saint Misericordia's driving home a startling fact. ("And after old Judas Iscariot betrays Our Lord, boys, the sap goes and hangs himself! He didn't even get to spend those thirty denaras of silver.")

"Bullshit, Panna."

"No, I ain't lying to you, Santos. I'm just saying what I know. He whipped them Redcoats right there in that focken fort."

"Who told you that?"

"Whatchu mean, who told me? You ignorant? I been here before, lots of times. I grew up in this park."

He picked up a small stone and pitched it hard at the fortress. "So don't tell me what I know and don't know. Everybody knows it, except you. Where you been at, stud?"

"You're jiving me, Panna. You lie."

"Okay, I'll betchu."

"Who, you? You ain't got no money."

"That's fine with me," he said. "I can pay you back tomorrow. But I ain't gonna lose. *You* is. I'll leave you broke you bet with me."

"Forget it, Panna. I don't wanna take your money."

He was always broke. His spending money came mostly from empty bottles and from tips he got delivering groceries on Saturdays. But he always managed to spend it all on candy and the movies by the end of the day, because if he didn't, he had told me, his big brother would go through his pockets at night and steal it. "He steal me blind when I'm sleeping, Santos."

He turned his head toward the fortress. "You *know* I'm right."

"Go ahead, Panna, prove it."

"Come on, I'll show you. Just follow Panna the leader." He trotted off toward the old fort.

I hesitated. "I ain't going in there, Panna. Smells fishy to me."

"What the hell you scared of?" he said. "You turning into a lame or something?"

So I followed him down some rocks and onto a narrow dirt path thick with weeds. Below I could hear the traffic going in both directions along 110th Street, and smell the gasoline fumes.

We squeezed through a small opening that had been knocked into the stone wall, like the holes in playground fences, only this one must have been smashed with a sledgehammer. Inside there was nothing but tall grass, more weeds, a few commonplace bushes, and a strong smell of human shit. Not far from where I stood, close to the wall, someone had relieved himself and left it at that, uncovered. Now flies, hundreds of them, buzzed around the mess like Ancient Romans at a banquet. In the center of the fortress, rising from a jungle of grass, a shredded, faded flag with only forty-eight stars flapped on a thin white pole, like a pigeon flyer's bandanna tied to the end of a bamboo stick.

"C'mon," Panna called. He was several feet ahead of me, up to his neck in grass.

"Fuck you," I said. "I'm staying right here. There ain't nothing in there but shit."

"There's an old, whatchamacallit, plaque, around here someplace."

I could just about make out his head now, a huge, black, kinky-haired ball rolling slowly along the grass, like an immense sunflower minus petals.

"That's where it says George Washington whipped the Redcoats right here in this spot."

"All you're gonna find in there is a big lump of shit," I called. "There ain't no plaque. You'll fall in a hole and break your leg. Come on, let's go back."

I was getting hungry. The Mass I'd missed should have been over long ago, and I was anxious to change into dry clothes.

I leaned against the stone wall and waited for him to emerge. "Panna," I yelled, "let's go, man. Forget the fuckin' plaque. George Washington never came near this place, you jerk."

A pebble bounced off my head. I looked up and saw one, two, then four black faces. Their owners were standing and sitting on the ledge of the wall, staring down at me. The sun was almost directly overhead now, and I had to squint and shield my eyes to see them clearly.

"Whatchu doin' in there, white boy?" the tallest of the four said. He was about six feet, and he was tapping the wall with the heels of his sneakers and cracking his knuckles. I moved back a few steps for a better look. They were all very black, blacker than Panna even; the noon sun gave their faces a smooth, rubbery look.

"I'm waiting for my friend," I said. My legs began to sag

slightly below the knees. I couldn't have run more than a few yards before they caught me. But even a speed-runner didn't stand a chance in that trap.

"Where your friend at?" another one asked. He wasn't much taller than me, but he had the arm muscles of a professional athlete or a truck loader in the garment district. His pants were the color of orange soda; he was holding a stickball bat out in front of him like a fishing pole.

I pointed toward the tall grass. "He's in there." I realized my mistake immediately. Panna had probably spotted them before I did; that was why he hadn't answered when I called him.

When I squinted up again, only one of them was sitting on the wall. He was the smallest, an inch or two smaller than Panna. A blue beret, spattered with dust, was tilted dramatically to one side of his head.

"Don't move, motherfucker," he said.

I pressed my back to the wall and looked for a possible way out. The hole I'd come in through was impassable; they would be coming in any second. There was nothing but grass, the long white flagpole, and the pile of human shit with its frantic flies. If there was an exit, it would have to be across the field, on the other side. If Panna had found it, he must have escaped. That bastard, I thought. It was all his fault, and now he had copped out on me.

The three came in through the hole in the wall one at a time and surrounded me. I stared at the ground, waiting stiffly for the first blow and regretting that I didn't have a gun on me and that I had never taken Karate lessons.

The six-foot one stepped up to me and looked down for a few seconds. I listened to the roar of a crosstown bus far away.

"Where your buddy, stud?"

"I told you," I said. "He's in there somewhere."

"What he doin' there?"

"He's looking for a plaque."

The one with orange-colored pants stroked the grass with his stickball bat. "A what?"

"A plaque," I said. "My friend says there's this plaque in here that says George Washington fought the Redcoats here during the Ci-Ci-Civil War."

They looked at each other, shook their heads, smiled, and broke into laughter. One of them slapped the side of his head and came down on his knees, almost touching the ground. He had on a sleeveless white sweat shirt with CLINTON HIGH SCHOOL lettered across the chest.

"Man, you must be outa your fuckin' skull," he said when he straightened out. "Old Georgie never came near this fuckin' place."

"He puttin' us on," the tall one said.

"I ain't puttin' you on," I insisted. I didn't see what was so funny. "That's what my friend said."

The one in orange pants snapped his fingers. "Maybe he mean *Booker T.* Washington." He stepped up to me and tapped me on the shoulder with his stick. "You tell your friend to come on out here 'fore I go in there and get him out myself."

I hesitated.

"You better do like he say, son," the one from Clinton said. "He ain't playing witchu."

I cleared my throat. The strong sun was beginning to give me a headache. "Hey, Panna," I called. "C'mere, man."

No answer.

They all frowned. They thought I had lied to them about Panna and the plaque.

I called again. "Hey, Panna, man, come on out, you *lame!*"

Nothing. I was sure he was back on the block, or in his house stuffing himself with peanut butter sandwiches and very likely enjoying the thought that I was getting just what I deserved for having called him a black fuck.

The one with the stick started off in the direction of the flagpole. "Man," he said, "if I don't find your friend in there, I'm gonna crack your hea-ud with this stick, dig?" In a few seconds he disappeared. I could hear his stick stroking the grass.

"I didn't do nothing," I said to the tall one.

"Nobody say you did, Jack."

"How much brea-ud you got, son?" the one with the sleeveless sweatshirt asked me. He was flexing the muscle of his right arm and staring at it as if it were some abnormal growth that had suddenly emerged into full view. It resembled a large sweet potato. I didn't stand a chance.

"'Scuse me?"

"I said how much brea-ud you got? You know, *mmmoneh, honeh.*"

Before I left the house that morning, Mami had given me a quarter for the church collection. I had planned on treating Panna to a soda at Loui's Luncheonette, but now he could go screw himself.

"I ain't got nothin' on me," I said.

"Put your hands behind your head," the tall one commanded. I inched away from him. "For what?"

He grabbed my shirt collar and pushed me hard against the stone wall. A shock of pain shot through my spine. My legs felt like two pieces of lumber.

"Put your hands behind your hea-ud," the Clinton student said. He was standing so close now that I could smell his bad breath.

I lifted my arms and clasped my hands behind my head, the way I'd seen it done on the block whenever the cops were frisking a suspect.

The big one stuck his hand in one of my pockets, then in the other, and came up with the quarter.

His mouth spread in a thick-lipped smile. "Dig," he told his friends. He pinched the shiny quarter between two long fingers and held it up for the others to see. The solemn silver face of George Washington flashed in the sun.

"Maybe he got a wallet on him," the one sitting on the wall called down.

The tall one slipped the quarter in his pocket and patted my head. "Turn around, cracker."

I turned quickly and raised both arms high over my head, the palms flat against the warm wall, while he slapped my back pockets. Where was Panna? I refused to believe he had run off. Not that it made any difference. He was too small to defend himself against one of them, let alone all four. Only the gang from the block could pull me out of this mess, and they were all far away, ignorant of the trap I had walked into. This was strange turf for me; I was only used to dealing with Spiks like myself. On the block my name stood for something among my friends; here it was less than shit. It was useless to tell these black guys that I had many friends who would descend on them in an all-out war if they didn't release me unharmed. That kind of threat might only get me a busted head.

"Sheeet, he ain't got nothin' on him," the tall one told his friends after he had gone through my pockets. "Turn around."

I dropped my hands and turned slowly.

The Clinton student grabbed my right arm and jerked it upwards. A pain shot down my shoulder. "Nobody say to drop your hands."

I raised them again, stretching them to their limits, to show that I hadn't meant any harm.

"And keep them up, mother," the lookout man on the wall yelled down.

Suddenly the six-foot one stuck his long leg between my legs and rammed the heel of his hand against my shoulder. I stumbled, scraped my back on the wall, and collapsed with a squeal on something soft. A swarm of flies, thousands it seemed, exploded around me, and in seconds I was immersed in the odor of human shit. I sat there, too overcome with disgust and rage to move. And the flies swarmed and buzzed around me, as if they had discovered a newly laid mass of human excrement and had gone into delirium.

Not because I had been pushed around and robbed of a quarter, which had not been mine to begin with, nor even because I had been smeared in shit, which could be washed off, but because I had been humiliated without any possibility of fighting back, of standing up for myself—for that reason I began to cry. I didn't cry loudly or hysterically; only girls and women had the right to that kind of display. I cried softly, missing my breath once in a while and sucking in the thin, fibrous liquid that spilled like egg white from my nostrils. A slow accumulation of pain, brought on by the strong noon sun, began to tighten around my forehead. I dropped my head and waited for them to kick my face in.

But they just stood there, silently staring down at me.

From the grassy area, where Panna and his pursuer had disappeared, I could hear voices and a stick slashing grass. I waited, resigned to the stink of the shit I was sitting on and the sting and buzz of frenzied flies. The voices had the sound of calm conversation rather than conflict.

In a few moments, Panna and his captor emerged. I watched them through half-closed eyes. They were still talking. Panna was smiling.

When he saw me he stopped, clapped a hand to his mouth, and whispered: "Holy shit! Oh, lordie."

I rubbed two fists in my eyes.

"Who you got there?" the tall one asked the one who had found Panna.

"This here's Ramírez, my friend," he said, slapping Panna on the back. "We went to junior high. He all right. Foo! Whatchu-all been doin' to whitey here?"

"He pushed me in," I said.

The one with the Clinton sweatshirt kicked some dirt in front of me. "I make you eat that shit, too, if you don't shut your big mouth."

"He's my friend," Panna told him. "Right, Santos?"

The tall one sucked his teeth and looked him up and down. "So whatchu be hangin' out with him for? He ain't none o' your kind."

"We live in the same block," Panna explained.

His school friend held out the stickball bat to me. "Here, man, grab on to this."

I shook my head, suspecting a trick.

"Go on, Santos," Panna said. "Get up, man."

I grabbed the stick cautiously and pulled myself up quickly, in case he might decide to release his hold on it.

The seat of my pants felt wet. Repulsed by the stink, the others backed up a few steps.

"Man, you full of shit," the kid on the wall said. He was holding his nose.

The tall one stuck his hand in his pocket and brought out my quarter. "Here," he told me, "take your fuckin' George Washington back. I don't want your quarter."

I put out my hand suspiciously and let him slap the shiny quarter in the palm.

"Let me tell you somethin', white boy," he began. "This here's our turf, understand?"

I nodded, biting my lip.

"And it don't make no difference to me who your friend is, even if he black as an asshole. You stick to your side of the park."

I kept nodding.

"Otherwise I make you eat that shit. Just keep that in mind."

Then he turned to Panna. "And you, shorty with the big hea-ud,

don't think cause you black all over and ugly as sin you can bring
who you wants around here."

Panna nodded. "Okay, man, I keep him off of here."

A long silence followed. I stared at the flagpole and longed to
be back on my small block, where there were no territorial divi-
sions, no white and black bullshit.

"You better get on home, Ramírez," the school friend said to
Panna.

I let Panna go on ahead and tried to remain calm during the few
seconds it took to squeeze through the hole in the wall of the fort.
And just as I was about to emerge on the other side, I heard a voice
behind me: "Man, you full of sheeet," followed by a fit of laughter.

We walked slowly side by side until we reached the top of the
hill, from where we could see part of the baseball diamonds, and
beyond them the mansions of Fifth Avenue. I started down in a
half-run, then broke into an awkward, stumbling rush down the
steep hill until I was on the safe side of the little stream.

From somewhere behind me I could hear Panna calling. "Hey,
Santos, man. Slow down. Whatchu scared of?"

I ignored him and picked up speed. Near the baseball diamonds, I heard the reassuring sounds of Spanish and slowed down.
"Nothing," I said to myself. "I ain't scared of nothing." I stopped
and looked back for Panna. He was nowhere in sight. I continued
walking at a steady, brisk pace, leaving a strong stench behind me.

8: Stoopball

JUDGE DEGETAU'S THREE DAUGHTERS were the best-looking girls on our block. My brother, Tego, went out with Norma, the middle one, for almost a year, and almost married her. I had a crush on Delia, the youngest of the three. "She's what I want," I'd say to myself. But I didn't think I stood a chance. She was too good-looking and too choosy for someone like me, so I didn't make a play. Tego said I was too shy for my own good. He wasn't shy, and he didn't think Norma was too good-looking, or too good anything, for him. He was more self-confident around girls. But in the end it didn't get him Norma, or her him.

Delia looked a lot like the oldest sister, Amparo. When Amparo was nineteen, she appeared on the cover of *Picadillo,* a popular men's magazine, a Latin *Playboy,* a *tetas* publication that sold well. Even women bought it. It carried articles on all kinds of interesting topics, including hints on what the ideal young woman was supposed to look, act, and think like, even what she should eat, and what she was supposed to do with herself when she hit thirty and started sliding downhill. It also published advice for men: what, for example, a man, young or getting on, single or "domesticated," could do to get his hands and teeth on an ideal young woman of the *Picadillo* variety; how to hold on to her once he had her eating out of his hand; and how a *Picadillo* playboy could free himself from an over-thirty woman who was sliding downhill fast or, as one of the magazine's columnists put it, "when her beauty span is played out."

The *Picadillo* issue that displayed Amparo on the cover sold out fast. Tego stashed his copy inside the bottom drawer of the four-drawer dresser we shared. I looked at it five or six times every day for weeks. Then Mami found it and threw it out. When I got back from school that day, the garbage truck had driven off with it, and none of the newsstands I visited had any copies left. I was angry over that loss, but there was nothing I could tell Mami. I had to play it dumb. That's what she did.

Looking at Amparo on that cover had been like looking at Delia a couple of years older. They had the same face and build. The only significant difference in their looks was that Delia had a chipped front tooth, one of the upper incisors.

Amparo was smiling at the photographer. She had hazel eyes and long light-brown hair. She was reclining in a bikini on a fake beach. Maybe the sand was real; maybe it was only extra-fine saw-dust. But the solid-blue sea and sky behind her, and the sunlight spotlighted on certain parts of her—those were man-made *fakerías*. Her body looked wet, too, like the physiques of weight lifters in body-building magazines. Some kind of oil was supposed to account for that shiny look. One of my friends on the block, a barbell fanatic, said they sprayed them with Mazola. Whatever it was, Amparo looked well-done. Tego could have done worse with his thirty-five cents. I should have told Mami that after she junked Amparo.

"You know what you threw out, Mami?"

"Trash."

"That thing cost Tego thirty-five cents."

"You'd better not tell that to your father. He has a lot of debts."

That's how she would have answered me, with her gorge going up. So I kept it to myself.

A lot of good-looking and ugly guys, and men too old to be called guys, made plays for Amparo, but there was no way they could get their hands or paws on "Miss Picadillo," our new nick-name for her. (Before that, it was "Miss Tetas," because she had big ones.) She knew she was something special, and her father, El Judge, was a choosy man. And what did those "jung buns" and "old buns," as he called them and every other male in our neighborhood —what did they have to offer his Amparo? A Home Relief life on Willis Avenue? Half a dozen kids and sagging breasts by the time she reached thirty? Summers at Orchard Beach and City Island?

Sunday picnics near the baseball diamonds and mulch pile of Central Park? An early grave in a run-down cemetery? In other words, what the buns had to offer his Amparo was nothing, *nada*. And *nada* was what they were going to get from Amparo and the judge.

So they played it smart: She married the Cuban free-lancer who had taken her cheesecake for *Picadillo,* and the *gusano* got her a glamorous position as a steno-typist in that publication. He was a well-dressed, striking-looking man from Mother Cabrini Boulevard up near the Cloisters. Tego told me his dark hair and moustache were taken care of by Orlando of Miami Beach on Amsterdam Avenue, and that his fingernails were trimmed by Orlando's sister, Sarita. Whenever I saw him he was walking fast with his camera, in a big hurry, as though his day wasn't long enough.

Right after he and Amparo got married, they moved out to Corona in Queens; and after that we saw them around only when they came to visit her family on certain holidays (Thanksgiving, Fourth of July) and Good Friday. On Good Friday she always wore black; he always wore white ducks and Cuban heels, and he had a black Leica with telephoto lens looped around his neck. It looked to me like the biggest medal in the world. Jealous or not (and envious, too), some of us had to admit that they made a fine-looking couple, the kind that put others to shame in dance halls.

"So what, Santos?" Tego said when I told him something wasn't "fair" about the whole thing. "Some people have it made. Others have to ride the subway." He was the one who filled me in on most of the gossip about Amparo and the photographer.

Tego took his love affair with Norma seriously, I thought, but I don't think El Judge did; and it was the judge who wore the *pantalones* in his apartment. We—his friends and I—were sure he'd marry Norma after they both finished high school. Even Mami and Papi thought so, though they weren't exactly crazy over the prospect. They wouldn't do a thing to stop it, but they weren't looking forward to it, either. They considered the Degetaus a snobbish family who thought they had been condemned by God and circumstances to live on our block. In all the time he was going out with Norma, Tego never brought her home. I concluded that she didn't want to visit us. "I'll bring her up one of these days," he used to tell me. But he never did.

I was sure he was serious about her because he spent most of

his spare time up at her house dancing to LPs of Tito Puente, Tito
Rodríguez, Machito and his sister Graciela, and other salsa types.
He said those were some of her favorites, and he kept their records
stored alphabetically in our bedroom. He housed them in a shel-
lacked cabinet he'd made in Chelsea Vocational.

"You can play them any time you want, Santos. But don't mess
them up."

"I don't want to play them." I preferred listening to the kind
of music Papi played on his guitar in our dining room: Puerto Rican
hillbilly, the le-lo-lai stuff, which meant I was a hopeless case, out
of it.

Tego was the dancer in the house. He used to practice new and
standard steps by himself, or with Mami's broom, in our living
room, while I'd be sitting in our bedroom doing homework or
playing stoopball outside with my friends the Turbine Tots, or
flying a kite on a rooftop. He practiced five or six times a week, and
I could tell when he was going to Norma's house because he always
took a stack of records with him.

But it didn't work out between them, and when I asked him
why, he told me to mind my own business. That was his first
reaction. Then he reconsidered. I knew he would; he didn't want
to hurt my feelings.

"She just wasn't my type, Santos. That's all." Some answer.

"So how come you used to spend so much time up in El Judge's
house?"

"Why? She was a good dancing partner." But he sounded
depressed when he said it. He'd been seeing her almost every day
or night for a year, and all of a sudden she wasn't his type. What
had happened, I was sure, was that El Judge didn't think my brother
was fit to be his son-in-law, so he ordered his daughter to drop him.
This happened after Tego quit Chelsea and went to work in a
luncheonette in the garment district.

El Judge was a guard for Bowery Savings. We called him Judge
because he liked to tell gullible kids that he was "a justice in the
Applellative Division of the U.S. Supreme Court." He was also
very proud, and contemptuous of other Puerto Ricans. He wanted
his three daughters to marry men who could take them out of our
neighborhood into a "good" one. Men like that free-lancer with his
Leica medal. One of the things I heard him say on his stoop, after

his oldest daughter's marriage, was that *"los cucubanos"*—the fire-flies—"they put our people to the shame. They are more esmart, that is why. Very ambishows."

"And what does that make you, Judge?" the Tots' center fielder asked him.

"A very esmart judge," I said. I think I hated him.

He was a short man, he was going bald, and he had a froggy mouth. I also thought he was built like a walrus, round and hipless, and I began referring to him as "Your Honor, El Walrus," or simply "El Walrus." My friends on the Tots picked those nicknames up. They didn't like him any more than I did. Tego didn't think it was so funny, though.

"You're just being nasty, Santos."

"Maybe. But he asked for it."

"You're just playing his game."

"Why do you like him so much?"

"Who said I did? I just want to get a good night's sleep."

"Me too, but you keep sticking your feet in my face." I slept at the foot of our bed; he slept at the head, and he did kick my face a lot in his sleep. Sometimes I kicked him back, and we'd have a short kicking fight in the dark. Sometimes we ended up laughing ourselves to sleep, and sometimes we didn't talk to each other for days because of those foot fights.

"When I get a job," he used to say, "I'm going to get us a huge bed so you can stop complaining."

"No, you won't," I said. And I was right. He couldn't afford one.

His Honor, El Walrus had married a very attractive woman (it was her the three sisters took after), and I couldn't understand why she had picked him.

"How come Mrs. Degetau married that walrus, Tego?"

"How should I know? Women have weird heads."

"She does, anyway."

"She did. They've been married going on twenty-two years."

"That's a long time to be a walrus's wife."

"He's a good supporter. You should see their apartment."

"Yeah, he's a peeping Tom, too."

"Who told you that?"

"I saw him. I was up the roof with some of the Tots one night. He was looking down at windows."

"So what? Maybe he was just checking up."

"On what?"

"Crooks. Burglars. What else?"

"Women."

"So what were you and your friends doing up there that time of night?"

"Checking things out."

"Don't talk, then. You're another one."

"I'll tell you something, Tego. Just keep it to yourself."

"Go ahead."

"He was checking out his own apartment."

"El Judge?"

"His own house."

"So what? It's his house. He's the one that pays the rent."

"What's the rent got to do with it? He was looking down at Amparo and the *Picadillo* man. I don't have to fill in the details. Her room door was locked, and her light was on."

"You must have had a good front seat."

"El Walrus had a better one. They must have thought he was down on the stoop putting down people."

"And I think you're putting me on, Santos. Don't kid around like that."

"Forget it, then." How could he?

"Stay off the roofs at night."

"Don't get the wrong idea, Tego."

"What idea?"

"About Norma. We never saw her from up there."

"I know you didn't. You can't, that's why. Her room's on the other side of the building."

"That ain't why."

"You're telling *me* where her room is?"

"I wasn't talking about her room."

"So what the hell were you talking about, then?"

"I don't know."

"Don't go up there at night. I'll see you later." He was on his way to their house.

That topic never came up again, but for a while after that he gave me some extra kicks in the head. I don't think he was always asleep when he did. I complained about it. He apologized and said he'd been having "a couple of nightmares lately." One night I had to sleep on the floor, and when I looked in the mirror next morning, there was some blood caked in one of my nostrils.

"You see what you did, Tego? Just take a good look."

"I did that?"

"Yeah, *in your sleep.*"

"Hey, I'm sorry, man. I'll sleep on the floor tonight, all right?"

"No, you keep the bed. I like the floor. It's good for my back."

"I told you I'm sorry. You think I did that on purpose? To my own brother?"

"No. You were sleeping."

My way of rubbing it in. He had a delicate conscience.

"Why your brother quit the school?" El Judge asked me one day out in left field.

"He said Chelsea stunk. Didn't he tell you?"

He shook his head and smacked his lips. I imagined tusks and whiskers on his face. "No good now," he said. "Now he is a bun too."

"Yeah, well. This block's full of buns, Judge. They're all over the place."

"No more future for Tego now."

"Nope. He's had it."

"That is correct. Now he is a jung bun too."

"Maybe. But maybe you shouldn't call him that, your honor."

"And why not?"

"Because I'm his brother."

"So you are a jung bun too?"

"Sure. I got it made."

Right there I came close to asking him what he was doing up on the roof the night I was on another roof with my friends looking down at his Amparo and her *gusano* in her bedroom—with the door latched. It was none of my business; I just wanted to hit him where it hurt. But just then the opposing team's man-at-the-plate hit a blooper out to left, and I caught it to retire the side. When I returned to my position, he was gone.

Left field was my permanent position on the Turbine Tots'

stoopball team; it took in El Judge's stoop. Sometimes, while I was out there leaning on a railing, waiting for something to field, he'd be sitting on a neatly spread-out hanky on the top step of his stoop, looking at everything and passing judgment on the people and dogs who lived on our block. The sight of two dogs sniffing each other up or humping away was something most of us ignored or laughed at; but to the judge it was "a spectacle immoral," and he'd say that the two animals "should be sended away or gasséd to dead."

One afternoon a pair of them had just finished copulating and were trying to come unstuck. The male had dismounted and was attempting to get to Madison Avenue; the female was headed for Fifth. Neither was getting anywhere. After a while they came loose and trotted off in different directions. Next day they'd be at it again. No one could care less, except the judge. He said they should get the hot-water treatment: Somebody should pour a pot of hot water "in the place where they are stuckéd."

"Why don't *you* do it, Judge?" I suggested. "Run upstairs and bring the pot of hot water. I'll hold them for you."

"That is not my job," he said.

"He only finds them guilty, Santos," our center fielder said.

El Walrus agreed. "Correct."

"Ask him about Amparo and the *gusano,* Santos."

The judge heard that, got up, and disappeared in a hurry.

And yet, this bank guard who didn't see much difference between humans and dogs was a responsible family man. Tego himself told me so, and Tego wasn't the kind who went around exaggerating, as he said I did.

"I wish I had the judge's job, Santos," he told me after he'd quit Chelsea and was in a position to know what a lousy job was like.

"A bank dick?"

"Why not?"

"They all get it in the end. One day some hard-up junkie or something walks inside the bank with a stickup note, and the pot-bellied old dick has to draw his piece to protect the bread in the vault. Most of them don't know how to pull a trigger, so they get it in the gut or head and their widows collect the pension."

"Who told you that bullshit?" he asked.

"Mami. She read it to me from *El Diario* while I was having dinner. It happens all the time."

"It doesn't happen all the time. And even if it did, it's still worth it. They make better bread than a short-order cook."

"Why don't you get a better job?"

"Where? Doing what?"

"I don't know. Anything."

"Stay in school, Santos. Don't make my mistake."

"You know who you sound like?"

"Papi?"

"You must be getting old already."

"He's not always wrong, you know. Sometimes he knows what he's talking about."

"Oh, I don't know about that."

"That's why you should stick it out in school."

"You wanna cut the sermon short now? I already heard it from the judge."

El Judge went to Sunday Mass. He attended the 10:30 with Mrs. Degetau. They never missed it. His daughters went to the 11:30. He trusted them to do that by themselves. Maybe he shouldn't have. One Sunday morning, close to 11:30, I was walking with Tego down Fifth Avenue. We were headed for a big play-off game in the Central Park baseball diamonds, and we spotted Norma and Delia walking inside the Vanderbilt Garden; they were in a hurry.

"I thought they were supposed to be in church," I said. "Did they lose their faith too?"

"I don't think so, Santos. Sometimes they just lose their sense of direction and end up in there."

"For what, to pick flowers for the altar?"

"No, that's against the law. They just look at them. They have some nice flowers in there."

"So they're playing hooky from Mass, eh?"

"It looks like."

"If the judge catches them, their ass is cooked."

"He won't catch them," said Tego. "He trusts them. Why don't you go in there and say something to Delia?"

"Like what?"

"Anything you want, as long as it ain't nasty."

"She's never said boo to me. Why should I be nasty?"

"I know. You're supposed to say it first."

"What should I tell her? You know all about this stuff."

"I just told you. The first thing that comes to your head. She ain't stupid."

"I know she's not. I am."

"Forget it, then."

I couldn't. We walked to the diamonds in silence, and when we got there I had a hard time keeping my mind on an interesting game. He didn't, even though he had more reason to be distracted by the play-offs. His team had been eliminated a few weeks before, and he had been the starting pitcher in the fatal game between the Orocovis Shipping Co. Pirates and the Muñoz Meat Market Matadors. He had given up a barrage of hits, a slew of walks, and five runs before Millo the manager, all pissed off, walked up to the mound spitting tobacco juice left and right and asked him what the hell was the matter with his stuff.

"You're our ace hurler, Tego," he said, still spitting. (Tego told me what he'd said afterwards; the spitting I saw for myself.)

"I just ain't got it today, Millo." He had just split up with Norma, and he couldn't concentrate on his delivery. His curves were high and outside, his fastballs went into the dirt in front of home plate, and his breaking balls were extra-base handouts. So he told Millo to yank him out of the game. Millo clawed the mound with his cleats, shoved both hands in his back pockets, and nodded at the "bullpen," a roped-off area next to the cuchifrito and beer vendors.

"He said he made up his mind to pull me out ten batters ago," Tego told me, "and send me to the bush leagues, whatever the hell that means. He gets nasty when things are going bad for the team."

"You should have hit him one."

"Yeah, sure. That's how you cure everything, right, Santos? You hit 'em one. Maybe you should get those fists of yours insured before you break your knuckles on somebody's teeth."

"I was just talking. Norma really got to you, eh?"

"I told you she wasn't my type, dammit."

"Is that what El Judge told you? I'd like to hang him by the—"

"You better go play with your friends, Santos. I'm losing my cool."

"Don't let it get you, Tego. Fight it. See you later."

"Yeah, no hurry." He was like that on and off for about a month; then he met Amalia, a pieceworker, and got over it.

* * *

Delia was going out with two Conquistadores and a Wizard at the same time. The two Conquistadores wore glossy black jackets that displayed the name of their "action club" in white letters on the back. The Wizard's jacket was a Day-Glo-orange job with black lettering. The initials V.W.C. were printed over his heart. That made him the Vice War Counselor, the one who subbed for the regular W.C. when that officer couldn't attend a war council.

I never saw Delia coming home by herself; one of those three was always with her. As far as I knew, they never overlapped, so she must have had the situation under control. They walked with her as far as the stoop; then they'd sit there, chewing the rag between two old pillars. She smiled and laughed a lot. I used to wonder if maybe she wasn't overdoing it, just to show off her terrific chipped tooth; she can't be all that happy. Maybe she is. And her nonstop gum-chewing could have been a case of nerves, but maybe it wasn't. She had been a tomboy in grammar school; now she was a very successful flirt, from the looks of it. And she went in for "action-club" types, goons, like those three.

After five or ten minutes of talk (which I never got close enough to overhear), she'd yawn or frown, or give the air in front of her a sad, glazy-eyed stare, flick a look at her wristwatch, give the Wizard or Conquistador a see-you-later smile, and disappear inside the building. I never saw her take any of them upstairs with her. El Judge, if he knew of their existence (I think he did), wouldn't have been hospitable; she was still too young to be bringing boys home, and she'd never be old enough to bring home a bun, jung or not.

But going out with them was something else. Almost every weekend, before Tego and Norma broke up, Delia and one of the Conquistadores or the Wizard, accompanied them. They went to dance halls like the Palladium and the Taft, or to one of the three movie houses on 86th Street—"German Town," we used to call that street—where you could see first-run flicks fresh from Hollywood, if you had that kind of money. Tego, before he left Chelsea, had worked as an ice boy, delivering blocks of it in buckets to those neighborhood merchants who hadn't caught up with refrigeration; and with what he made from that part-time job he could afford to take Norma to high-class places like the Taft, the RKO 86th, and the Loew's Orpheum. Whatever good times they had, or how good they had them, I knew nothing about; I guessed at them. He didn't give me the details. I pictured them swinging to the salsa in those jam-packed ballrooms everybody talked about, and passing popcorn around in the German Town flicks.

"Why don't you make a play for Delia, Santos?"

I was sitting on the edge of our bed scribbling the first draft of a composition on mouth-to-mouth resuscitation for my swimming instructor at Franklin. It was a penalty he had imposed on me because I couldn't float. I could do everything else well enough to pass, but I couldn't float without treading water, which the instructor said was cheating. He finally gave up and told me my bones were too heavy, and the composition he'd assigned me was meant to compensate for my deficiency. "Maybe you should go in for wrestling, Malánguez," he had told me, and I had pretended to take him seriously.

"Why should I make a play for her, Tego?"

"For one thing, she likes you. And for another thing, she's a good-looking girl, which you shouldn't pass up."

"Did she tell you she likes me?"

"She wouldn't come right out and say that to a guy, Santos. But she told it to Norma, and Norma squealed."

"What else?"

"She said she likes the way you play stoopball. In my opinion, you're some kind of show-off on the outfield. You make easy catches look impossible, but maybe she likes that, which I think is a big hint."

"I've never caught her looking at me showing off on the field."

"They got sneaky ways of taking in an outfielder, Santos. The time to look you straight in the eyes comes later, after they get to know you. I'm talking about *her* type, though. The others are another story. Types like Delia have to protect themselves from *Picadillo* types like you. At first, anyway. Otherwise, you'll think she's an easy lay."

"Who said I thought she was?"

"That's not the point, Santos. Stop playing stoopball with me."

"I'm not. What's the point? Tell me."

"Forget it."

"No. What's the point?"

"I forget. Do what you want. I can't help you."

Maybe he thought we were all born with the same making-out

talent. He had it, so he couldn't see why everyone else didn't. That's how it looked to me.

He said he couldn't help me, but I think he tried. I think he talked to Delia about me. He probably told her she'd have to make the first move, "because Santos is a shy guy. He's nice, though, even if he's my brother."

I was covering left field; she looked me in the eye and asked me if I was "Tego's kid brother." She was playing it as dumb as she could, which I appreciated. I felt nervous, but I controlled myself enough to play it straight.

"When your hands are shaking and your heart's going like crazy," Tego had told me, "play it straight. Don't even try to make a joke. It'll flop."

So I played it straight. "Yeah, he's my brother."

She was smiling and chewing her Chiclet; I stared at her chipped tooth.

"You ever go out, Santos?"

"To where?"

"Anywhere. Dancing, the movies. Things like that."

"Sure. Some of the—sometimes." Her eyes, as I put it to myself later, were "very hazel," and there were smile wrinkles at the eye-corners of her nose.

"That's nice," she said, and waited for me to go on from there; but my mind had gone blank. "Nice" was a word I had trouble dealing with, anyway. Brother Fish back in the seventh grade took off points for "nice" whenever it showed up in our compositions. "It's an open-ended word, boys. Doesn't mean anything, doesn't lead anywhere. Be more specific."

All this lasted two minutes at most. She checked the time on her wrist, shut her mouth without letting up on the chewing, and lost or took back her smile. Then her eyes got glazy, and a line drive caromed off my shoulder. The opposition's man-at-the-plate had caught me napping out there, and all I could do was watch the rubber ball bounce toward third, a manhole cover. The Tots' third baseman one-handed it at the same time that the runner on second was sliding into the "bag." It would have been a putout, but a careless driver in a Chevrolet coupé came along just then and almost creamed the runner, who was saved from a permanent putout only because he overslid the bag. And I got chewed out by my teammates.

"Santos, goddammit," screamed the third baseman, "either you're gonna play left or you're gonna bullshit with the broads!" The second baseman nodded and said I couldn't have it both ways.

"Who said I did?" I said, just to say something face-saving. In my shoes, Tego would have told them to find a sub for him, and spent the time talking to Delia on the stoop. But I didn't even have the time of day to offer her; she had her own watch.

She was still there when I turned around. "That could have happened to anybody, Santos." Maybe so, but so what? It had happened to *me*. In her opinion, she said, I was "a very good stoopball player." I thanked her; she smiled; I couldn't. She said she'd see me around sometime, then turned and climbed up the steps of her stoop.

She saw me around sometime, all right. She saw me lots of times, whenever she was coming or going and I was out there manning left field. Usually the Wizards' V.W.C. or one of the Conquistadores was waiting for her on the stoop, taking in our stoopball game. Sometimes, coming and going, she said hi or hello, and sometimes she said nothing, depending on her mood. I always returned her one-word greeting, and the smile that went with it; and her companion of the day always looked me up and down with a threat in his eye. That was it; I'd had my chance.

One day, chasing a fly ball backwards, I crashed into one of the Conquistadores. He was sitting on the spot where El Judge alias Walrus liked to sit, and I knocked him on his back. I forgot about the ball and started to help him back up; he slapped my hand away and told me to watch it.

"Watch what?" I said. "The ball? It's down the basement. It went down there for a ground-rule double."

He didn't like that, and started removing his Conquistadores jacket. I backed up a couple of steps and waited for him to hang his garment up on the picket fence. He was wearing polished shoes with pointy tips, tassels, and leather soles; I was in sneakers, which gave me the advantage. I'd keep moving around him and tire him out, then move in on him. But the Tots stepped in and yanked me away. The center fielder wanted to know whether I was crazy or something. He said I had to have flipped to be messing with one of the Conquistadores, who outnumbered us about nine to one and who specialized in warfare.

"I don't care," I said. "He started it."

"So what, Santos?" the third baseman said.

And the second baseman: "He started it, and he's gonna finish it, too."

And the first baseman: "You better apologize to him. If he goes get his boys we're gonna be in for a wasting, and then what difference does it make who started it."

So I walked up to the Conquistador, who was waiting for me, and told him I was sorry, though I didn't know for what. "The guys said to tell you I'm sorry," I said. "They don't wanna mess with your boys, and I don't blame them. I don't either." I held out my hand and asked him if he wanted to shake.

"Go shove your handshake," he said.

I nodded and walked off while he removed his jacket from the picket. A couple of minutes later, while waiting for my turn at the plate, I saw him and Delia walking toward Madison. They were going somewhere in a hurry.

I think it was sometime in her high-school senior year that she got involved with Cisco Barcelo, the third baseman of the Orocovis Shipping Co. Pirates. Cisco was tall, wiry, and fast on his feet; he also had a neat Emiliano Zapata moustache and a missing front tooth on the right side of his upper jaw from a hot grounder that had taken a bad hop on wet grounds. He couldn't afford to replace the knocked-out tooth (and never would, I thought, because he was another high-school casualty. I think Tego's entire team was a high-school casualty). He was one of several Orocovis Pirates who had tried out for the Yankees' and Mets' farm clubs, but he didn't make it. Tego said he hadn't come anywhere near making it. We all thought it was too bad, because we'd always wanted one of the guys from the block to make it to the majors, and of all the guys on the block, Cisco had stood the best chance of playing in Shea or Yankee Stadium, or wherever. We would have settled for Philadelphia.

El Judge must have gone into mourning when Delia told him she was going to marry Cisco. Tego said he didn't think Mrs. Degetau would mind Cisco for a son-in-law. "He's a nice guy, even if he ain't going nowhere." But the judge was less interested in nice guys than in successful ones. I pictured him pulling his hair and asking her, *"Porqué, mija?* Why? Why this jung bun? Why you did not find a photographer, like Amparo?" And she: "Because he's a nice guy, Papá, and he's cute and he knows how to give a girl a nice time, too."

If anybody had bothered to ask my opinion, I would have said it served El Judge right. After what he'd pulled on Tego, he deserved a bun with a missing tooth in his family, somebody to offset the *gusano*. The judge had gotten his at last. Maybe God had given it to him. Maybe "circumstances" had.

"How come Delia married Cisco, Tego?" We were in the dark; he had just kicked me awake.

"I don't know why. Go back to sleep."

"Maybe she liked the hole in his teeth."

"What's bugging you now, Santos? You had your chance."

"I don't think he's her kind."

"That's not up to you to say."

"A lot of guys had the hots for her."

"Yeah, except you."

"To tell you the truth, I did too."

"So what stopped you?"

"I don't know. How many girls with a smile like that you think have a chipped tooth?"

"Twenty million. Maybe thirty. You talk like she was born with that broken tooth."

"I don't care how she got it."

"She liked you, too. But all you did was play stoopball."

"Yeah, well, that's under the bridge now."

"I told you, Santos, don't let 'em come to *you.*"

"Okay, but stop kicking me in the face."

"Next time, you make the play. It's the only way. Take it from me. Now let's go to sleep."

"Not if you keep kicking me in the face."

"I'm not kicking your face."

"Who the hell is, then?"

"Nobody. It's all in your head. See you in the morning."

He had to open up the luncheonette early. He had to start cooking breakfast by seven for those workers who didn't make it at home. One of them was a seamstress, his future wife.

9: Digging In

"THE BEST WAY TO FIND a position, Santos," Papi used to tell me, "is to stumble into it." That was his way of leading into the story of how he found the gondola job with an Italian construction crew shortly after he and his brother Mito and Mito's wife, Agripina, arrived in New York.

"I didn't have to pay a penny, Santos. Nobody asked me anything about my past. Not until I was hired, anyway. I just walked in off the street."

Wandered in, he meant. Lost. Freezing his testicles. He got off at the wrong stop on the Broadway local. He should have gotten off at 96th Street, taken another local back up to 110th and Lenox, a crosstown bus to Lexington, and walked down to his "home." He lived in a rooming house, a single room occupancy near Saint Misericordia's R.C. Church, his other home.

But he fell asleep that day on the local and got off at 137th Street, a long walk from home. All the money he had on him was some loose change and he didn't want to waste it on another token, so he decided to get back to his SRO on foot. It would do him good, this walk, if it didn't turn him to ice.

Up the cold hill he goes, not sure whether he's heading in the right direction or toward New Jersey, and not caring, he's that lonely. He's also recently unemployed. Burdock Bride Frocks down on Thirty-something and Seventh has relieved him of his duties as an assistant packer for misaddressing one shipment too many. The head packer has been lying on his behalf all along, but now he's had it.

"There's a limit to how many mistakes you're allowed in this life, Geránimo," the headman tells him, making it sound like a moral lapse on Papi's part. And all Papi can plead in self-defense is that he had a "meegraine" at the time he made his fatal error.

"So buy a bottle of Bayer's," the head packer tells him. "On your time."

"In other words, Santos, I am fired. This head packer is polite, and doesn't like to use filthy language like 'fired' and the other things he called me when he was urinated off. I don't argue back. I was expecting for it." Urinated off? Sometimes he liked to coin a euphemism.

The day he got off at the wrong stop, he had been at his brother's and sister-in-law's apartment on Fox Street, East Bronx, taking advantage of their hospitality and their handouts: another free meal (Agripina gets high marks for her cooking, some of the best in the Bronx), guitar music, and singing (solos, duets, and trios). He'd had himself a good time, and returned the favor with his talents. But freeloading has its limits, and he's too polite to push them. Besides, Agripina wouldn't care for his hanging around the apartment too long. Her sense of privacy is strong. He understands. Nobody has to tell him about privacy. So, before he'd like to, he leaves.

He's not looking forward to that SRO on Lexington. It's a lonely place, and it's noisy. His most valuable possession there, aside from his gold-tipped pen and the stationery he uses to write his wife and sons, is a pawnshop radio his brother gave him. He keeps it tuned to *La Voz Hispana,* like someone on hurricane watch. First thing he does when he gets in is turn it on, then the light; then he takes off his secondhand army coat (a Catholic Charities discount), hangs it up on the nail on the door, puts the coffeepot on the hot plate, takes his customary leak in the communal john, and then, with a cup of coffee at his elbow, starts in on his latest letter to Lilia and the boys. His gold-tipped pen was a farewell present from Octavio Cardona, Chuito's godfather, who gave it to him the day he and Mito left the island, and he can't bring himself to pawn it, much as he's tempted to at times.

"My dear Lilia! You have a lucky husband. I fell asleep on the subway train and found a job with some Italians. I push a wheelbarrow. Let me tell you about it, since I have all the time in the world. . . ."

At the top of a cold hill on Amsterdam Avenue, he sees a crew of Italian-looking men working away as if this weren't the coldest day of the year. Some of them are singing in Italian; and at first, in his ignorance, he wonders if maybe they're not a company of professional singers rehearsing for an opera.

He walks up to a couple of them and asks in broken English if they need some help. They take one look at him and laugh—who is this little iceman in the army coat? But he gets the job anyway. Out of compassion, he thinks afterward, since they seem to be all filled up. Maybe they can use some extra comic relief on the job, a butt of jokes during lunch break. For a steady job, he'll put up with whatever ridicule they want to throw at him. "Let them kid me all they want, Santos. For regular work, I'll stand on my head." Maybe he did.

They give him a wheelbarrow and throw in a quick lesson on what to do with it. He fills it with frozen sand on this side of the site and shoves it to that side. A sand-and-rocks man. "The Malánguez Cadillac," some of the men call his wheelbarrow. He calls it his Italian gondola. They get along all right. He keeps his mouth shut, follows orders (everybody's), and keeps to himself. Sometimes the kidding comes close to getting out of hand. How come he doesn't look too much like a Spik? What's he going to do with himself when he grows up? And others of that kind. Some of these questions, and the answers he retaliates with (smiling), he wouldn't repeat in public. It's everybody's way of letting off tension, he thinks. No hard feelings. They were kind enough to give him this job, after all. He opens a savings account and begins putting a few dollars into it every payday. For four plane tickets. Lilia and the boys. And for an apartment, and furnishings.

His Italian colleagues teach him some opera lyrics and explain what they mean. *"Amarilli, mia bella, non credi O del mio cor dolce desio . . ." "Sebben, crudele, mi fai languir Sempre fedele ti voglio amar . . ."* He sometimes hums himself to sleep with these; and years later he would sing them to himself in our dining room, alternating bel canto with the le-lo-lais of our old village. A confusion of cultures, mild in his case.

But there was to be a time limit to this wheelbarrow windfall. It was seasonal work, and at the end of spring they let him go. Then he moved on to a laundry, a comedown. They put him to pressing shorts and folding shirts nine to five. During lunch breaks, he looked around for something cooler. One of his co-workers told him to try the Hotel Roosevelt. "They're hiring dishwashers this week." But when he applied, the man who did the kitchen hiring told him he didn't meet their qualifications, their height requirements.

"To wash the dishes?" he asked.

Yes, he was told. Besides, it wasn't just his height; it was also his eyesight.

And since when, he wanted to know, did one need the eyes of a hawk to wash dishes?

"Since I said so," the man told him. "Listen, Mr. Malan-guéss, I don't have to defend our hiring policy to anyone who walks in off the street looking for a job."

"You mispronounced my name," Papi tells him.

"So scram," he's told. He scrams, before the police are called in.

That night he punches the walls of his SRO, damaging private property as well as his knuckles. His neighbors bang on their own walls to shut him up. He swabs the back of his right hand with iodine and spends most of the night blowing on his bleeding knuckles. He doesn't repeat this outburst. Bad for his handwriting, for one thing. "That last letter you wrote us," Mami writes back, "was almost illegible. What's the problem, Gerán?"

"I was in a hurry, Lilia," he answers. "I was on my way to a job interview."

A steam-room colleague put him on to the American Combining Company, a textile place in Brooklyn. He took the New Lots by mistake, then switched to the Flatbush when he discovered his error, and got there at about the time he should have been back in the laundry. But it ended well; he got the job. The man who did the hiring for the ACC misspelled his name: "Malanga," after a former employee who had gone back to the island after twenty years on this job. Papi didn't correct the misspelling until it made no difference how they spelled his last name.

From his ACC paycheck he had deductions to make: his wife

and sons, the savings bank, his father-in-law (installments on a dead mule), and a dentist on Fox Street, who had put a gold crown in his mouth. This was to be a surprise for Lilia, something special.

He was disappointed when we weren't impressed by this gold tooth. Why, Mami asked him once, had he turned his mouth into a gold mine?

It was for her benefit, he told her. "I wanted to look presentable." The sweat of his brow had gone into it. Wasted sweat, it seemed.

He should have asked her first, she said.

"It's my mouth," he told her. He had pushed a gondola for this tooth, and his own wife was ridiculing it. It was the only luxury he had allowed himself during those SRO days. Single Cave Occupancy, he might have called that period of his life.

Even when he had to step outside that room for a trip to the toilet, or for a rapid shower in temperamental water (sometimes lukewarm, usually freezing, and always mixed with rust and other disgusting impurities), he locked his door. Not that the lock was going to keep anyone out. But he didn't want to tempt his neighbors. Besides, Octavio's pen, his brother Mito's radio, his Catholic Charities army coat, were precious possessions, think what anyone would; so were the letters from his wife. He numbered and dated the envelopes, he tied them in a bundle and kept them "locked" inside a shoe box. He reread them often, had memorized some of them, didn't want them stolen by a neighbor.

The place was noisy, a lot of fights broke out on weekends, and it was lonely in there. Always that, the hardest of his problems. Mito and Agripina had just had their first baby, Genoveva, an unattractive name in his opinion. It didn't go with the kid's looks, at any rate. Whatever they called her, this baby picked up his mood. But Agripina was one of those jealous mothers who don't like people handling their babies too much. "Let me have her back, Gerán, before she forgets who her mother is. She needs my breast." He took those remarks as hints: time to go.

His other home, Saint Misericordia's Church, helped some. He went there every morning, including Saturdays, when even the priests looked bored; the altar boys fell asleep on their feet, the parishioners on their knees. He pinched himself to stay awake, considering it sinful to fall asleep during the service. Afterward, he went back to bed. Fire trucks, police sirens, neighbors, bad dreams, woke him up from time to time. He didn't recommend that kind of life, he told me, whispered it to me, as if ashamed of the experience. "Stay away from the SROs."

Eventually, against his better judgment, he made friends with one of the people who lived in that rooming house, a woman in her twenties from Orocovis or Morovis, some place not far from Bautabarro. This young woman, whose name he couldn't recall, he said, worked for Linens of the Week or Month; she washed, starched, pressed, and folded all week. Not exactly a vocation. She had a couple of friends from the island there, but they were all married women with husbands, kids, and other lookouts. So, like him, she was by herself. She had come to join her fiancé, El Prometido, who had disappeared somewhere in the Hunts Point section of the Bronx. Needle in a haystack. She hadn't heard from him going on six months. Something horrible must have happened. Her telegrams and letters were wasted, unacknowledged. So she decided to come and find him herself. She was in love.

After a lot of detective work, including ads in *El Diario* (a waste of money), she found out that El Prometido was living with a divorced woman who had eight or nine kids from previous husbands and lovers. Now she was pregnant by El Prometido. Very fertile, this woman. A cow type. "Which I don't mean as an insult, Santos," Papi said. "Far be it. But—well, I can almost hear her mooing. She was trapped by her own fertility, and whatever else. Those men in her life, for one thing.

"And this El Prometido had the *cojones* to suggest to my friend, La Prometida, that she take up with him by moving to her own apartment on Simpson Street, near that police precinct we've all heard about. The Apache one. That was the same block El Prometido and his pregnant woman were living on. He tried all kinds of tricks to talk La Prometida into going along with this proposal."

He offered to find her a better job in a dress factory and to pay her rent until she got on her own. Some of his friends on Simpson would paint her new apartment. The way El Prometido put this proposal to her, it was as if she had no choice, as if she couldn't wait to jump into it. He's coming on like the head of a numbers syndicate. Big man, a take-charge type. Just leave it to me. Easy Simpson Street. Like a personal friend of Genovese or Costello. When what he is is a big mouth, holes in his pockets, he can use a new pair of heels, but he can't seem to afford them: He's up to his nose in easy payments.

So what does she think of his proposal? "You're going to hell," she tells him. He laughs, she leaves, and ends up in the same rooming house where Papi lives.

"What was her name?" I asked him.

"I can't remember. It's not important." He usually had a good memory for names. "We became very good friends, that's all."

He said he tried talking her into going back to her home village, but she wouldn't. She had been shamed by her fiancé; to go back home would be a disgrace. Maybe she was exaggerating a little, but that was how she felt, and he understood. His own situation was similar, if for different reasons.

What, I asked him, had gone on between the two of them? Nothing, he said, looking embarrassed enough to be holding back the truth. She went to live on the West Side after a while; a lower-rent SRO. He hoped she was married and happy. They'd lost contact. He switched topics quickly, told me about the "tragic" telegram he received one day from "Lilia."

The telegram said she was arriving at La Guardia in two days, Wednesday morning. That made no sense to him. But the name of the sender was Lilia, and he knew only one Lilia. Maybe her father had given her money for plane tickets. Maybe he had died and left her something. Hard to believe, but no less hard than this incredible telegram. Maybe she'd gone insane.

He hardly slept that night, and he was so confused that it didn't occur to him to send back a telegram demanding an explanation. Next day and night, same sleeplessness. He must have smoked a pack of cigarettes in a couple of hours; he went into a bar and grill and got drunk on three beers. Wednesday morning, looking like the original insomniac, he headed for the airport hours before the plane was due to arrive. He took a bus and train, then a cab. The driver took him for someone who didn't know his way around and made him pay for his ignorance, left him close to broke; and Papi was too polite to refuse the thief a tip: two quarters.

He got there a little past sunup and spent close to five hours abusing his stomach and nervous system with cup after cup of black coffee, waiting for the airplane to land and clarify that mysterious telegram. ". . . Starving, but the last thing on my mind was food, if that makes any sense . . . my nerves." The waitresses kept a close eye on him, as if they thought he was going to steal something. They put the salt, pepper, mustard, and ketchup out of his reach; the cream was under the counter, the donuts and turnovers on the other side of it. They had him all wrong.

The plane was late; when it finally arrived, there was no sign of Lilia and the boys, only strangers walking into the arms of waiting loved ones. He was about to break down when this woman with high cheekbones, her face almost a mask from all the makeup, a bony woman, close to breastless, swished up to him as if she had invented sophistication, and introduced herself as Lilia Tapia de Cardona. Her middle name was Pompilia, and he must be Gerán. Doesn't he remember her?

"No," he says, embarrassed. "Almost yes, but no. Forgive me, I had short sleep last night. Fire engines . . ."

She explains that they're second cousins, or maybe only third. "You know how backward they are about keeping birth records in our villages. Some of them have never heard of the twentieth century."

He nods politely. Who is this woman? "Whoever she is, in less than a minute she's talking like an old friend."

"Whatever cousins we are, Gerán," she's going on, "I'm on that side of our family that has a few successful members." And when he asks her what she means by that, she wastes no time telling him about the medical doctor in Mayagüez, the "classical" pianist in Ponce (a poverty-parish organist, he can't help thinking), the schoolteacher in Santurce and the other one in Hato Rey, the parish priest in Caguas, the cement executive in Bayamón. . . . She goes on with this list of family notables he's never heard of; she's sounding more desperate with each name dropped,

"What she wanted, Santos, was a place to stay." So he asks her cautiously, as politely as he can put it, whether she'd mind spending a day or two at his "apartment. My broom closet, I meant. But I didn't want to offend her with language like that."

She wastes about ten seconds pretending to be thinking it over, and while waiting for her guaranteed yes, he sizes up her outfit: a thin purple dress decorated with nondescript tropical flowers, something out of a San Juan bargain store, he can't help thinking;

and a pair of white shoes, imperfectly dyed high-heelers, some of
the original black showing through the white.

"Very well, Gerán," she tells him nonchalantly, as if doing him
a kindness, "maybe for a couple of days until I can find a decent
hotel." He tells her she shouldn't have any trouble finding one, and
off they go.

"I thought you were my wife and kids," he tells her on the
subway back.

"Do I look like her?" She must think he's trying to flatter her.

"I meant that you both have the same name."

"I know," she says.

"You do? May I ask who told you?"

"Octavio's Calpurnia. My cousin. I stayed as her guest before
taking the plane."

This Calpurnia must be running her own rooming house. "She
must have put this Lilia Pompilia up to the telegram trick. Talk
about *maromas*. All kinds of stunts to get something for nothing,
Santos."

"Did you sleep in the same bed?" I ask.

"Who, me? What are you getting at?"

"Nothing. One bed, two people. That's always a problem, depending."

"No problem. I slept on the floor."

"I think you're too generous sometimes, Papi. That's one of
your—"

"It was good for my back. I was her host, anyway. Where else
can I sleep?"

"How long did you have to sleep on the floor?"

"Two weeks."

"Did she leave you a tip?"

"I wouldn't take a tip even if she had anything to tip with. She
was almost broke when she arrived."

And he went broke feeding her, taking her to old Mexican
movies (he slept through those, he said) and to employment agencies. It turned out she had secretarial skills, so she wasn't all helpless, and she finally found a position (he found it for her) with a
Latin American import-export outfit. He got docked for taking off
from work so he could escort her around the job agencies. And
when he came home from work one day, looking forward to a little

companionship, all he found of her was a note pinned to his pillow. It said a friend of hers from work had put her onto a "decent hotel" downtown (no address) and that she had decided to move in right away before someone else took it. She promised to come around as soon as possible, either next day or the day after. "But you know how it is," he told me a long time later. "I never saw her again."

"Did you try to track her down at least?"

"What for? She was on her own now. I have a feeling some man in that import-export place fell in love with her, and that was that."

"And you weren't even angry?"

"For what?"

"For being taken in by this Pompilia Lilia."

"Lilia Pompilia."

"All right."

"No, I wasn't. What for? It happens all the time."

Not angry, he repeated, but frustrated, impatient to get his own family over. "Desperate, Santos." The lonelies hit him hard again, and not for the first time he considered pawning Octavio's gold-tipped pen and Mito's old radio with it; he also thought of giving up his SRO and sleeping in basements for as long as he had to, a small saving. Except that was just another way of committing suicide, a major sin. So he controlled the urge and went to his brother instead. "But only after trying everything else. Mito and Agripina had next to nothing themselves, and I didn't want them to think I was turning them into Household Finance."

Somebody at work put him on to this HFC, and he went to them, the local branch, but they didn't even ask to see his Social Security card; he had no collateral. Same for the two savings banks he approached. "Let me put it to you this way, Mr. Malánguish," one bank manager told him. "It's not what our bank can do for you, but what you can do for our bank, if you see what I'm getting at." No collateral, no loan. The alert guard's eyes followed him to the exit, holding his head up. The revolving door almost brought him back inside, he was that upset.

His favorite confessor at Saint Misericordia's Church, a benevolent old Irishman who had worked his way up to the priesthood ("I spent my boyhood shining shoes, my son. I worked on the docks before I joined the seminary"), suggested he try Catholic Charities, which specialized in emergency cases. "And you look as though

you belong in an emergency clinic, Germán. No offense meant."
None taken.

Catholic Charities told him they had no money. "We don't
dispense cash, Mr. Málangas. Only household items, secondhand
necessities. Look around and pick out a few. Take your time." He
took as many pawnable items as he could carry: two secondhand
shopping bags stuffed with used pots, pans, dinnerware, a pair of
shoes without laces, a shadeless lamp shaped like a jug of whiskey
with a four-leaf-clover design and some green words in a foreign
language, two pairs of pants too big for him, and a couple of shirts
he wouldn't be caught in, no matter how desperate. The third
pawnshop he approached with these handouts gave him three dollars for both shopping bags and asked him not to come back. He
promised not to.

He visited *bodegas* and asked if they could use a part-time
delivery man, but they were either all filled up or they had no
deliveries. "We're strictly cash-and-carry here, Malánguez," one
grocer told him. "Try Don Matos down the block." Don Matos
down the block laughed him out of his hole-in-the-wall, and suggested he try shining shoes. Which he considered, but the competi-
tion in that field was already fierce; an amateur like him trying to
move in on the pros would get swamped, go bankrupt overnight.
Same for selling the Sunday *News* Saturday nights. He tried doing
that and came back home with five unsold copies. From eight P.M.
to two A.M. he had succeeded in selling all of one copy to a heavy
drinker in a bar.

And finally, before hitting his brother for an interest-free loan,
he discovered empties. There were refundable bottles all over the
streets: milk, soda, beer. You didn't even need the entire bottle;
from the neck up, an empty bottle was worth two or three cents.
Weekends, armed with a potato sack one grocer gave him, he went
around collecting discarded empties. He found them in the gutters,
in garbage cans, on stoops, in empty lots, and in Central Park. That
park was a gold mine of empty beer bottles, each one worth three
cents. Grocers and candystore owners began referring to him as
"The Empty Bottles Man," "Señor Refundable," "Don Deposits,"
"Mr. Bottleneck," and other tributes. He couldn't afford to defend
himself, a choice between hard cash and swallowing his self-respect.
He swallowed the respect, for the time being.

Then the Law, in the form of two mounted policemen, put an end to this scavenging. They caught him coming out of the 106th Street exit with his stuffed sack. This was about two hours past curfew. "Let's see what you got in the sack, Chico," one of them said.

"It is just bottles, officer," he answered, and they said that they'd believe his story as soon as he showed them. So he had to pull every empty out of the sack (some of them were only refundable necks) and upend it to satisfy the officers that there were no jewels or illegal drugs inside: only insects (spiders, a couple of Japanese beetles), but these didn't count as contraband, so they had to let him go. Another nut, they concluded.

"Let's not catch you in the park after curfew." And they confiscated his flashlight (borrowed from someone at work), a burglar's tool.

As usual whenever the cops stopped someone for any reason, spectators had gathered around the scene of the frisking ("I felt like a bum, Santos, which maybe I was just then") and he decided to give up exchanging bottles for our plane tickets. There had to be a less humiliating way, and a faster one: Mito again.

Mito had about fifty dollars in the bank (for his children's education, he had said), and something more important: collateral. The chef at the hotel where he worked—a fancy one on Park Avenue—and the chef's steward, and a couple of other men with impressive titles all vouched for Mito's honesty. Good enough for Mito's savings bank and the local HFC. "We'll pay them back any way we can," he told Papi, as if there was nothing to worry about, as if this weren't the first time he had pulled that stunt. As if he weren't peeing in his own pants.

Papi didn't have too much trouble finding a furnished apartment for us. He did a lot of asking around and taped hand-lettered signs on storefronts. Within two weeks he got a response from an old couple who couldn't wait to move back to the island as permanent guests of their grandchildren and others. Their apartment was furnished and they wanted a hundred dollars in cash, but that was just a bluff. He had no trouble knocking them down to fifty—a steal, but he had no choice—thirty cash and twenty in installments. They'd just have to give him their new address and trust him to come through. (He did.) They were impatient to leave. "This whole thing has been a big mistake for us, Gerán," the old man told him. "But you're still young." He guessed he was; it didn't always feel like it.

And that was what we moved into: fifth floor, five-and-a-half rooms, a huge hospital one block away to the south, Central Park less than a block away to the west, the Home and Hospital for the Sons and Daughters of Israel on one corner, Mr. Cohn and Son's Farmacia on the other, and, spanning two windows, a fancy fire-scape for just in case. "Not bad, Lilia, eh?" he told Mami.

She wasn't too sure about that. "Is this what we left Bautabarro for?" she said. "I don't think I want to spend the rest of our lives here, Gerán."

"Don't worry, Lilia, we won't. This is just the beginning." He was hurt. She was disappointed. They'd have to work it out.

It was a strange neighborhood: crowded, littered, smelly, loud. Men, grown, growing, and declining, sat on stoops doing nothing special, just talking or staring into the distance, as if expecting something. They played sidewalk cards and dominoes, using garbage cans as chairs. The table was a piece of rescued plywood resting on two pairs of knees. One wrong move and the whole game would come crashing down. "It's different, all right," Mami concluded.

Then there was Papi's problem with Tego and me. We didn't take to him right away. I found his face only vaguely familiar, thanks to those snapshots of himself he'd been sending us twice a year. He hadn't wanted us, he said, to mistake him for a stranger. But we did, anyway, I more than Tego. Couldn't be helped.

In the evening he came home from work with what we called "sugway candy": coin-op chewing gum and Life Savers, Hershey chocolate bars. Big treats. We got hooked on them. But why did he always come home looking so tired, half-corpse, half-human? He tried to cover up his fatigue with grins and smiles, but it didn't work too well. We could see, through his act, his real mood.

"What were you talking about in your sleep?" Mami asked him once.

"*I* was talking in my sleep?"

"All night. You sounded like a master of ceremonies, but I couldn't make out a word."

"Don't look at me, Lilia. I was asleep."

"I wasn't."

He ignored that, or pretended to. He went to the dining room. He had to write Chuito a letter, explain that he was doing what he could to get him over. Chuito hadn't replied to his last two letters. Maybe he felt betrayed, and Papi couldn't blame him, he said, "but that's how it is. He'll just have to be patient."

"When hasn't he been?" Mami said. "I hear some people die from this patience." And once again he ignored her.

"I think," she told him another time, "that we shouldn't be spending so much money on picnics. We could be saving it for Chuito." When spring came, we began going to the park Sunday afternoons, after Mass. We took cheap food with us, mostly frank-furters, processed cheese, Taystee bread, chicken wings, and home-made lemonade. Mami cooked everything in the house before we set off for the "picnic" grounds, a grassy hill near the baseball diamonds. At the bottom of the hill was a winding trickle that drained into the artificial boat "lake" at the north end of the park. Our tablecloth was an old bedsheet that the repatriated couple had left behind. We took our time eating. Nobody bothered us.

But one day, after we hadn't heard from Chuito in a month, Mami began to complain that we were wasting money, and Papi took it as an accusation that he was doing this on purpose, that he didn't really want Chuito, another dependent, to join us; or at least that he was in no hurry to get him over. He lost his temper and denied it, an argument followed, then complete silence. Tego and I were told to go to our bedroom and stay there till they called us. But they forgot about us, or pretended to, and we blamed it all on him. We wanted to go back to the village, without him. He must have known this, but pretended things were coming along just fine.

But then—mainly because of those misunderstandings with Mami—he began coming home later than usual. First an hour late, then two, then close to bedtime. Then one night (the first of many) he didn't come home at all. Mami would dump his food in the garbage ("A sin," she'd say to herself), and when Tego asked her where Papi was, she said he was working overtime, and disap-peared inside their bedroom. She did a lot of reading in there. And praying. Tego and I invented games to use up the time.

Papi's explanation for those overnight absences was that he'd been visiting Mito and Agripina in the Bronx. I don't think he expected us to believe that, but he had to say something. "Before you knew it," he'd say, "it was almost midnight, so I decided to stay over." He said he and Mito were composing a couple of songs. Maybe they could sell them and make some money on the side.

Mami began referring to him as The Composer, and made jokes about his musical talents behind his back. "Compose himself is what he should do," she told us one day. "And I'm ready to go back home."

So were we, even if we had to change bottles for our tickets. We rarely left the house. We took trips, the three of us, to the grocer around the corner, to the public market five blocks away, to church on weekends, and we hurried back home; we avoided our neighbors, even those who tried to befriend us. One reason was that Mami was afraid they'd find out about his overnight absences and spread the word. That would amount to a disgrace she wouldn't be able to live with. So she kept to herself, even though she could use a couple of companions her own age, instead of a couple of sons who were too young to understand what was going on, and so had no trouble blaming everything on "him."

One day, when she couldn't take any more, she got ahold of him in the kitchen and told him off. "I know you're spending your nights with another woman. A *trapo.*" A greasy rag. The Prometida he was to tell me about, discreetly, years later? Lilia Pompilia? He denied her accusation, and proved the truth of that denial by banging on the table and overturning his coffee.

Tego and I ran to the dining room and positioned ourselves on either side of the entrance. If he laid a hand on her, we were going to make him regret it, we thought. He was no more capable of laying a hand on her, on anyone, than she was of walking out on him, but we didn't know that then. Right now he was calling her names: ". . . ignorant and jealous, Lilia." And before she could answer him, he noticed us standing guard at the entrance and told us to go back to our bedroom. "This is not for you," he said.

"Or for me," she told him, and walked with us back to our room, leaving him there with his spilled coffee and the cup on its side.

"I'll hit him," Tego said, back in the room. So would I, I said.

She couldn't help laughing at that. Then she became serious and said, "Don't you dare. Don't you even say it." Whose side was *she* on? They were getting us all confused.

A little later the front door slammed and he was gone again. Another twenty-four-hour break. For two of us, anyway. She was crying in their bedroom, and when we went in there to ask her what it was, the only reason she gave us was that she missed Chuito, and wanted to know whether we didn't miss him also.

We said we did, and I for one felt there must be something wrong with me for not crying over him all the time. I tried forcing myself to, but it didn't work; it worked at other times, when I wasn't trying too hard. But it usually took the form of sadness, not tears. It used to hit Tego, too. "I'm sad, Santos. I miss Chuito." He might be dead by now for all we knew.

And all along, behind our backs, Papi was busy raising the money for that plane ticket. Through Octavio and Calpurnia, he had tracked Chuito down. ". . . Still living in your old home, Gerán . . . working for Lilia's father . . . waiting for the plane ticket, he tells me . . ."

"Why doesn't Octavio buy him that plane ticket?" Mami asked. "He has an army pension, doesn't he?"

"His rent is high, I guess," Papi said.

"I guess godparents aren't what they used to be."

"I'll get him the ticket, Lilia."

"When?"

"Next week."

"You have the money?"

"Almost."

And when she asked him how he got it, he said he'd tell her someday. There may have been a connection between his overnight absences and Chuito's plane ticket, but he never said. I wouldn't have put it past him to spend those missing nights in Central Park, collecting bottles in a potato sack, playing hide-and-seek with the mounted patrolmen. Whatever it was, he got the money and mailed it to Octavio, who was to do him the favor of turning it over to Chuito, who arrived a couple of weeks later.

Tego and I were disappointed. He looked as though he'd been living on bread and water since our departure. And he was evasive about what he'd been doing back in the village all this time. "I

worked for Papagante," he'd say, and leave it at that. Mami and
Papi turned the dining room into his bedroom (the bed came from
Catholic Charities, as did a used print of the Sacred Heart, which
he never got around to hanging up). And after the first two weeks
with us, that was where he spent most of his time after dinner.
Another recluse.

"So why did he come?" Mami asked Papi one night.

"Give him time, Lilia. He's only been here a few weeks. This
is a big change for him. You know what that's like."

"It's his silence that bothers me," she said.

"That's part of his adjustment."

But she insisted it was more than that. "I think it's a grudge, is
what it is," she said.

And Papi insisted the grudge was all in her head, but he probably agreed with her, in secret. "Whatever it is, Lilia, we'll just have
to live with it for a while."

Chuito grinned a lot, no change there, so it was hard to tell what
he was hiding, if he was hiding anything.

Tego and I acted as his chaperones for a while, during his period
of adjustment. We took him to the *bodega,* the candy store, and the
farmacia on Madison. And when Mami took all three of us to the
public *Marqueta* on Park, the mobs made him nervous. They made
all four of us nervous, but he couldn't wait to leave, suspicious, on
his guard, as if someone were out to get him.

After a while he began to take walks by himself, mostly in the
park, and little by little he began making friends with others like
himself, recent arrivals. One of them found him a job as a packer's
assistant downtown, and he began bringing this friend and others
to the house. They spent most of the time in his dining-room
bedroom, door closed. Beer, music, joking, sometimes a little
noisy, then a little noisier, first a couple of hours, then four, five.
Neighbors began calling out from their windows to shut up and let
them go to sleep. Papi and Mami, who must have been feeling
guilty about something, took him aside to discuss some ground
rules. And he stopped inviting his friends altogether. Now he went
to their houses, or someplace where they could pay for the noise
they made. And when Papi and Mami talked to him again, this time
about coming home at "indecent hours," he grinned and said he

was thinking of finding his own place. His friends, he said, were helping him find one.

But before he did, the Army found him out. "I don't know how the hell they tracked me down," he said, grinning.

"It must be all that noise he and his friends were making," Mami told Papi.

"Yes, maybe somebody complained to the recruiting center. This might be good for him, unless God stopped working in strange ways."

The night before he left for Fort Dix, he disappeared. After dinner he said he was going out for a can of beer, and we didn't see him again for four months. During that time in training camp, the message of his short and infrequent letters to us was that the place was cold in winter, which was the only reason he objected to getting up at four in the morning for maneuvers in the forest, and that some of the K.P.'s in the mess hall kitchen would stick their filthy, greasy boots inside the cauldron of scrambled eggs as a way of getting back at the Army. "They're trying to poison the rest of us just to get back at the C.O. But I'm adjusting."

He didn't bother explaining what he meant by "K.P.," "C.O.," and other Army initials and names. As if he didn't care. And when Papi asked him, in a letter, about when we could go visit him, he wrote back saying that they didn't allow visitors in training camp, "and they don't give us any leaves, either. Yoyos don't get leaves." What was a "Yoyo"? He didn't explain that either. He was picking up all this new language and keeping it to himself. Papi and Mami had a lot of reading to do between the lines, and by the time Tego and I got their interpretations of Chuito's cryptic and stingy letters, we hardly knew what it was all about. Not that we cared that much anymore. He wasn't the same person we had left behind in the village.

"People change, that's all," was what Papi had to say to that. Mami said nothing, not out in the open, anyway.

At the end of those four months, he came home on what he called "a very short leave, just long enough to get a good home-cooked meal in my system." He had gained weight, he looked tough, self-confident, somewhat impersonal. It was a two-day leave, but we hardly got to see him. He spent most of it looking up the few friends he had made ("D.P.'s," he called them) before the draft got him. Then he was gone again, before he and Mami and Papi could sit down and have a serious talk about anything.

"I guess there's nothing to talk about," Papi said.

"We must have done something wrong, Gerán," she said.

"Like what?"

"I don't know, he didn't say."

"Maybe he's still adjusting, Lilia."

"I think he has, that's just it. He's a fast learner."

"Something else," Tego said, a new expression he'd picked up in school.

The next time we heard from Chuito, two months later, he had just finished something he called "my specialty training" someplace in the South—without telling us what this specialty was—and was on his way to Korea "to get a personal look at the Chinese."

"Are Koreans Chinese?" Mami asked Papi.

"I don't know, Lilia. He doesn't say."

The next letter we got from Chuito, about a month later, this time from Seoul, "the capital of Korea," answered Mami's question: "Another thing I found out right away was that Koreans are not Chinese. They only look alike. At least that's what the barrel-crackers in my barracks say."

Maybe his next letter home might tell us what a "barrelcracker" in the barracks was. It didn't. He sent us snapshots of himself and a couple of buddies with "geishas," another new word, undefined as usual. "I'm thinking of re-enlisting," he wrote.

"Maybe they will make him a general," I told Tego.

"How they can make him a general, Santos? He don't even have got a high-school diploma. He don't even speak English too good yet, like me and you."

"He speak it better than you, that is for sure."

"That is how much you know, is what it is."

"I *know* I know."

"You don't know nothing. General Chuito. Ha!"

General Chuito came home a buck private. "Not even a first-class private, Lilia," Papi said to Mami on the sly.

Over a substantial welcome-home dinner, Chuito explained why, after two years in the service, he still had no stripe. "Actually, I had one, but I lost it in a game of friendly dice." Some barrelcrack-er had been cheating, and when Chuito caught him and took his losses back, "every penny," the cheater reported him to the C.O. The C.O. in turn asked him to turn in his stripe. "He stripped me of my stripe, and when I told him the whole story, he told me I had no rights anymore. I was a yoyo again, and yoyos don't count for nothing." Now we knew what a yoyo was. "I guess it's like that all over. Get me another beer, Santos." He was the only one drinking at that table. He put a whole six-pack away, and a good deal of Mami's home-cooked meal before he got up and left. He had some old pre-Army friends to look up in the neighborhood.

Within two weeks of his discharge, he was throwing parties in our apartment. Old friends and new friends, both sexes, all hours, as if he were trying to compensate for all those months he had spent by himself back in the village before Papi sent for him. When his discharge money ran out, in less than a month, he had no trouble finding a job as head shipping clerk in a Seventh Avenue factory. Something Frocks. In the Army he had worked for the quartermaster, which explained why his new bosses gave him the top position, over others who had been on the job ten or more years.

In no time, he was making a lot more than Papi, and those weekend parties he threw at our house were becoming more elaborate (Seagram's 7 and 7-Up were added to the beer, then Don Q rum and Coke) and noisier. Neighbors' complaints couldn't be heard over the phono's volume (his phono, brand-new). This went on for about six more weeks after he found his job. Instead of complaining, Papi and Mami let him have his way for a while. We took to spending Saturday nights at Mito's house; we slept over.

"I wouldn't put up with it if I were you, Gerán," Tío Mito would say. Agripina, put upon by four overnight guests in their crowded apartment, would nod; and Mami, embarrassed by the whole thing, would pretend she didn't hear what Mito had said.

"He'll get over it, Mito," Papi would say. "He's still readjusting to civilian life. One of these days he'll grow up and get married."

Tío Mito would shake his head. "I just don't understand this patience of yours, Gerán. Or Lilia's. But I guess you know what you're both doing."

"We do." They didn't look like it.

In the meantime, Chuito and his friends were sleeping in our beds. Mami would spend most of Sunday afternoon cleaning up the mess, stripping the beds, scrubbing the sheets; Papi would take the garbage down; Tego and I would sit in our smelly bedroom, doing Monday's homework for the nuns of Saint Misericordia's school. Chuito was always gone by the time we got back; he wouldn't show up till next night, for dinner; then he'd vanish again. Sometimes we didn't see him for days. We didn't miss him.

One Sunday afternoon, after Mass in the Bronx, we came home to find one of Chuito's friends sleeping in our bathtub. There were about eight inches of water in the tub. The faucet had been turned off; otherwise she might have drowned. She had her clothes on and was snoring peacefully. Chuito and the other guests were gone. They must have overlooked her when they left, or else they'd figured Papi and Mami would look after her until she sobered up. She had a miserable hangover. She told us later that she wasn't used to all that 7-Up. Mami lent her one of her own dresses, a little small on this guest, who was well-built—very well built—but there was nothing Mami could do about that. She gave her breakfast, part of which consisted of two raw eggs for the hangover, and Papi fed her aspirin. Our guest explained, in a contrite voice, that she had intended to take a bath and had fallen asleep.

"In your clothes?" Mami asked.

"I guess I wasn't sober, señora. I don't want you to think I always take a bath with my clothes on."

"Too late," Mami said. "Now I'll spend the rest of my life thinking you always go to the bathtub with your clothes on." I think she was more amused than angry.

As she was leaving, Papi asked her to give Chuito a message from him and Mami. "Tell him I said enough is enough. If he throws another party, I'll call the police. Or maybe I won't. Tell him the penance is up."

She wanted to know what penance.

"He'll know which one," Papi told her. They'd both been very polite to her.

Chuito must have gotten the message, because we didn't see him again for another couple of weeks. He didn't mention the message, though. He acted as though no one had been left behind that particular Sunday. He came with a suitcase, to pick up his things. He had found an apartment.

"I'm glad you haven't been sleeping in a rooming house," Papi said. "I don't recommend those."

· Chuito thought Papi was putting him on. "You wouldn't catch me in one of those, Papi." Then he left, after a cup of coffee. We didn't have any beer in the house.

A week later he came around to break some important news to us. "I'm getting married in a month." We congratulated him. This time Tego and I were sent to the *bodega* for some beers, and we all had a nice time celebrating the event. If we didn't attend the wedding, he said, he'd never talk to us again. Mami and Papi had no intention of not attending the wedding. It would be a farewell of some kind, they said; in more ways than one, they meant.

The four of us went, first to the church on a street called Tinton, then to the reception hall on another street called Dyckman. Those who hadn't attended the church ceremony were already there, and in a short time it was crowded with people, mostly strangers to us. Some of the faces were familiar, though, from the apartment parties, those who had slept in our beds. They were good dancers. The music was live, a sextet. All six could sing. Some of the guests took turns going up on the stage and joining in, but their voices weren't as polished as the sextet's. Nobody minded, though. It was a festive occasion, not a concert.

And there was a good deal of food, and for starters, a bottle of Seagram's 7 and another one of 7-Up on each table. On the immense food table, which also contained extra bottles of Seagram's and soda, was the wedding cake, right in the center. It was a white skyscraper, ten tiers high, and on top of it, in plaster, were a midget bride and groom. From where they stood they had a good view of the hall. I wondered what would happen to them when the cake was cut.

ı In addition to the alcohol and the food, every table came with a special treat for each guest: an almond wrapped in mesh. Also a shiny dime. You pinned this gift to your lapel or your dress. Boys and girls went around collecting these from the grownups. "There must be at least fifty dollars' worth of those dimes," Papi said, amazed.

"Not to mention the almonds," Mami put in.

"Yes," he said, "enough for one month's rent. At least."

Tego and I got sick on sips of Seagram's. Mami had to take us to the washroom. "I told you to stay away from that," she said. "I said stick to the soda." We were sorry we hadn't. Our first hangover was on the way. She washed our faces in cold water. That helped some. Then we left, long before it was over, long before they cut the cake.

We said goodbye to Chuito and his bride. They worked in the same factory. He said she was a first-rate seamstress. She was also good-looking. He had good taste. He told us so, right in front of her. She blushed, but I could tell she agreed with him. There was no reason she shouldn't.

"A good choice," Papi told Mami on the subway back home. She had to agree that was true, and that was all they said on the way back. We were all tired.

We got a thank-you card from them for the wedding gift, a pop-up toaster on easy payments. After the honeymoon they came around on a courtesy visit. This was on a Sunday afternoon, another cloudy one, tailor-made for this kind of visit. Tego and I had no trouble escaping into Monday's homework (a mixed blessing, the nuns' homework; it imprisoned us in our bedroom much of the time, but it also saved us from situations we could do without). Mami and Papi, as usual, were very polite to Chuito and his wife, and patient. They fed our guests well; Chuito had his usual dose of beer, "cold enough to cut one's teeth," he said, his old grin still very much there.

Subsequent visits from Mr. and Mrs. Chuito were infrequent and uneventful. She was pregnant. He was doing well on the job. His only anxiety was that the people he worked for, two old men from Long Island, were talking about retiring and selling the business, or closing it down if the right buyer didn't come along. In that event, which Chuito insisted was inevitable, imminent, he might buy into the business, go into partnership with some of the other more ambitious employees of this frocks enterprise.

"I think he's turning into a dreamer, Lilia," Papi said.

"Maybe not," she said. "He's anything but dumb."

"I didn't say dreamers have to be dumb. Just the opposite."

"He has a savings account."

"Of course he has a savings account. He's successful."

This was just before Chuito and his wife moved up to Co-op

City, where they had bought themselves a co-op apartment. "A coin-op apartment," Tego called it. "They live in a coin-op apartment in Coin-Op City."

Mami told him to be quiet. "That's calumny," she said, "and calumny is one of the Seven Deadly Sins." But I think he was too young to understand this calumny business.

Chuito became treasurer of his co-op building's tenants' association. If he could rise to the top so quickly, thought Papi, maybe his talk of buying into his bosses' factory wasn't just talk. "Let's wait and see."

In the meantime Chuito was becoming religious. Papi said he guessed that went with his new position in life. Whatever it went with, Chuito told us he wouldn't miss a Sunday Mass for anything, he and his wife. They both received jointly. They also went on religious processions organized by their pastor. Chuito was one of the people who helped organize them. He carried the cross through the streets of the Bronx, to remind others of what this life was about, why we were put on earth, and where we were headed. In one of these processions, he told us, he had dressed up as Christ and carried the cross all the way to Castle Hill, a long walk from the church. "I wore a crown of thorns," he said, "and sandals. The cross and the crown were made of plastic, so please don't get any ideas that I was bleeding all the way to Castle Hill." We hadn't. There were no scars on his forehead.

He made special house calls for his church as representative of some parish group that specialized in reconverting lapsed Catholics. He and a partner gave these tenants special talks. He said we'd be amazed how many people had reconsidered their apostasy (his word) and returned to the sacraments. He also played Pontius Pilate in one Easter passion play put up by the pastor. The following Easter, in the same play, he played Saint John and his wife played a pregnant Mary Magdalene. They knew that Mary Magdalene, as far as the Gospels were concerned, had never been pregnant ("They must have had their own kind of birth control in those days"), but that made no difference. "This was only a play, not real life." Besides, a pregnant woman was a sign of fertility, and fertility was a virtue. And birth control was going to become one too, he said. It was only a matter of time. "The Church evolves," was how he explained that up-and-coming virtue.

He gave us a plot summary of the Easter passion play before he
and his wife left, and we were asked to attend the next passion play,
which was still a lot of months off. Papi and Mami said they would,
but they forgot to. None of us had ever gone to see a play, so it
was easy to forget.

"Santos," Chuito told me one Sunday afternoon. We were in
their house this time, a return courtesy visit. They had a lighted fish
tank to which an oxygen pump was attached; otherwise, he said, the
fish would "drown." Some of those fish were fancy-looking; some
of them came from Australia. On one wall was an embroidered
peacock. You bought a kit and followed the numbered instructions,
and in a week's time you had this majestic-looking bird with
an immense tail that looked like a glorious sunset. His wife had
made it.

"Santos, you're old enough to be an altar boy. Why don't you
try it?"

The nuns at school had already approached me with that offer,
and I had chickened out the day before I was supposed to report
for the first rehearsal. I had felt bad about that; I had felt stupid.
And when Chuito, unaware of my failure, reminded me of it, I got
angry and said, "Why don't you?"

"I'm too old for that," he said. "That's for boys."

"I'm too old too," I said.

"So don't, then."

I didn't.

We didn't see much of him and his wife and their two kids after
that. They were busy with their own affairs, we with ours. They had
a boy and a girl and then a third was on the way. After that one
was born, he told me, his wife was going to get her tubes tied, or
he was going to get his cut, or both, just to play safe. A fourth child,
they said, would upset their budget. He still had that factory in
mind.

10: Maromas

In spite of his poor eyesight, Papi was a farsighted man. He was also thoughtful, responsible, and concerned for the future of his two sons. "Too late for mine," he would say. He wanted us to do well, without specifying what we should do. Instead of telling me and Tego, "I want you two boys to become airplane pilots or army generals," he would say, "You're both going to finish school," by which he meant high school. He thought college was only for geniuses, men like this Einstein he had heard about, and Tego and I just didn't have that kind of brains. There were plenty of good jobs open to high-school graduates.

The time Tego hinted that he wouldn't mind getting a summer job at the American Combining Company ("Just so I won't have to be asking you and Mami for movie money all the time"), Papi cut him short: "The ACC is my problem, Tego. I don't want you to go near that place. Just study. I'll give you the money for the movies."

Tego hated print. The sports pages of the *New York Post* were okay (he read them slowly, as if he were just learning to read), but anything else was boring. So instead of books he studied gambling. He owned about five packs of cards; he carried a pack of Tally-Ho's in his pocket at all times, and practiced winning pennies, nickels, and dimes from his friends on stoops, in basements, on rooftops, wherever the cops weren't likely to show up. Papi couldn't have known about this "vice." If he had, Tego would have been put under house arrest for at least a week and his packs of cards confiscated, his movie money (with which he gambled) cut off, his smallest move surveyed. Keeping track of his moves would have been hard, though, short of locking him up in our bedroom. He was very secretive about his vice (he wouldn't even tell me about it; I was too young for that, he said), and he had private ways of disguising his scent.

Mami may have known about the gambling, but if so, she must have figured that boys have to have hobbies. What she didn't know was that this hobby was turning into a passion, an addiction, a vocation that would eventually take Tego, along with his wife and their baby son and daughter, back to the island. "Back where we started," Papi was to say, not too thrilled, when it was too late.

He had done what he could, though he would have been the last to admit it. He was strict about our choice of friends. He didn't want us to bring home any "hoodlums," or his idea of hoodlums. Almost any boy who didn't go to a parochial school was a hoodlum. Better yet, any boy who didn't go to Saint Misericordia's parochial school. There was another parochial in the neighborhood, a dingy-looking version of Saint Misericordia's, named after an Irish-American airman or seaman who had been killed in the Second World War. It was situated in a block that Papi called "a street of vices," and he was against our making friends among its students. A graduate of that school had been written up in *El Diario* and the *News,* front page of *El Diario,* page forty-something of the *News.* He had been caught burglarizing the Park Avenue apartment of a famous Italian-American nightclub tenor, sent to the Tombs before sentencing, and found hanged in his cell, with his own belt, the morning after they put him away.

"Even a Catholic education," Papi told me and Tego (in the preachy way we disliked), "is no guarantee that a man won't hang himself. With his own belt, too! Why don't they remove their belts when they lock them up?"

"They do," said Mami. "Maybe they forgot this time. You never know."

Tego and I excused ourselves before this turned into a sermon on the evils of breaking and entering. We had our own cynicism going for us on the side. Sometimes we overdid it. We also kept most of our friends a secret. The more interesting ones went to public school, and we never brought any of them home. The way they talked and acted would have given them away as students of P.S. something or other, and Papi might embarrass us with stares and frowns, until our friends got the message and left.

One of his regrets was that he couldn't go with us to the nine o'clock Mass every weekday morning. If his job had been a good one, he told me, he would have the time go with us to church. If only for that reason, we were glad he didn't have a better job. The other students would have laughed at us—except for those students whose own parents went to church with them, the ones everyone avoided.

It wasn't always easy to get on with a man who didn't want his two sons to make what he called his "mistakes." (I never knew what he meant by this word when he applied it to himself.) But we respected him from a distance. It was hard not to. For one thing, he wasn't the kind of parent who believed in smacking his children around. He couldn't stand violence. He couldn't understand, he said, how the Old Testament tolerated it, why it "glorified" it. An eye for an eye was a disgrace, he used to say.

What didn't occur to him, though, was that his tongue compensated for his hand. So did his disapproving looks whenever Tego or I got out of hand. With his stares and frowns, he didn't need slaps or kicks or his belt to get the message across. That was the way his mother's father had brought up him and his brothers—or had been bringing them up before he died—and it was the way he was going to bring up his own two sons.

He took after his grandfather in other ways. He kept our supply of rice and beans going no matter what. He was making fifty-something a week at the ACC, a cheap outfit that was always threatening to move down South if the union acted up. No problem. This union Papi belonged to was a corrupt local, he told us. Some of its officials, if not all, were members of organized crime. "They are in the cahoots with the bosses," he said.

To supplement his fifty-something, he had to enroll us on Home Relief one year (pronounced by most of us as "real-if"). "This disgrace may have to go on," he said, bunching his mouth, "until Tego finishes school." (He didn't suspect that Tego might never finish school.) This real-if enrollment was an example of what he called a little *"maroma,"* a caper, an acrobatic stunt, walking the tightrope, saving oneself from drowning.

A lot of people on our block were enrolled in this real-if, but no one was shameless enough to admit it—only certain men when they got drunk and became suddenly confidential and indiscreet. "Lend me your ear a second, Tito. I am one of those elements who is on the home real-if. Don't tell anyone about this, above all your wife." Tito would promise not to, and then go on to tell his drinking partner that he too was one of those "elements." And next day everyone on the block would know about it. It was like a small village in that sense.

On the long-awaited morning when real-if checks were due, all kinds of "clients" (mostly women, old people, and unemployed men) gathered on the stoops to discuss the weather and the unfeeling landlord (most of the buildings on our block were owned by an anonymous syndicate whose name ended in Associates, Inc.), certain news items they had heard over the radio or read about in the omniscient *El Diario,* and Americans in general (the "enemy"). There was also a great deal of talk about the day when I and You, We and Us were going to save up some money and go back to the island, because this New York experiment was a mistake. But most of that was just talk. The majority of us knew we weren't going back. Maybe to the Bronx or Brooklyn, but not much farther than that. And then, if one had the luck, and the money, one could get decently buried in the city-sized cemetery out in Queens, on the way to the airport: close to the airplanes, but close didn't count.

This grabbag gab on the stoops would go on until the mailman arrived, his shoulder pouch stuffed with perforated green checks, Department of Welfare, State of New York, which he refused to hand out to the clients out there on the stoop.

"You'll just have to wait till I put 'em inside the mailboxes," he'd tell them firmly. "That's the law. You want me to lose my job?" He had passed a tough civil-service test for that job, he explained; he was working his way up the ranks to a sitting position; he had his own dependents to consider, his self-respect to uphold. At least half the mailboxes in our building had no locks; some had no doors, but that made no difference to him—rules were rules, the law was the law, no special favors. So the clients would just have to wait. "Line up," he'd say. "The line starts here." And he'd point to the spot where he wanted the clients to position themselves single file. "No sneaking up."

Papi, always self-conscious, disapproved of those twice-a-month stoop conventions. "This is supposed to be a private disgrace," he told Mami. "An embarrassing necessity, a humiliation I'll never live down. Not a public spectacle. Don't you agree, Lilia?"

Yes, she did, though not necessarily in the same words. She used fewer words than he did. "Your father," she used to tell me, "uses more words than he has to. I think he likes to hear himself talk too much."

She was the one who pulled our real-if checks out of the mailbox, as if they were dead mice. She held them by one corner, between two fingers, like a mouse's tail. And then she would go and wash her hands. Her method of approaching the mailbox for those checks was also peculiar. She'd wait for the other clients to disperse (she could see them from the front-bedroom window), and then sneak downstairs with the mailbox key. She was so ashamed of those checks that she couldn't bring herself to open the envelope. Papi had to do it. That was a man's *maroma* as far as she was concerned. So was cashing the thing at Matamorros's *bodega*, La Flor de Mi Patria, or Al Arentzky's semi-kosher establishment (a holdout from the old days).

"Here, let me have the check, Lilia," he'd say, putting on the self-confidence. "This isn't exactly my idea of a *maroma*, by the way."

"Whatever you call it," she'd tell him back, "I want no part of it." She was always afraid we'd be found out, someone might stool on us, and we'd be arrested for defrauding the government. So was he, although he pretended there was no way they could catch him at that *maroma*, "as long as we keep our mouths shut."

If "they" found out he was putting in forty to fifty hours a week at the factory, Tego and I thought, they'd send him up the river. At the least, they'd sue him for stealing public funds; he'd have to pay interest on that debt. Or they might deport all four of us, and we'd end up depending on Mami's father to survive. If that happened, Papagante would never let us live it down.

"Don't worry," Papi said. "We'll pay it all back. Every penny. The boys will help when they finish school." A lot depended on our finishing school.

"Is this something we should confess to the priest?" Mami once asked him.

"It's up to you," Papi said, "but be careful which priest you tell it to. Some of them look like informers to me. The secret of the confessional doesn't mean a thing." And he gave her the names of those priests he thought were potential stool pigeons. "We don't want one of those announcing it from the pulpit one Sunday, Lilia. God may approve of what we're doing, but priests don't always see eye to eye with Him." But she wasn't all that sure God approved.

Most of his *maromas* were a mystery to her (and to me and Tego), and she wanted to keep it that way. Some of those stunts, though, were too obvious to conceal: things like borrowing simultaneously from banks and loan-shark agencies in order to replace the floral-pattern carpet in our living room, or the last-legs sofa left behind by the previous tenants, whom he was still paying back, via airmail, in interminable installments.

"Don't wear your shoes in the house," he told me and Tego. "It uses up the leather and scuffs the carpet. Wear your sneakers. Or better yet, walk barefoot in here. It's good for your feet." It also saved money on shoes and sneakers.

He had to buy most things on easy payments, the notorious layaway plan, which sounded to him, he said, like an ad for the funeral director, Don Gonzaga of Madison, one of the most thriving entrepreneurs in the neighborhood. So, for that matter, was the tacos and enchiladas vendor, a bona fide Mexican, who sold his homemade products to mourners coming and going out of Gonzaga's establishment. Two smart businessmen. Maybe they, too, were in the cahoots. Many obvious jokes made the rounds concerning the source of the Mexican's tacos meat. "He gets it on the layaway plan," Tego used to say, convinced by now that the only way to keep from drowning was to manipulate this layaway plan racket. And for that you didn't need a high-school diploma, just smarts, connections, angles.

Tego was already set on dropping out of Chelsea Vocational and finding a job "somewheres." "To help Papi pay the interest," he once told me.

"Are you going to break the bank of Montesinos, or something?" I said.

"What Montesinos, Santos? Where's that at? I never heard of this Montesinos."

"That gambling joint somewheres in France or Italy."

"That's Monte*carlos*. In Spain. *Carlos*. You read too much, Santos. You get things all confused."

I'd been reading *Gone with the Wind* for two straight weeks, and it was making him nervous. He had flipped through it. "Trash, Santos. Waste of time." More than one book a year, as he saw it, was too much, self-indulgence, a sign that one wasn't practical. At Chelsea, he said, they stuck to reading manuals with more diagrams than print. He was good with his hands. His ability to shuffle his decks of Tally-Ho's always amazed me. When I tried it, at his suggestion, "just to see what it's like, Santos," I littered the floor with the pack. "I guess it takes a special aptitude," he said. "You read; I deal. It all comes out to the same thing in the end, I guess."

Once I caught him reading Mickey Spillane. The cover, depicting a half-stripped blonde with tits the size of beachballs, must have been responsible for that purchase. He didn't finish it, though. He had dogeared it on page 30 and left it inside our bureau. When I asked him why he hadn't finished it, he said, "The sex sucks, Santos. That's not the way it is. Don't waste your time."

I tried to give him a short lecture on the difference between life and literature. After all, anyone who had read every word of *Gone with the Wind* should know. But he wasn't interested. "And another thing, Santos. You shouldn't be wasting Papi's money on them paperbacks. Use the library. That's what it's for. Papi's working his ass off paying off them Third Avenue crooks, and you're wasting his dough on cheap books. They got him by the balls. You know how I'd like to get them?" He didn't have to tell me. We had that much in common.

Every merchant on Third was out to suck one's blood, like Gonzaga with his corpses. No exceptions, as far as we were concerned. Some of these crooks were members of our church, the aristocracy of our parish. They sat in the balcony, counting their beads. "So they won't have to catch our bad breath," Tego used to say. A few were good friends of the pastor. More cahoots. *Sindicatos*. But most of them lived in other parishes and other boroughs.

It was Tego who came up with a name for what Papi brought

home from their establishments. *"Fakerías,* Santos." Fake furniture, cardboard shoes, synthetic clothes, warped carpets, shoddy curtains, imitation bedspreads. You name the shit, Third Avenue had it. The furniture, always "antique," came with names like Colonial, Provincial, Imperial, Baroque, Rococo, Revival, Quattrocento, Victorian, Edwardian, Renaissance, and others. A style for every epoch, "custom-made" period stuff. Pine or plastic, pine and plastic, pine, plastic, Formica, inlaid *junkerías,* cedars of Lebanon, mahoganies of Shangri-la, Duramicas of Arcadia, marbles of Ancient Greece, evergreens of Utopia. Crap of Third. You had to be careful how you sat down on the armchair or the Colonial sofa (Papi's choice, after much window-shopping and showroom testing): one of the springs might pop up and stab you, just as you were about to relax over some TV, or shut your eyes to go over tomorrow morning's homework.

"Fakerías," Tego and I used to chant every time something broke down, usually before it was paid. *"Todo* is fake." We kept these remarks to ourselves. Papi and Mami would have been hurt if they'd heard. They would have lectured us. "They wouldn't understand," Tego told me. I wasn't so sure of that. But they would have pretended they didn't. It was either that or sticking their heads out the window and howling, baying the moon over Central Park.

Over our Colonial sofa was a big blank space; the wall was warped and cracked. Old plumbing and the seasons had done that to it. "Unleavened plaster," Papi once termed some white flakes on his head, droppings from that wall, as if trying to bring the New and Old Testaments up to date. He laid fresh plaster and paint on it in thick coats, but he couldn't keep the cracks from coming through. They were out to get him; they began reproducing as soon as he turned his back on them. This was a humid, stubborn wall; it broke out in year-round sweats: cold sweats in winter, steaming sweats in summer, and lukewarm sweats in the spring and fall. No matter what the season, the paint went on peeling and the plaster went on splitting. We could always rely on that. And Papi, always patient with a hopeless situation, felt obliged to conceal the cracks for a while, as if not doing so would amount to a sin. The reason he gave us, though, was that these cracks were an embarrassment to the eye, anybody's eye, ours and the occasional visitor's; and all visitors, as he and Mami saw it, were potential critics, even his own brother, who liked to keep his criticism to himself.

So this wall became an obsession with him, as if his self-respect depended on how well he dealt with it. Maybe his life, too, he seemed that desperate. He used to curse it when he thought we weren't listening.

"He's talking to the wall again, Santos," Tego would tell me, while shuffling a deck of cards.

"I hear him, Tego. Is it talking back?"

"Not yet. Give it time. He just called its mother the great whore. He'll have to confess that one."

"Lay off," I'd say. "That's calumny."

"Calumny, shit. Your head's still in parochial school."

Papi discussed it with our janitor, Don Bartolo, a man who liked to nip a little vino once in a while. Nobody condemned him for it; it helped him get through the day. "I never think about the week," he used to say. "Not to mention the day. Now what about this wall, Don Gerán? What's wrong with it?"

"You can see for yourself, Don Bartolo."

"Those little cracks? Don't let that keep you up at night, Don Gerán. Every wall in this building—but if you can't stand the sight of it, let me suggest a little solution. . . ."

Papi tipped him something for the suggestion. "An inspiration," he called it, and attributed it to Don Bartolo's sips of wine.

The inspiration was a large mirror. Don Bartolo had seen it in a Third Avenue window, on sale. A clearing-out sale, one of those Everything Must Go temptations. And if he were Papi, Don Bartolo said, he'd get his coat on right away and go take a look before someone else took it away. He put his mouth up close to Papi's ear and told him the name of the dealer who was selling it. "One of a kind, Don Gerán."

By this time Papi's obsession with the wall had gotten out of hand, and almost any suggestion would have sounded like a solution, as long as it wasn't made by someone in his own family. Mami had told him many times to forget it, it would go away by itself, or not at all; it wasn't important. But he told her she was too close to the problem to see it as an insult to all four of us, and he had drawn the line. So she told him to go ahead and do whatever he thought he had to do, but not to look at her afterward.

He went ahead and bought the mirror, on installments. Household Finance chipped in. Fifty bucks, twenty-five down from the original price. There were no other mirrors like this in existence, the dealer told him. A collector's item. On purpose the manufacturer had broken the only mold. Someday it would be worth something. An investment, an instant heirloom. Easy payments.

When Mami asked him how much, he said he'd tell her if she promised not to panic, and he told me and Tego to go inside our bedroom for a few minutes. But Mami insisted we stay. "If they go," she said, "I go. How else are they going to avoid our mistakes?"

"Don't pass judgment before you look, Lilia."

In front of me and Tego, he told her he'd paid fifty dollars for it, cash. HFC's cash. Interest on the loan, he said, would double the value of the mirror. It was an illustrated mirror, one flamingo on the left and one on the right, facing each other, one leg in the water, the other bent at the knee, or what the artist had tried to pass off as a knee, a long stem with a joint and something like claws at the end.

"Those things don't look like flamingos to me," Mami said, after he had hung it up. It covered most of the wall's cracks.

"What do you mean, not flamingos, Lilia?"

"That's my opinion, Gerán. Ask the boys."

We said we didn't want to take sides, but he insisted. So we told him. Tego thought they looked more like a pair of big pink chickens, and I picked condors, just to pick something.

"You're all ignorant," Papi said, feeling betrayed. "No eyes to see."

"I wouldn't talk if I were you," Mami told him.

Later, in our room, while their dialogue continued in the living room and then in the kitchen, Tego, shuffling a deck of Tally-Ho's desperately, said, "He got carried away with that wall. Some *maroma.*"

"You couldn't have done any better," I said, "so shut up."

"I'll play you a game of knuckles, Santos."

"Get out of here with your cards. Go play with your friends."

He did. He didn't get back till close to midnight. They didn't tell him anything. "Goddam flamingos," he said under the blanket. "Pink chickens, vultures."

We had to live with those pink chickens, or whatever they were, for a couple of months. Then, before Papi was finished with the installments, the mirror's frame came apart at the joints. Papi tried prolonging its life with Elmer's Glue, but he might as well have tried prayers, for all the good that solution did. And he refused to admit his expensive mistake. At least he wouldn't admit it openly. Mami suggested he give it to the super, who she thought deserved it for misleading him into making one of the worst mistakes of his life, maybe *the* worst.

"That's your opinion, Lilia," he told her. "And I'm not giving it to Don Bartolo. It stays where it is."

She didn't want to waste time arguing with him—his self-respect was on the line again—so she left him alone with what she began calling his "illusion," his high-priced *maroma*.

He finally did take it down, when he thought none of us was looking, but only after the home real-if investigator embarrassed him over those flamingos. She came around on a routine inspection, to see how our standard of living was coming along, and immediately wanted to know where Papi had gotten the mirror. He was ready for her. "I won it in a church raffle. It's the first time I ever won anything in a raffle."

She didn't look convinced. "What kind of birds are those? What species?"

"Flamingos," he said. "Florida's full of them. The pink species."

"Aren't they all pink, Mr. Malánguez?"

"I don't think so." His eyes were giving him away, cornered. "I hear there are black ones, too."

"Black flamingos? You must mean swans." She was enjoying this. "I've never heard of black flamingos."

"I don't think it's important," he said, offended. This woman, this impersonal private eye, was trying to embarrass him in front of his wife and sons, and she had succeeded.

"Well, whatever they are, Mr. Malánguez, maybe the church raffle should have given you cash instead of a mirror."

"They don't give cash," he said.

"Why not?"

"I don't know, I'm not a priest. They don't have any money. It's a poor parish."

"Well, who paid for the mirror?"

"I don't know. I didn't ask."

"I think it was a donation, Señora," Mami said.

"Maybe you can sell it. Do you really need a mirror like that on your living-room wall?"

"It hides the cracks," he said.

"Cracks?"

"The cracks on the wall," Mami said.

"Isn't that what plaster's for?"

"It's supposed to be," he said, "but it doesn't work on this wall."

"Why not?"

"It's damp, it sweats. The plaster won't hold. This is not an ordinary wall." And he went on to tell her the whole story of this wall, inventing details here and there to make his point: that this raffle mirror was a necessity, and not, as she suspected, a luxury. I don't think she was convinced by his explanation, but by the time he got finished, she looked too tired to continue the cross-examination. Either this man was a liar, she must have concluded, or a nut, and she left in a hurry, shaking her head.

Next day he took down the mirror—carefully, so it wouldn't collapse on him—and left it at the entrance to Don Bartolo's basement apartment. "Let him live with it," he said, "for deceiving me."

Mami was furious. "I don't think he's the only one who deceived you."

"Just what do you mean by that, Lilia?"

"Nothing. I don't want to talk about it." And she found a quick excuse to visit the drugstore.

Next week he took us off the home real-if. "No more handouts," he said. "Let's try starving. It may help." What wouldn't? Eating?

"I think I'm going to get a job soon," Tego told me privately. He was a junior at Chelsea, and the thought of spending another year in that school, "in any school, Santos," was "messing with my sleep."

Papi had insured himself for a thousand dollars, "just in case anything happens to me," he explained to us the day he signed the contract. This had been another illegal *maroma,* but also justified as far as he was concerned. "For one thing," he said, "we may have to fly back home someday. And this policy will pay for the plane tickets and a few other things."

"Another illusion," Mami said, but not to him. "What does he think we'll do when we get there? Raise chickens? They'll laugh us back to here."

He tried talking the insurance collector into giving us an advance on the premium. "I have to pay off some debts," he said.

The collector said he sympathized—maybe he did—but that there was nothing he could do. "There's no such thing as an advance on a premium, Mr. Malánguez. I'm sorry."

So Papi would just have to wait until the policy matured; that wouldn't be for a long time. "In other words, Lilia," he said, "we'll just have to rob a bank."

"Anytime you're ready," she said, and nobody laughed.

So he continued pulling his *maroma* stunts whenever he had no choice, which was most of the time, and justifying them on the grounds that someone in his situation had to do something dishonest from time to time. "Otherwise I'll have to answer for it someday." He believed in divine retribution.

One of my favorite of his *maromas* was something he called *El Pícaro.* This was a thick, short black wire that stole electricity from the light meter, an antique gray box between the kitchen and the bathroom. He attached *El Pícaro* to the meter in such a way that the current wouldn't register. He hooked up this thieving wire for a couple of hours every day after sunset. Someone at work, another *maromero,* had shown him how to do it. "It's a sin," he said, "but what's another sin?"

"Show me how to work this *Pícaro,* Papi," Tego asked him once. "Maybe I can sell this stunt and make a killing for us."

But Papi would have none of that. "You're asking your own father to show you how to steal?"

"From those buzzards? Why not? It's them or us. You said yourself God doesn't mind."

"I said for me He doesn't mind."

"How come you're special?"

"I'll tell you why, Tego. Because I don't have a HIGH-SCHOOLDIPLOMA! That is why."

Tego, unconvinced, reminded him of the quickie diploma offer he'd seen in the subway. "Easy payments, Papi. Why don't you get one of those if they mean so much?"

"I don't want to buy a diploma, Tego. That's one reason. You're supposed to work for it."

"I understand," Tego said. "I think I do, anyway." And I could tell from where I sat in our bedroom, studying history, that he didn't mean a word of it. "Let me go do some studying," he said. Then he came inside the room, looked over my shoulder, and asked me how I was coming along with "them books."

"Not bad," I said. "Some of it's boring."

"Don't go blind, Santos." He pulled an old pack of cards out of our bureau.

"Don't let him catch you," I said.

"No problem. His eyes ain't so good no more. That's all he needs now, blindness."

"He'll ship you back to the island."

"I ain't going back to no island."

"To the Tombs, then."

"Don't be funny. See you later."

And he was gone again, to some gambling den in a basement. I was asleep when he got back. On the way to school next morning, I found two quarters in my coat pocket. Part of his winnings the night before. I wished he'd given them to Papi instead, but that would have led to questions, and lies, and might have given his gambling hobby away.

"There has to be a way," Mami said, daydreaming. But there wasn't. So she stopped talking like that.

Then Don Baldomero, one of Papi's fellow-workers, offered himself as a solution. He had a legitimate *maroma* in mind, he told Papi. It was called the Tenement Syndicate. He came from a village called Las Piedras, which immediately put Papi on his guard: Anyone born and raised in a place called The Rocks should be suspected on sight.

Don Baldo had been "kind" to Papi at work ("He talks to me"), and Papi, in a gesture rare for him, once invited him to dinner. Mami went to the *bodega* and came home with a bag full

of food, all of it on crédit. She cooked two kinds of plantains, green
and ripe. She cut them into thin wedges and fried them carefully,
in oil instead of lard. And there were pork chops instead of chicken,
long-grain rice cooked slowly in saffron; chick peas *and* bean sauce,
instead of one or the other. Black bean sauce, because Papi had told
her this Don Baldo was crazy about black beans. Some Cuban at
work had turned him on to them. She had bought them raw and
soaked them overnight, and first thing next morning, throwing in
spices, she put them on a low burner. And there was beer, a six-
pack, and homemade egg custard, and all the demitasse Don Baldo
could drink. She had put a lot of hours into this meal, and the grocer
had put a lot of arithmetic into the price of it.

The invitation had been a crazy impulse, Papi told us afterwards. "For a special guest. A man who knows how to enjoy a good
meal, too. He's the one who showed me how to hook up *El Pícaro*.
He's a clever man, but he also has some crazy ideas sometimes."
Just the same, Don Baldo's *Pícaro* scheme had been saving Papi as
much as five dollars a week on light bills, and the least we could
do for the man was treat him to a well-cooked meal.

"Let him come and eat his five dollars' worth, then," Mami said,
and went to work.

Before he arrived, Papi told us that he was a father of five or
six in his fifties, that he was one of the senior workers at the factory,
but that the boss had never even considered promoting him because he was too outspoken on wages and working conditions, and
that he was hard at work saving what he could in order to buy a
run-down tenement on St. Ann's Avenue, the Bronx, and fix it up
to show the American landlords how to run a decent tenement. The
janitor of the building in question was, he said, a man with a good
business head. The only problem was that, like too many janitors
nowadays, he drank a little more than was good for his health. He
drank something called Vino Bravo, which was the same as taking
poison, as Don Baldo saw it.

"Wasting his time and talent, Don Gerán," Don Baldo told
Papi at the dinner table. "And that's why he has to live in the
basement. No rent, you see. Free utilities. His wife and children ran
out on him. And now he lives down there with a dog that catches
rats and mice for him. He uses linoleum and cardboard to fire the
boiler. It saves on oil."

This man, whose name was Pipa something, was a cousin of Don Baldo's wife, and he had put Don Baldo onto this five-story tenement that was up for sale cheap. "I think we should own this building," Don Baldo told Papi. "But unfortunately I don't have all the cash on hand." So he was organizing a syndicate of men like himself to take it out of the landlord's hands. "And what I'm proposing to you, Don Gerán, is that you join us. We need one more partner, someone intelligent and progressive . . . one of our own kind." And he went on to talk about integrity, doing what one could for one's own people, trustworthiness, and the courage to take risks, even though this tenement scheme wouldn't be much of a gamble. There was no way it could fail, once they had the money to buy. "And I don't hesitate to say, Don Gerán, that you are a perfect candidate for this syndicate. To be honest with you, I think you're the best candidate for it." What kind of snowjob was this?

"Maybe I fit your description," Papi said, "and maybe I don't." The rest of us were too embarrassed to look up. Tego finally excused himself and left the table. He must have had a card game that couldn't wait. And Papi, looking inspired, went on with his reply to Don Baldo's scheme. "But I can tell you in all honesty that I don't have the capital—or cash, as you put it. I still owe our grocer twelve dollars for last month's bill, and this month is almost over. In the second place, I don't have a head for business like your wife's cousin Vino Bravo."

"Pipa," Don Baldo corrected.

"All right, Pipa. Whoever he is, he's a brave man. I also don't share your interest in tenements. It's bad enough we have to live in one. I don't think I'd enjoy being the boss of that super who keeps sticking pieces of carpet in the boiler to save money on real fuel. The smoke poisons people."

And so on for a few more minutes. He had spoken. All Don Baldo could do was stare at him while he was improvising his speech; he was getting a close-up look at a side of Papi that had been in hiding all these years. At least at work it had. And from the look on Don Baldo's face, he didn't want to get another look at this side again. We couldn't blame him. He went back to his meal and the tall glasses of cold beer that Mami kept pouring for him. He ate in silence, squinting at his plate like someone who wasn't used to this kind of food, until Papi tried to open up a conversation on something safe: old folksongs.

"Have you heard that old rendition of '*Lamento Jíbaro*' over *La Voz Hispana?*" he asked Don Baldo.

"Sure I have," said Don Baldo very seriously, almost grimly. "How can I help it? It comes on at least six times a week. I think they should try something different once in a while."

"Not for my money," Papi said.

"Your money? What money?"

"That's just a way of speaking, Don Baldo. I forget what it's called."

"It can't be important, Don Gerán. May I have another glass of cold beer, Doña Lilia?"

So much for the old folksongs. I wanted to join Tego, wherever he was, but it was the wrong time to run out on Papi, and Mami, who was doing her best to save face for all three of us. The beer helped.

Afterward, Papi brought out his guitar ("If there's nothing to talk about," he used to say, "try music") and played some old tunes. Don Baldo, buzzed from the six-pack, only pretended to listen, until it was time to give us a polite goodnight. He didn't want us to think he was just a common, crude, eat-and-run type, so he put up with Papi's singing and playing for a while, then got up, thanked Mami for the meal ("The best cooking I've had in years, Doña Lilia." She smiled, pretending to believe him), belched a couple of times, and left. I went back to my room, to work on a crude translation of *El Gibaro*, partly to keep up my dying Spanish. But I had trouble concentrating. He and Mami were having a little disagreement in the living room.

"Did you have to give him a speech?" she was asking.

"Yes," he said. "Yes, I did." His voice was cracking. "This wasn't the first time he pulled that *sindicato* proposal, Lilia. It started months ago at work. Maybe he was trying to humiliate me in front of my own family. Where's Tego?"

"He escaped," she said. "He couldn't take any more."

"I'll talk to him later. Where's Santos?"

"He's in their room. I guess he's trying to avoid our mistakes. Maybe he's just hiding, I don't know. Why couldn't you just say no to this Don Baldo? You're good at saying no when you want to."

"No, I'm not. And besides, I tried the straight approach already. At least thirty-six times. But in my house I draw the line, even if the walls are cracking. Did you notice the way he was looking at that wall? I'm sure if he were our landlord, he wouldn't put up with it."

"Now they'll laugh at you at the factory," she said. "He looks like a man of gossip to me."

"So let them laugh, Lilia. It won't be the first time. That's their problem."

"You win," she said. Then she went back to their bedroom. She was reading Volume I of the *Wonderland of Wisdom*. He went straight to the dining room, to work on his new hobby, leather-tooling.

In a little while I went back there to see how he was coming along. He didn't notice me looking at him. "Your *maroma* paid off that time," I said.

He looked up. He was wearing his thick lenses. "What *maroma?*"

"The way you told Don Baldo off. Put him in his place."

"That's not a *maroma*. Maybe you don't know what a *maroma* is. That was more like a disaster. And if you don't believe me, ask your mother. She'll tell you what it was."

"Maybe she misunderstood what you were up to."

"No, she didn't misunderstand. She understood it perfectly. Maybe she understood it better than I did."

"Well, it's a matter of opinion, then. He put that six-pack of beer away pretty good."

"I guess he needed a six-pack after my speech. Some speech."

"It was a good speech, Papi. Don't knock it. It was honest."

"I could have done better, but he caught me by surprise. My fault. I should have been expecting it. *Sindicato!* Schemers . . ."

I fixed us each a cup of coffee and sat there with him for a while. He worked away on the leather and hummed to himself. Old folksongs were coming out of his nose. He was cutting the leather with an x-ACTO knife as if one mistake might get him hanged. His cutting hand was shaking and he had to go easy or ruin the leather. I had to look away. Those pieces of cured calfskin might start bleeding any second. Then I couldn't take any more and left with my cup of coffee. I don't think he noticed.

11: Malánguez and Son

PAPI ONCE TOLD ME he'd done a lot of drinking before he married Mami, but that wasn't true. Maybe he only wished he had, and wanted to impress me. Instead, I winced. Nowadays, he'd go on, the only drinking he allowed himself was a couple of swallows of beer, *fría* High-Life, whenever he couldn't get out of going to a function of some kind because a member of the Holy Name Society, Puerto Rican sodality (basement branch), had heard him deliver a discourse one morning to the members of that middle-aged brotherhood and wanted him, if he didn't mind, to do another one like it at the upcoming wedding of a nephew or niece, the First Communion of a son or daughter, or the birthday of a bedridden grandparent. This didn't happen often, and he never said no. It was his duty, he thought, and he also liked making speeches. He prepared hard for them, night after night, in our dining room.

But the social side of those functions didn't interest him anymore. After his speech, followed by a big round of applause, pats on his back, congratulations and compliments on his eloquence, he just wanted to head for the subway, disappear. But he was too polite to leave right away, so he stuck it out a little longer. He'd stand in one spot, sip a little beer (wine and the other stuff were out) with the host and hostess and the other guests, flatter the bride and groom on their choice of spouse, and wish them all the children they wanted. Then, a little self-conscious, though he was trying hard to look as casual as possible, he'd sneak a squint at his Timex, smile at all the blurred faces around him, and slip out of the function quietly, like somebody's second cousin, the one who hadn't been invited. He'd take the can of beer with him, so people would think he'd be back in a minute, and drop it into the first garbage can he came across.

Back home, a little tired and close to cranky, he might call the function he'd just left a "malfunction," but that was only to keep from taking himself and his formal speeches too seriously. (I think he also wished he'd stuck around a little longer, made some friends.) Sometimes he came back wishing he'd taken up the law or teaching, instead of "textile-combining," the fancy name for what he did. There was only so much you could do with a specialty like that, and it had been some time now since he'd lost his passion for coating the backs of fabrics, plain and fancy, with a species of glue called "Bulldog" and turning them into a different kind of fabric without wrinkles or air bubbles.

He had always liked oratory, but his passion for it didn't come out of the closet till he picked up a handbook for orators, A. Calleja's *Manual del Orador,* on impulse, at El Siglo, a Spanish-language bookstore on the border of Black Harlem and El Barrio. It was already brown and flaking off at the edges when he bought it for a quarter; its print was so tiny that he had to screw on the strongest pair of lenses in his special eyeglasses whenever he sat down to study it, and since even those lenses weren't strong enough, he assisted them with a magnifying glass. And he didn't just study Calleja. I think one of his private ambitions was to memorize every page of that handbook, including the table of contents at the back: five pages of it. That was a lot of Calleja to get by heart. He put ninety or more intensive minutes a night into it, right after his nap and before he pulled his guitar out of the dining-room closet.

The *Manual* had a long subtitle: "Discourses for Patriotic, Social, Political, Cultural and Civic Feasts; for Toasts, Congratulations, etc.; Biographies of Celebrated Persons; Instructions for the Orator; Poems, Addresses." Published in Mexico, DF, 2,000 copies, all remaindered or burned, I thought. About the only occasions it left out were earthquakes, sudden coups, and states of siege, but the gloomy tone Papi declaimed in most of the time made up for that omission.

First he'd read the selection silently, then lip-read it to start shaping the words in his mouth and to hear the sounds in his head. Then, when his heart and head were comfortable with the contents, he'd start reciting out loud to the walls.

One of his favorites was called "Discourse on the Anniversary of the Death of Emiliano Zapata, 10 April."

"Fellow Mexicans," Papi would start: "All of us gathered here preserve in our souls the tragic memory of the loss of the most renowned figure of the Mexican Revolution." (Immediately I'd think of Marlon Brando and his impersonation of Zapata. I'd seen the movie three or four times.) "But his death has not surprised us in the least, since infamy and base assassination will always dog the steps of those who give all they have on the altar of their beliefs; and when they have nothing left to sacrifice, they are sacrificed by their enemies . . . the dispossession that the natives suffered during the reconquest. I have spoken."

Papi always stuck in that I-have-spoken tag. Calleja prescribed it. He said you had to let the audience know when you were finished, so they wouldn't start applauding too soon.

As soon as Papi started, Mami would drop whatever she was doing, look around her as if her nose had caught something strong downwind, and say, after making a little clucking sound, *"Por Dios,* there goes my husband again with his Mexican speeches." And she'd beat it to their bedroom to read *El Diario,* her *Wonderland of Wisdom,* or one of the *Life* magazines he used to bring her: "For reality, Lilia," he'd tell her, "because those other things distort your sense of it."

In the summer months, when our dining room turned into a strong hint of Purgatory, and he had to open the window or die, dogs all around the alley went to town on him. They barked and bayed as soon as he started in with Don Calleja. Some of our neighbors joined in. "There goes that lawyer Malánguez again." "Turn up the volume while he's winning his case." They drowned him out with their radios and phonographs. One amateur musician somewhere gave it to him with a trumpet. But that didn't stop him. They didn't know this man Malánguez too well, a man who wouldn't quit—or come to his senses, depending on how you saw the situation.

"If they don't want to listen," he said, "they can close their windows and minds and turn on their air conditioners." (Their refrigerators, he meant.) Those dogs in the alley had at least two heads, he said. And the neighbors who turned up their volumes and slammed their windows shut were *canallas,* riffraff, whose ignorance and lack of curiosity would keep them in the dark all their lives. Same for their children, unless God intervened. Those neighbors never ridiculed him to his face; some of them probably respected him from a distance. But at the same time they must have taken him for a weirdo. You couldn't blame them too much. Don Gerán Malánguez, the man who couldn't see two feet in front of him and who talked to himself out loud at night in the dining room in fancy Spanish, like a judge or a preacher or a politician or a lunatic, one of those.

"To Congratulate the Governor of a State upon Taking Office":

"Señor Gobernador: I come as a messenger, on behalf of my fellow-citizens, to congratulate you on this auspicious day. . . . You may count, Señor Gobernador, on the modest cooperation of our . . . carrying out the program . . . which deserves the support of those of us who . . . true saviors of our Mexican homeland. . . . I have spoken."

Or this one, dedicating the statue of a sage: "Señores: Of all the attributes of human nature, none is so elevated and worthy of the most profound admiration as intelligence . . . distinguishes man from . . . the naturalist Carlos Linnaeus . . . *homo sapiens* . . . the other animals . . . the monument you are beholding a symbol of . . . life of this man pure and honorable . . . true sages always children. . . . I have spoken."

He'd always had what I thought was an exaggerated respect for public speakers—of any kind, including the kind I distrusted as soon as they opened their maws. But mostly he looked up to those who used their gifts of tongue to help the helpless and fight *el diablo's* honchos; only he couldn't always distinguish between the honest ones and those who were out to help themselves. He admired President Kennedy's precooked eloquence, although he did think the man's larynx had betrayed him: weak and reedy; the blue jays of Central Park sounded something like that. It was the *canalla* Nixon who had come equipped with a better voice box, but he had the look of a rent-controlled landlord and the heart to go with it. (Maybe the *canalla* should have studied Calleja.) He also had a certain amount of admiration for that heavyset TV lawyer in the wheelchair, and for glossy priests like Bishop Sheen, though not for his smile, which Papi suspected of something; he couldn't put his finger on what—just instinct. Then there were those who, with a little wine in their heads to get their gizmos going, stood up at social functions and ad-libbed away with tongues on fire until they came down with hoarse throats, and sat back down to heavy applause and crocodile tears.

In Papi's opinion the law was the most useful profession because it gave one the opportunity to defend one's people against the Judas Iscariots and others, including members of one's own people, like that so-called schoolteacher who had sold Mami the twenty-four-volume *Wonderland* of endless installments while he was out in Brooklyn sweeping floors, fetching coffee, donuts, crullers, and muffins for his associates; and against those who accused the innocent of crimes they never committed.

"Señor Judge," I imagined him saying in court, "Señoras y Señores of the jury: This is a travesty of the rent-control law, and anyone who denies it is in league with the accuser and the prosecution. The burden for nonpayment rests with the landlord, a crook, a sharkskin Procurator of Judaea, a simoniac who undoubtedly devours raw eggs, shells and all, for breakfast, and raw fish, with their intestines intact, for dinner, while my client here and his family have to settle for government-surplus powdered eggs, powdered milk that tastes like ground glass, and processed cheese that smells like sulphur paste, except on those lucky days when they can land a goldfish or two, instead of a flat tire or a used prophylactic, in that Central Park swamp miscalled a boat lake, and risk getting arrested for fishing in public waters. A churchgoing man is my client . . . welfare check, a bribe to keep the poor in their place, stolen from mailbox day before rent was due . . . junkies with crowbars and screwdrivers . . . varicose veins the size of tire tubes . . . nervous attacks on locofoco express home from factory . . . half-blind, burning bladder, *fuego* in the *vejiga*, dizzy spells, *jaquecas*, a euphemism for *migrañas* . . . landlord who should be on the dock fishing for compassion . . . insult to our common human . . . throw the Scriptures in his face, make him memorize both Testaments . . . I have spoken . . . humbly rest my case."

After the applause and the tears, his client was exonerated, and the two were photographed for front-page headlines. The landlord stood no chance; he was tried on the spot and sentenced to five bitter winters in his tenant-victim's cold-water flat, with a two-headed dog standing guard outside the door just in case he tried breaking out in the middle of an avenging blizzard. Some people, champions of "the little man," proposed a statue for Papi down on Central Park South, next to those of Martí, Bolívar, San Martín, and vindictive Sherman, who was out of place among those Latin liberators.

But he shook his head and said they should wait until he had made his quietus, "because, my friends, the living should not be honored that way, not until they've cashed in their chips. It makes for vanity, and I have better things to do with myself than strut around like a vulgar rooster signing autographs. Besides, the public respects monuments, but has little love for them." He had spoken.

As much as he was hooked on Calleja, when a boxing bout came on the tube, there went the Mexican master and his exercises in oratory; there went the discourses on all those worthies: Zapata, Bolívar, Martí, Benito Juárez (I pictured Paul Muni doing him in the old movie), Isabel Católica, Cristóbal Colón, Cauhtémoc, Francisco I. Madero, José María Morelos y Pavón, Álvaro Obregón, Bernardo O'Higgins; there went the statue of the sage, the speech to the girl who had just turned fifteen ("the splendid blossoming of a flower"), the one against alcoholism on page 190, and the other one denouncing Communism on 192, the eulogy at the burial of a fellow-worker killed on the job, the one on the Day of the Tree, the inauguration of an artistic club, the funeral of an artist who had died with the brush in his hand, the agrarian question, the dedication of a Masonic lodge, the one on strikes against exploiting businessmen, the one from the fulsome worker to his boss on behalf of his fellow-workers, the one on the heroes and heroines of independence, the birthday of Benito Juárez, the death of Benito Juárez ("one of our bravest paladins"), the execution by firing squad of Padre Hidalgo, the one to a much-loved man of letters ("fill in name"), the all-purpose felicitations in verse (to a mother from her son-in-law, and from a brother to his second cousin); there went the poems and recitations: return to one's homeland, my flag, salute to America, the *charro*'s ballad, the deserter, the bread of the

Indian, the trees, and a translation of "Woodman, Spare That Tree" by someone called Jorge P. Morris (". . . don't ruin it now with your cruel and barbarous axe"). And more.

They had to take a break, because the boxing matches came on only once a week, for no more than two hours. If you missed the elimination bout to decide the next crack at the Junior Lightweight Title, say, you missed it for good, no replays; but Calleja's *discursos* and tributes to the great dead and the undistinguished living weren't going anywhere; the dining room was their permanent place of residence, their eternal SRO, until we fled or the building burned down or Calleja crumbled, whichever came first. (Papi had laminated the *Manual* front and back, because the weather conditions in that dining room would surely turn it to dust in a short time, and this was the only copy left, he was pretty sure. "And I have a feeling," he said solemnly, "that Don Calleja is dead.")

So a minute or two before the fight came on, he'd rig up his binoculars with the long-distance lenses, fix himself a good strong eight-ounce cup of black coffee with a long curl of medicinal lemon peel (just in case), and position the armchair right in front of the sixteen-inch tube. During commercial breaks he analyzed the preceding round and whispered snatches of Calleja to himself. Sometimes he mixed them up. "If that Kid Paladín doesn't pace himself more carefully, he'll knock himself out by the fifth round. And without begging the question, whatever that means, I can tell you that our radical reforms have been accomplished with amazing moderation, unless I don't know what I'm talking about." That one, minus his editorial doubts, was about the Mexican Revolution, about which none of us knew anything, except what he recited to make-believe audiences from Calleja.

The night Kid Paladín, a compatriot, lost the elimination bout to another kid called Peacock, or Paycock, of undisclosed origins, I was reading Dr. Alonso the folklorist's account of how he and about thirty others, a mixed group on mules and horses, celebrated the Feast of the Epiphany out in the countryside, in the home of some very hospitable people, the kind of ghosts I'd only heard of.

This custom of the *trulla* was something I'd missed out on completely. I'd left the island too soon and had, as compensation, spent most of my Christmases in the homes of friends (Papi and Mami didn't throw parties—too much disorder for their taste), getting high on Vino Bravo (two bucks a gallon) or vodka slipped inside a half-filled bottle of 7-Up (a Molotov, we called it), making out with the girls of the block, somebody else's sisters, on our poor hosts' "dance floor" (as if this were some basement hangout), on sofas and armchairs and wherever else there was room for the limbs, and then coming home with a vino-Molotov hangover, right into the arms of an intense cross-examination that began with some familiar reference to the 23rd Precinct and one's not-so-secret whereabouts. I always promised not to do it again next Christmas, and I always meant it at the time; my head hurt, hangover contrition. And I could picture my friends making the same confession and the same promise to their own parents, with all the conviction in the world. But we all relapsed anyway. Twelve months was a long time to get over the headache and the contrition and the promises those extracted from us.

Alonso by comparison was bland and formal, courtly, decorous, an old-fashioned *caballero* from the middle class that held on to certain Spanish customs. They still danced the quadrille in his day, which gave the whole thing away. This "quadrille" sounded French and perfumed, but it was only a Spanish square dance with airs. I'd seen it done in musketeer-type movies with periwigs, shirt sleeves with puffs, collars with frills, patent-leather footwear with buckles and lavender hose, and women with moleskins the size of a quarter. Some of the men had these moleskins too, but Alonso himself wasn't the type: too down-to-earth.

In the Epiphany celebration, the troupe gets off its mules and horses and stands outside the invaded premises while the musicians among them sing the Three Kings carol composed by one of them for the occasion: their admission price. The man of the house comes down the steps when the song is over and invites them all inside, where an oversized table stacked with food and drink is waiting; and in about thirty minutes there's nothing left of this abundance. They've also danced a couple of quick quadrilles, in which the host and hostess and the children of the house have taken turns. Then the troupe has to make way for another troupe that's been waiting outside with its own Three Kings carol.

They don't go back home just then, though: still too early, only just got started, more of same still to come, other hosts and hostesses lined up for this all-night *trulla* fest. And by the time the

backwoods roosters have started to scatter the night away, the
whole group is bombed out and snoring in somebody's house.
Alonso has worked up something with a girl along the way, the
beauty of the group. He calls her Rosa. She was with her aunt, her
chaperone, whose mule is pregnant, a coincidence. The mule Rosa
was to ride on has hurt itself just this afternoon, a lame leg; her two
brothers and her sister have already ridden off on the other three
family mules, so she's stuck—*"tengo que quedarme por ese moti-*
vo"—unless she can hitch a ride. This is Alonso's big chance, his
cue to make out. He takes it, dives in, offers Rosa a ride on his
horse. "Señora Doña Pepa," he says to the aunt, "my horse has
room in the back and is very steady; so if Rosa wants to stay behind,
it's not for what she's told you, because she can ride with me." With
pleasure; he's got himself a deal. Only the future lies ahead.

He's discreet about just what happened that night between him
and Rosa, whether the aunt, sticking to the old custom, kept an eye
on them or made herself scarce. All he does is round off his account
with "mouths that sighed like those in sleep," "total languor of the
body," "light pressure on my back," and something else about "la
Rosa came nearer and closer and appeared more passionate." He
cuts the reader off just as Rosa's aroma is about to relieve him of
his breath—his last one?—and left me wondering what ever happened to the aunt. "Where's Doña Pepa?" Fell asleep on the job.

Alonso's chronicle came out in 1849, "the fruit of many hours
stolen from sleep and rest," written in Spain seven years after the
events. Studied medicine in Barcelona; went home for Three Kings
fest; family had money, source undisclosed.

The book was given to me by a former neighbor, Iñigo Bolu-
chen. He was a dropout from Fordham U.: There went a full
scholarship and possibly a future monsignor with miter and staff, or
our first P.R. nuncio. He fled New York, his birthplace, to go see
for himself the island of his ancestors. He told me he'd wanted to
do "a little digging" into his forefathers and mothers ever since the
death of his father, a self-respecting carpenter who had been slain
by mistake during a cops-and-pushers shootout on 103rd and Lexington. At the time, Iñigo was attending Saint Misericordia's Grammar School, a formerly all-Irish "academy" for boys and girls from
Catholic homes, three blocks from the shootout that finished his
father. And now he talked as if he was all set to dig up a cemetery,

the one where his ancestors were supposedly buried, to find out something; he didn't say just what. I don't think he was all that sure himself. He had replaced, it seemed, one obsession with another, theology with anthropology, and now he was off to do his field work alone.

"I didn't feel like spending the rest of my life burning incense," he told me, sounding cynical, "and slapping Communion wafers on people's tongues. And turning California burgundy to blood," which sounded to him like "an appetite for carrion. *Necrophagia* it's called."

Then he recited some lines from a strange poem: "'Not, I'll not, carrion comfort, Despair, not feast on thee . . . scan / With darksome devouring eyes my bruisèd bones? and fan, / O in turns of tempest, me heaped there; me frantic to avoid thee and flee?' "

"I don't think I follow half what you're talking about," I told him.

"Never you mind that, Malánguez," he said. "Just take the Alonso—and read it."

I said I would, and took it. He put it this way: "If you read this one, Santos, you'll be miles ahead of everyone else on this gloomy block." Speak for himself: another label maker. But he was generous, too. Along with the Alonso, he left me a thick anthology of poetry, from Chaucer to Eliot, plus his personal copy of *Webster's Collegiate Dictionary,* also much used. "The real, bona fide Webster's," he called it. "*Noah* Webster, 1758–1843. Springfield, Mass., not that *New World* crap you've got upstairs." Whatever he said. I took it, and the others he pushed on me, no questions.

Something had snapped inside his head, maybe all those years locked up inside his room, reading all night, and wondering what this was all about. Why, for example, did he have a "vocation" for the priesthood? Because his mother, a widow who dressed like a nun, had told him so? Because he was supposed to be grateful to the professor-priests who had given him, a dark-skinned boy on welfare, a four-year scholarship to a top Catholic college? I should have asked him, but this didn't occur to me till he was gone, looking for ancestral bones. I should have asked him about that, too, his sudden, unexplained fit of ancestor-worship.

"I'm taking the next Eastern Airlines Jumbo out of here," he told me just before disappearing, "so the field's all yours, kid." He made it sound like an impossible responsibility; and I still didn't know what he was talking about. I wished him all the luck. And for going on two years I kept picturing him lost in the mountains of his ancestors' home village—*looking* for the village, actually, and never finding it, because it didn't exist anymore, and asking people who'd never heard of it or of his remote beloved dead if they could tell him how to get to the San Juan airport on a borrowed mule.

"The music of Epiphany is one of those customs that don't need any reforms and that deserve much praise," Dr. Alonso says, to close his chapter on the mounted revelers. I thought that was a line Papi would have gone for, but he was all caught up in the battle between Kids Paladín and Paycock.

Paladín the Puerto Rican lost a decision, which may have been close. Close or not, Paladín had lost his shot at the title, and Papi took it hard. Paladín's opponent had certain physical advantages, so there was no need for Papi to take it personally and feel disgraced, but he did just the same; he almost insisted on it. As soon as the ring announcer with the nasal diction called the defeat unanimous, the partisans of Paladín went berserk, bilingual; so did Papi. He jumped to his feet, said it served Paladín right, and slammed his thumb into the off-button when the screen changed from a screaming all-out protest to a singing beer commercial. He paced around the living room for a while, working off his disappointment, and consoled himself a little by telling the walls that anyhow, "At least we went all the way. That was a lot of endurance for one man. Just the same, Santos, I think he misnamed himself. Kid Desgracia or Chapucero would have been better names. Take his pick."

"He'll get another crack at it," I said. "You win one, you lose one. There's always tomorrow."

"Maybe, but I'm not going to watch tomorrow. It uses up a lot of energy, and I have better things to do with my time." He must have been thinking of Calleja again, and leather tooling, and his immortal mountain music.

He went and washed up and didn't say goodnight to me. In bed that night he tossed around a lot and talked to himself while Mami snored. He was mumbling Zapata again: "synthesizing the aspirations of the rural masses" and other good causes; while in her sleep, I figured, Mami was turning the facts of *Wonderland*, Vol. 3, into personal fantasies; and I knocked off the next chapter of Alonso, a letter in verse to his late friend, Señor Francisco Vasallo, who had cashed in his chips and made his peace with the Almighty following a "massive inflammation of the blood."

The night after the rout of Kid Paladín, Papi was listening to his favorite recording of Hernández's *"Lamento"* on the radio when the record cracked in half, said the disc jockey, right on the turntable. It sounded more like a circular saw to me: a high-pitched buzzing shriek followed by a few seconds of silence, and then some unintelligible exclamations in the background. For a while Papi took *that* personally. Another humiliation. He came close to kicking in his antique radio-phonograph. He might have, too—and I wouldn't have blamed him—but this was one radio-phono you couldn't replace: this was a one-and-only, a pawnshop heirloom from pre-World War II, an electric fossil. His brother Mito had given it to him for his first birthday in New York. Ten bucks. Try getting it for that now. His sole consort in the SRO, while he wrote Mami those long letters on nothing new. It had a strep-throat speaker and tubes that did a credible imitation of a whistling teakettle, or a dog whistle, depending on its mood. Its mood most of the time was something plaintive, inconsolable, lamentable, a deep fundamental sadness. I never touched it, and not just out of respect for its sentimental value, or out of fear that I might catch its sadness if I did. I had my own radio, a high-school graduation present from them. It was a blue plastic Philco, free of knocks and keening whistles. So I had no need to touch Papi's Fada, which was always tuned, maybe stuck, to the only station he and Mami put their chips on, *La Voz Hispana del Aire.* It seemed to be a strictly Puerto Rican enterprise, *La Voz* (but you could never be sure whose hand was pulling the strings).

La Voz broadcast just about everything it could crowd in: baseball from the island, a pastime Papi didn't care too much for; the latest bulletins from San Juan, from R.I.P. Don Calleja's Mexico and the rest of South America ("Peronistas trying to stage a comeback . . ."), from Washington, D.C. ("quoted the late President Eisenhower that 'only the future lies ahead' . . ."), from El Barrio and El Bronx ("Another five-story tenement burned down last night on Simpson Street, a five-alarm blaze. But would ten alarms have saved this one? Details after this message of importance from

Busch Jewelry, where we have a ring for every finger in your family"); soap operas backed up with music from French and Russian ballets, Italian bel canto, and Spanish *zarzuelas;* an amateur hour apiece for children, teenagers, and people over forty; and poetry readings that kept us in touch with our culture, present, recent, and remote, but mostly remote, and with our "aspirations," public and private. "My country!" for example. ". . . I can feel the blood in my veins freezing, / Unblesséd by the rays of your sun. . . / Let me return to your lovely regions. . . ."

I listened to those poetry readings myself some nights, but not nearly as much as Papi and Mami did, especially Papi. The subject matter, and even the disc jockey's dramatic-nostalgic voice, were closer to their own experiences, good, bad, and commonplace, although I had my own share of nostalgia—dangerous stuff, strychnine, nightshade, nux vomica. I also had my own easily ridiculed attachment to fictions and chronicles, and to poems that contained alien lines like "The spacious firmament on high," or "While the Cock with lively din, / Scatters the rear of darkness thin," or "Old Yew, which graspest at the stones," and lots of others like them, some better, some as good or bad, others worse, but almost none of which sat well with a room overlooking an alley where dogs with their overnight barking and cats with their *cosi fan tutte* gave me back their reactions straight from the hip—politeness wasn't *their* forte—and neighbors carried on simultaneously about turning down that volume, *carajo,* and turning up the heat, son of a bitch.

I had quit a part-time job assisting a packer in a girls-and-ladies' frocks factory down in the garment district, because it cut into the time I could be spending with the Keatses, Alonsos, and Concolor-corvos (another hybrid). So Papi and Mami were doing all the hauling in the house now. He paid the rent and the installments on whatever we needed, or thought we needed, and paid for the food; Mami bought the food, did the cleaning and cooking, and read some *Wonderland* every night to justify the installment payments; and I read. I was not pulling my share of the load, and justified it by telling myself that this was the way it had to be for a while. "First the books, then the *real* responsibilities," I told myself, and added, looking left and right for support, "Like that recluse Flaubert said, 'this idea of "happiness," incidentally, is the . . . cause of all human misfortunes.' " Yes, and I wished *me* all the luck, too. I might need it.

Papi's Fada: "Oh, my country! sublime Eve, host of the soul, chalice of life, whoever can forget you forgets God himself! But he who takes communion in your temple redeems himself!" I had nothing to add.

My anthology: "A hand that can be clasped no more— / Behold me, for I cannot sleep, / And like a guilty thing I creep / At earliest morning to the door." Or: "Befil that in that seson on a day, / In Southwerk at the Tabard as I lay, / Redy to wenden on my pilgrimage / To Caunterbury with ful devout corage," and so on. Sometimes, distracted by a barking dog down below or a neighbor in agony somewhere across from my window, I'd feel like a fat boy putting away a box of Schrafft's gift-box chocolates behind closed doors and I'd shut the book, sometimes slam it shut, in the middle of a line that seemed to be leading me nowhere, or off the track, whatever the track might be. Then, no matter what the time of night, I'd take a slow walk down Fifth Avenue—we lived right next to it, not far from what I called "the mansions of Mammon"—or I'd walk inside Central Park, ready to take on the muggers, who'd get nothing from me anyway except a hard time, or to make tracks and dust if I was outmatched or outnumbered. I always went in sneakers, playground Converses, which meant I could be taken for a "criminal element" myself and treated like one.

I had to take those walks to get over "the funny feeling," the disparity between the contents of my hand-me-down anthology and the dramatics of that alley over which in my own way I was going blind, crawl-reading something every night, even on those nights when I couldn't stand my room, the apartment, or our block itself.

Sometimes I lit out for one of the local movie houses: the Star on Lexington, close to the Italian bar and near the SRO where Papi had once roomed alone. Or I'd go to the Eagle, a Mafia-controlled flick with sticky floors: "3 Features, Always a Western." The other two features were either a gangster and a horror, or a gangster and a comedy, or a horror and a comedy, a menu of crackling old rheumy reruns. Or else I'd go to the RKO or the Loew's on 86th (Yorkville, also known as Germantown), two pleasure palaces with rugs in the lobby and up and down the stairs and patriotic etchings in the john. As soon as a star of many fronts, like Frank Sinatra, Bob

Hope, Gene Kelly, or Debbie Reynolds, ambushed the audience with an unctuous pitch for the Will Rogers Fund to aid old actors put to pasture, and the ushers started passing the tin cans around, I'd get up with my Goobers and go look at those etchings, or engravings, in the gentlemen's john. One of my favorites was George Washington in a tight outfit, holding in one hand a scrolled document that must have been headed for the Smithsonian Institution; the other hand was hidden inside his tailcoat, checking out his Founding Father's heartbeat or tumescence.

The neighborhood itself reminded me of Marlene Dietrich's prewar Berlin, *Der Blaue Engel,* Lola Lola, Joseph von Sternberg, Professor Unrath, accordion music coming out of little bars and nightclubs with curtains in the windows and private blue lights inside. Sign on one window: THIS WEEK ONLY: GUSTAV GUZZELBERGER ON THE ACCORDION. Behold the man. He must have packed the place. The pastry shops packed them in, too. Piles of it—cheese delights, chocolates, roasted slivers of almond, cherries dipped in chocolate with their stems still on, glazed fruit, *confituras,* strudels, tortes, cookies, fruits of all kinds disguised as something else: all of this inside unscratched, spotless windows. You couldn't be sure there was glass between you and the heaven of sweets unless you put your hand to it, which I did, on impulse, my fingertips, when I thought no one was spying me out. I never went inside any of those *"bakerías"* to buy myself something; it would have felt like trespassing. So I'd walk off empty-handed, like a shoplifter who's lost his nerve at the last second, having left my fingerprints on the otherwise stainless storefront as evidence: Malánguez was here.

Back home I'd read something, a ritual like Mami's and Papi's night prayers, before knocking off for the night. "Awake! awake! Ring the alarum bell! Murder and treason! . . . Malcolm, awake! Shake off this downy sleep, And look on death itself! up, up, and see The great doom's image! . . . As from your graves rise up, and walk like sprites, To countenance this horror!" Enter Lady Macbeth, playing it dumb: "What's the business, That such a hideous trumpet calls to parley The sleepers of the house? speak, speak!" And "Trojans' trumpet" in that other play. Little in-jokes for slow midnight readers. Like doing a crossword puzzle. Or this, from John Milton: "Hence loathed Melancholy, / Of Cerberus, and blackest Midnight born, . . . Find out some uncouth cell, /

Where brooding darkness spreads his jealous wings, / And the
night-Raven sings . . ." Or: "Or likest hovering dreams / The fickle
Pensioners of Morpheus' train." More midnight in-jokes. Free
sleeping pills.

While in their own room, my sleeping parents snored and went
about their own dreaming business: Calleja and the *Wonderland* of
Morpheus and the Layaway Plan, though they must have had other
things to dream about. Our home village? My brother, Tego? He
had married the good-looking seamstress, worked as a short-order
cook after working as a messenger boy after dropping out of high
school in his junior year, then turned himself into a packer of
girls-and-ladies' frocks on Seventh Avenue, moved to the South
Bronx near Simpson, where they had a boy and a girl, the girl hers
from a previous marriage to a homesick Filipino who went back to
Manila or Samar or wherever. Then they, Tego and his wife, who
had her own gold cap put in about the same place Papi had his, went
back to P.R. with the kids. Her uncle, a professional gambler, got
him into a croupiers' school, job guaranteed, Caribe Hilton, then
the Sheraton, stickman, blackjack, the wheel, late-night work only;
coming home at three A.M., sometimes later, out with the boys,
living in a cement-block suburb, pebbles in the lawns and *coquí*
froggies in the shrubs. He never wrote. Christmas cards in her
handwriting. If that was what Papi and Mami dreamed about, as I
sometimes did, hooking it up in some confused way with "the death
of the family," they never said; kept the pain to themselves. So did
I, since talking wouldn't do a thing for it.

One night, during what I called my disparity walks (I'd just
finished reading the one about the child being father to the man,
and wishing all his days to tie in each to each and so on), a prowl
car from the 23rd pulled up in front of me; it screeched—to draw
attention to itself, I guessed. It was as if the two bulls inside had just
left something starring Cagney or Bogart and hadn't yet gotten
over the influence, which I could understand, being subject to that
kind of illusion myself. They looked tough, too, a couple of gun-
slinging, itchytriggerfinger bouncers in dark blue, with pink com-
plexions and bulbous noses. The bulls of the 23rd always looked
tough in excess: half-man, half-bull, minus horns, hooves, tail, and
extra pair of legs, but that didn't fool me. They were handpicked

for rough turf, although this particular turf I'd grown up in—was still growing up in—was becoming less interesting to the reps of law and order, and to the natives for that matter. Its criminal and other dramatics were diminishing from month to month as the housing projects crowded out the crumbling old fire-gutted tenements with the scrollwork facades, grinning gargoyles under the parapets, and chimneys that shot out blackest midnight soot at drunken angles. The one on our roof was shooting out the burned refuse at that angle when the two circuit riders with badges screeched up to me. Hands-up time.

Both of them got out of the prowl car. One walked up to me, hand on holster, OK Corral style; the other one, rear-regarding, stood by the car, his back to the flung-open door just in case some cop-car klepto happened to be passing through.

The one who walked up to me, caterpillar brows touching, told me to hold it right there. Unnecessary: I'd already been paralyzed by their brakes. He ordered me to back up against the stone wall that separates Central Park from Fifth Avenue and the rest of the city, almost directly across the street from the two sister hospitals, Fifth Avenue and Flower. Then he told me to clasp my hands behind my head. No problem. I was tempted to ask him, old-movie style, just what was the idea, whether this was some kind of practical joke, and to tell him he'd nabbed the wrong perpetrator, he and his sidekick. He was shining his flashlight in my face, attracting night insects. I must have had a guilty look, or he must have been seeing a criminal element where there was only a frightened pedestrian.

When I began to squirm from the heat, he told me to freeze. It was between ninety-five and a hundred that night, and muggy (July again). And my face, thanks to the flashlight and the sweat, must have invited every insect in the park to come have a sting and a salt lick. From where I stood I could see the light on in my parents' bedroom, fifth floor, third and fourth windows to the right. Mami must still be reading Volume III of the *Wonderland*, Papi declaiming against exploiting landlords in the dining room.

Hands behind my head, my back against the stone wall, flies, gnats, and mosquitoes competing for my face, I was slapped and patted from my armpits to my ankles; and I was found to be carrying a pencil on my person, a Mongol No. 2 in one of my back pockets.

The point had snapped off. I must have been sitting on it in my room. The frisking officer wanted to know quickly just what the hell I was doing with a goddam pencil on the avenue that time of night.

I told him the truth, everything I knew. "I think I put it in my pocket without thinking," I said. "Maybe I was going to the lavatory." The *lavatory?* I must have been trying to impress the man. "Or the kitchen, I'm not sure." In no time I'd be contradicting myself, and then—the clink, the hot lamp, the bail bondsman, the seedy, loitering lawyer offering his services for a fee to get me out of this. I'd seen it all in the movies.

In the meantime the constable wanted to know whether I was a numbers runner, a pervert of some kind, a graffiti nut (the type who goes around putting his "Handcock" on public walls and subway cars), or just the hell what. I said I didn't know. He asked me for my list of numbers, where was it, had I swallowed it when he and his partner (still with his back to the open car door, and looking around him) pulled up to me with a screech that must have roused all the patients in the twin hospitals? Or had I ditched it in the bushes behind my back, on the other side of the wall? I said I didn't know that either, I didn't have a list, just the pencil. Was I, he went on, swiping at insects, thinking of stabbing somebody with that Mongol, or mugging one of those people who were coming out of the hospital because visiting hours were almost up? No.

After five minutes of this he got bored with himself, or with me, and told me to take a quick walk and not let him see me prowling around the avenue again. "Any time of night. Go do it in your own neighborhood. And stay off the park."

I said I would, but I was also feeling a little insulted, and stuttered something about pressing charges against him and his *socio* over by the bullsmobile. I didn't know how to begin pressing charges against anyone, or where (the D.A.'s office? the mayor's mansion? the local precinct?), but I thought a little outrage was in order, if only for self-respect; and I let him have it. It almost got me wasted.

He bared his teeth, a little growl, then a louder one; he made as if to slam me across the mouth with his holster hand. I flinched, still holding on tightly to the back of my head, pressing hard against the knob of bone connecting spine and skull, and waited, squinting, for the detonation. He didn't deliver it; he was just kidding, was not in the mood all of a sudden. He said he had a mind to, though, and who could blame him, but he didn't want the people across the street to get the wrong impression.

I must have turned suicidal all of a sudden, because without thinking twice I told him to go right ahead and give those hospital visitors the wrong impression. "Go ahead, officer. I don't give a damn."

And he almost did. He said what he'd rather do, "if I had more sense about me, is kick your little balls into a pair of omelettes, you little—" But even that might give the pedestrians across the street the wrong idea. So he checked himself and told me to beat it. No omelettes this night.

The people across the street, after seeing their sick, had been waiting for cabs and chauffeurs when the prowl car ran over an empty bottle and pulled up in front of me. The driver was now busy checking the tires for a possible flat, and telling motorists to pick it up or get ticketed; some of them had slowed down or pulled over when they saw the grilling of a skulky-looking suspect in sneakers in front of that stone wall. Another witness was the hospital's doorman, in parade uniform, who kept blowing his whistle for taxis nobody seemed to want at the moment, and then gaping our way.

When I was half a block away, about halfway home, I felt the self-confidence coming back and unclasped my hands to slap at the insects that were still trailing my face. No pencil; the patrolman had confiscated it. It might end up tagged and labeled, with my fingerprints on it, among other confiscated weapons. He hadn't taken my name. Maybe they'd only been kidding, a joke on impulse.

At home I junked the anthology first thing: dropped it inside the big brown garbage bag in the kitchen. While I was giving it this dramatic good-riddance, people were out in the alley, neighbors, screaming away at each other and at God knew what, crying and cursing, a shriek or two now and then, accusations, moans, and howls. Dogs barking, radios, TVs, and phonographs, cats making the kinds of noise that explained why some people still connected them with witches and the devil.

That disparity between the life in the alley and the poetry in my anthology was over my head. So I simplified it by telling myself one had to take sides. "You can't have it both ways; you're not supposed to; oil and water." But next morning I'd wake up siding with the anthology, and that same night I might turn against it again after reading a couple of sentimental selections.

Mami next morning wanted to know what *el libro de poesías* was doing in the brown bag of garbage. "If you don't want it," she said, "other people can use it." Goodwill Industries, for example, would take anything. Better yet, she said, "I think you should hold on to it, because you never know."

I knew already. I told her I'd dropped it in the garbage by mistake, and she gave me a head-tilted, eye-squinted look and said that that was a strange mistake to make. No comment.

"How does one drop a book in the garbage by mistake, Santos?"

"Yeah, that's a good one. Here, let me have it back."

She turned it over. I took it back to my room and looted it that night, looking for odes and sonnets to self-pity. ". . . a drowsy numbness pains My sense" was one of those I found useful.

Papi's own run-in with law-and-order was a little more dramatic than my own. They stopped him one late afternoon for looking like the pervert in a mouse-gray suit who'd been going around molesting little boys and girls. This particular psycho didn't care about their sex as long as they were the right age and height and had the look of innocence and a sweet tooth. The day they nabbed Papi, he happened to be wearing his only mouse-gray suit and maybe looking a little like someone who would do a thing or two like that to little boys and girls because he had a rush-hour headache. His usual look in public, slightly misleading, was that of an intense daydreamer, a man whose tie you could cut off or unknot, no hurry, and walk off without attracting his attention. "Behold, this dreamer cometh. A dreamer of dreams. Let us slay him. . . ."

They caught the real pervert, a man from Yorkville, not long after they let Papi go, but it took him a while to get over the humiliation, helplessness, and depression. The bulls with badges shoved him up against a parked car, in view of a lot of people coming home from work. Many of them knew him by sight; they knew where he lived and roughly how, whose husband and father he was, and more or less how much rent he paid and how much he owed the grocer that month. They probably didn't know about the encyclopedia installments, because that was a well-kept family secret, though they probably had their own secret installments and so wouldn't have been surprised. They saw the two patrolmen make him reach for the sky, something he wasn't used to doing; it must have looked awkward, unprofessional. And they watched him remove everything from his pockets, including a roll of Tums.

What the cops found in his wallet, including a handwritten copy of Brau's *"Patria!"*—coffee-break reading—might not get him sent up for ten-to-life or longer; and the six-inch comb that came to a point very likely wouldn't hold up in court as a murder weapon, unless the D.A. or one of his assistants stretched definitions. But what they found in his shirt pocket might: an unopened stick of Wrigley's Spearmint Gum.

What's this stick of gum for? they demanded to know. What are you planning to do with it? Chew it, he said. Don't give them that, they retorted. But it's the truth, he replied, confused, frightened, and outraged all at the same time. *Who* chews it? they pursued. I do, he said. Don't give them that either. This Wrigley's was, wasn't it, what he used to entice the kids he molested into alleys, behind stairways and into the bushes, up to rooftops and under whatever? Chewing gum: a pervert's tool. He didn't deny this was so, but what did that have to do with me? he wanted to know—demanded to know, feeling excessively insulted. He insisted that he had never, never once in his life, used chewing gum for immoral purposes, against anyone.

But they were convinced he was lying and hauled him to the station house anyway. It was only half a block away, so there was no need to get the paddy wagon. They went on foot, one officer on either side of him. They had one potential witness already: the blind news vendor from whom he bought his sticks of Wrigley's and rolls of Tums a couple of times a week, when he surfaced from the Lexington Avenue local. Other witnesses would be easy enough to find, once they got the ball rolling on this creepy perpetrator.

But when they cross-examined him with the help of a hot lamp, they found him to be too boring and bewildered to qualify as their man—a real disappointment. "His pit was empty, no water in it." They'd picked up a stray yokel, a nervous little illiterate with a gold nugget in his mouth and bad vision in his sockets. That was some tooth he had there, Malánguez. How much had he paid for it?

He couldn't remember just then; his memory froze on him just

when it was being tested. But he had paid a lot. A Dr. Alicate up
in the Bronx; not that he was recommending the man, but it helped
to document one's alibis. Out of an incurable sense of politeness,
he overdid it and translated the dentist's name into English. "Dr.
Ply-ers." What, was he putting them on or something? That tempted one of them to give him the back of his hand across the nugget,
but he let it pass. The lamp was turned off, and he was told to
get up.

"Show's over, Malánguez. Put on your jacket." They walked
him outside, and on the central steps of the station house they gave
him a couple of friendly swipes on his shoulder padding and ad-
vised him to stay clean. He said he'd do his best—cautious about
committing himself to something he might not be able to live up
to—and when he got home he was very thirsty. No appetite,
though. So he put his meal in a pot and put the pot in the refrigerator for next day.

"A lot of people in this world go to bed hungry," Mami
told him.

What was that to him just then? "We'll get their names and
addresses and send them this pot before it spoils," he said.

She let it pass to keep the peace. Let him sleep it off.

He was tired but too rattled to nap, and not up to any of his
dining-room hobbies. After he changed into a different set of
clothes (and junked his troublemaking gray suit: fuel for the boiler), he sat down with a cup of black coffee and watched Perry
Mason for a while. But he had seen that case already, so he switched
off the set and turned on his Fada.

We knew it would be useless, but we tried to cheer him up just
the same. "It happens to everybody," I said.

"Sooner or later," Mami said, and added something about taking the bitter with the better and not letting little setbacks sink us.
I added that there was no evil that didn't come to good in the end,
one of their own old lines.

But he wasn't having any of that this time; he wasn't listening;
he wanted to be left alone. So we left him alone, and put up with
his silence and dejected looks for a few days. He was still up,
tooling leather, the night the Fada newscast informed him that the
child molestor had been apprehended with a pocketful of Hershey

bars (some with almonds, some without) on his person and a little girl in tow. Then he listened to the nightly poetry recital, a litany.

As a boy in the grammar school of Bautabarro, he used to tell me, he'd had to memorize many stanzas from the works of his country's classic poets, and a few from Spanish poets, whom he hadn't cared too much for (too snobbish for his "peasant taste" was one reason). This homework was all to the good, he admitted, except that Señor Malconsejo, the man who assigned his students those stanzas, a bachelor, was also, unfortunately, gifted with a streak of malice; maybe his mother hadn't given him enough of the tit, a terrible deprivation. Or maybe he felt cheated because he'd been born too late to get a job with the Spanish Inquisition as a thumbscrew specialist or a master of the garrote. In one hand he held a book of poetry, a well-thumbed anthology, and in the other a fresh switch, *la varrilla,* for cruelty to his fellow man, in this case boys and girls, timid children who were only too willing to swallow his definition of laziness—"sloth," he called it, a deadly sin—and misbehavior, a lack of "decent domestic influence," as Señor Malconsejo put it in his elegant way. But none of this had strangled Papi's love of poetry.

He once tried setting Brau's *"Patria!"* to guitar music. He had some composing talent, too, although it didn't come up to his oratory. He was the first to admit it was derivative. ("Originality is a full-time job—it demands too much solitude, and I don't have the time and patience.") At one time, when he still had the energy of someone much younger, he'd made a practice of singing all of six stanzas of Brau's long poem right after his nap. But then he had come across Don Calleja's *Manual* in El Siglo (fate, not chance), and oratory gradually crowded out Brau's 104 alternate-rhyming tercets, a lot of hexameters, before he could polish up the melody he'd set it to: an ingenious (to me) stockpot of *aguinaldo, seis chorreado, danza, plena,* and other Puerto Rican dances. *"El Sancocho de mi Patria"* was his working title. "The Stew of My Country." "My Country Stews of Thee," I called it one night in the dining room, while waiting for our fix of coffee to warm up. He asked me to leave.

"Keep your insults out of my *estudio,* Santos," he said, offended.

But since he'd never learned to read music, a big regret, he hadn't been able to write it down, and now he couldn't remember what his own music sounded like. That wasn't his only unfinished project. "A bad habit, Santos," he told me. "Finish what you start."

"Of course," I said, "but suppose it's something that wasn't any good to begin with?"

"Then don't start anything until you're sure it's good." The point, he said, in case I'd missed it, was that I shouldn't take after him.

"No problem," I said. Just trying to be agreeable.

"Well," he said, looking less than pleased now that I'd said it, "but you never know."

"And what good's it doing me if I don't know? Eh?"

"You'll find out."

I let that pass: something ominous? An object lesson of some kind? He didn't explain. And as for Brau and his tercets, maybe the 104 stanzas of elegy, or whatever it was, had begun to bore Papi, possibly to depress him with its laments in rhyme; or it could have been the sound of his own singing voice, which wasn't strong, and which hit a lot of wrong notes that startled and irritated him, like a basketball player who keeps messing up lay-ups. In any event, whenever he tried recalling the melody he'd sweated so hard to compose, it came out sounding like somebody else's stew, something resembling a mix of our four native anthems (three of them off the books): *"La Borinqueña"* by anonymous, Rafael Hernández's *"Lamento Jíbaro,"* Noel Estrada's *"En mi viejo San Juan,"* and Ramito of the Mountain's *"Que bonita bandera,"* plus traces of bel canto from his gondola days. None of which, he was the first to admit, went well with Brau's lyrics. "What you can't cure, eh, Santos?"

"I guess. Don't look at me."

"Why not?"

"I don't know."

We couldn't help him out with his recall. "It's like a man forgetting his own name," he said, punching his own hand.

"One of these days he'll remember it in his sleep," Mami said. "He'll wake me up in the middle of the night and send me to the sofa. But it will be worth it. He's taking the loss of that music too seriously for my taste."

But it didn't come back to him, in the middle of the night or any time, not while we three were living together. Still, it wasn't his lost melody that meant the most to him; that honor went, hands down, to Hernández's *"Lamento,"* which he said was "our authentic anthem," our rice-and-beans-with-chicken lament. Not that the other three anthems weren't masterpieces. "They just don't come up to *el 'Lamento'* is all, nothing personal."

His version of it was a scratched, gritty one that sounded to me as though it had been recorded inside a tin-can studio, a tiny Quonset hut, something from the nostalgic times of Nelson Eddy, Rudy Vallee, and other nasal specters. This was the version that cracked in half over the Fada one night. The man who sang it was a tenor with a sinus condition—an asset in his time—whom I imagined as a pair of neatly trimmed and pomaded flaps of very glossy, very black hair, a polka-dot bow tie, an inflated-looking white suit with collapsed cuffs, and patent-leather shoes with stiletto tips and raised heels. He was backed up by a full orchestra containing violins, a muffled trumpet, a small eight-string guitar, maracas, bongos, a cow bell, a notched gourd, and drums. Papi had never heard an arrangement of this species before, "but you have to take into account that this is an unusual song, take my word. So the arrangement itself has to be unusual."

It's a song about an exuberant subsistence farmer who takes his produce to town one day on a smiling mule, looking forward to buying his wife a new dress. But when he gets there the whole town is not only deserted, it's "dead," washed up. The big Depression has hit the island. Now he knows firsthand what it means; he's run right into it just when his scrappy patch of land has thrown up a bag or two of tubers.

It was played on *La Voz Hispana* about five times a week, sometimes six, as Don Baldomero of the Tenement Syndicate had said, the same version he had taken issue with: too nostalgic, sentimental, for him, and he may have been right, up to a point. It was a big favorite with listeners of the generation that had lived, somehow, through the lean old days, and who would have set up statues of Muñoz Rivera and his son Muñoz Marín alongside those of Bolívar and Martí if anyone had offered. These people called in all the time requesting the disc jockey to play *el "Lamento"* once more for nostalgia's sake. Some berated the man for not playing it seven nights a week; who did he think he was, the Pope himself or something? ("I'm only human, my friends," he'd reply. "Don't confuse me with the Holy Father. I never even went near the priesthood.")

And Papi himself would have liked to call in and request that the station play it, as if by law, every Sabbath afternoon after he got home from Mass and had had his Sunday lunch of boiled green bananas, codfish, avocado slices, and onion rings in olive oil, with Alka Seltzer or Brioschi on the side just in case. But he was phone-shy, feared and hated that faceless apparatus, so he confined himself to the scheduled fare of *La Voz* (the children's amateur hour) and to hoping the disc jockey would wise up and learn to read the minds of certain listeners: "The best they've got, the majority."

"And now," the solemn-voiced D.J., El Locutor, would tell his audience at night, "please lower your voices, *damas y caballeros,* make the children sit still for a while, if they don't mind, but don't chase them away. And let's all marshal our nostalgia, because it's time again to play our beloved *"Lamento,"* our favorite national anthem. Start lighting your candles, and if your electric lights are still working, turn them off. They're not compatible with the sentiments of this song we're going to hear, which by the way is brought to you courtesy of Busch Jewelers," where there was a finger for every ring in the family, "and by the Cophresi Travel Agency, which has been taking our people for a plane ride since the time piracy at sea was abolished" (one of his stale jokes).

"Gerán," Mami would call from the bedroom, "El Locutor is talking about pirates and rings again. Whatever you're doing, drop it. Last chance." No need to tell him. He'd thank her from all the way back in the dining room, a formality, and walk into the living room, his binocular specs still on. First he'd turn up the volume on the Fada, take a seat on the armchair next to it, or lower himself to one knee on a linoleum of scuffed birds and nondescript flowers, and then lend el *"Lamento"* both good ears (deafness wasn't one of his problems). His voice was no match for the nasal tenor's, so he didn't make an attempt to compete, but he hummed along in a low, plaintive voice, a faraway look in his magnified eyes: hypnotized, the kind of look muggers must have dreamed of. "Behold, this dreamer cometh."

*　*　*

The night the record split in half I was reading an overdue library copy of a little blue book called *The Bible in Spain,* which had about as much to do with the Bible as Alonso's *Gibaro* has to do with the American Combining Company, even less. I'd borrowed it because of its catchy title, and because I thought it might contain some hints on our missing links. If it did, I was blind, but I read on anyway. "We are frequently reminded of Gil Blas," went a quotation in the preface, "in the narratives of this pious, single-hearted man. As a book of adventures it seems to us the most extraordinary which has appeared in our own or any other language for a long time past." And I, leading at the time the most uneventful life of anyone I knew, was a sucker for this kind of thing.

Mami in the meantime, while *el "Lamento"* was coming over la Fada, was talking back to some entry she had found incredible in her *Wonderland* of useless facts, and wondering out loud whether this two-dozen-plus so-called encyclopedia wasn't really an endless collection of fabrications, horse manure.

Then the sound of the circular saw interrupted us, and the Locutor, sounding like the keynote elegist at his best friend's funeral, announced to his dear friends, the listeners out there in *La Voz Hispana*land, "Ladies and gentlemen, I have the sad duty to inform you" that *La Voz's* only copy of *"Lamento"* had just passed away—"tragically," he said—right there on the turntable, and no amount of epoxy or Elmer's Glue-All was going to put it together again and beam it into our living rooms, our *bodegas* and candy stores, our car radios, bars, grills, pool halls, to our stoops, sidewalk domino-and-checkers tables under blinking lampposts, rooftops with tilting smokestacks and low-lying peeping Toms.

That was it, finished, R.I.P., let the dead bury the dead. "I don't have to tell you, my friends," the Locutor went on, "that this is—well, how can I put it?" Who was he putting on? This man never lacked words to suit the occasion. ". . . a night of sorrow for us here in the studio," as it must have been for his listeners out there. "As a great poet put it," he concluded, " 'In many ways this was a dream indeed.' " What great poet?

"Carajo!" Papi said. Then he turned off the Fada and went to the dining room, where he sat down to compose a letter to *La Voz,* c/o El Locutor. It was an emotional appeal for the two halves of the split record, his own memento. He drafted the letter four times that

night (Mami found the shreds in the garbage bag next morning),
and read each draft aloud to himself. Something like: Señor, As one
who had been listening to *"El Lamento"* since the first time *La Voz*
had played it, he was saddened by the loss of that collector's item,
easily his favorite, and was requesting the two pieces for his personal memento-mori collection. He went on about its sentimental
value for people like himself, "for many of us in the self-expatriated
boricuan community—not that we had much choice, as you well
understand, being an expatriate yourself." And he offered *La Voz*
a postal money order plus shipping and whatever other charges
they wanted for it. He wasn't above C.O.D., if that was their policy.
Whatever they wished. In an afterthought (Calleja here behind the
scenes), he said he understood perfectly if they didn't want to part
with the "remains of that record," but that no one he knew could
possibly, "could remotely care for it better than I would if it were
in my charge"; so they had nothing to worry about on that score.
He finished off his (embarrassing) letter with elegant thanks, for
their prompt attention. All for two pieces of cracked plastic with
grooves. Memento mori, all right.

Mami's comment to me was that she wished he'd get over his
dead past as soon as possible. *"Lo más pronto posible,* because it's
going to cut his life short," she said, "as if he can't wait to join his
ancestors," who would probably laugh at him if they knew. But it
wouldn't do any good to tell him that. He'd only hit her back with
more retorts than she could field. So she told me instead, and I kept
it to myself. We'd just end up arguing the pros and cons of nostalgia, with him outnumbered and his two opponents feeling bad
about themselves afterward.

He didn't mail the letter to La Voz that night or next morning
because he didn't think the stationery he had on hand was high-
quality enough for that. This was a very formal request and needed
paper to match it. Next evening, after his nap, he sat down again
and recopied the fourth or fifth draft with his pre-World War II
fountain pen. He had brought home an expensive-looking pad of
Haines letter paper, the best he could get his hands on, two matching envelopes, in case he messed one up, and a bottle of Parker's
Turquoise Quink, his favorite, a fancy bottle in the shape of a
diamond. After he got done transcribing it, sometime after ten P.M.,
his eyes bloodshot, his writing hand looking—and probably feeling

—arthritic, he went out to mail it, though he knew the next mail pickup wasn't due till after he got to Brooklyn next morning.

But it was too late; he should have called the radio station. By the time it reached El Locutor, the two pieces of the disc were out in the Atlantic. "To that listener," said the disc jockey two nights later, "that fellow *boricua* whose name I prefer not to divulge over the airwaves, who wrote us a request for what was left of 'El Lamento,' and offered us a blank check for it, I have the sad duty to inform Señor Malánguez that his request has reached us a little late." He explained that one of his colleagues in the studio had junked it by mistake the night it kissed off. And to console the anonymous Don Malánguez and his kind, he played the Los Panchos version of the song, the one Mami preferred; so did I.

But that didn't console Papi. "I have nothing against it," he said. "Those Panchos are excellent. But it's not the same, so don't try converting me to your taste, Lilia."

"Well, why didn't you call the studio, then?" she said. "Before they gave it to the garbage collectors."

"Because I don't like the telephone," he said. "I happen to despise it, in fact."

"So do I," she said. "Just the same—"

"You can't see a person's face over it," he said.

"You're not supposed to," she said.

"You can hear their voices," I said.

"That's not the same thing," he said. "You're supposed to see their faces. It's like talking to a ghost." Which he did all the time anyway, as far as I was concerned.

"It's still faster than a letter," she said.

"I think El Locutor was lying," he said. "That's my opinion."

"He could have been lying," she said. "For the benefit of nostalgic types like yourself. Radio stations are in business like everyone else. But I still say you should have called. That's *my* opinion."

"Of course," he said. "I respect it." But that was all. And from then on it was Los Panchos over *La Voz*. "I can get used to anything," he said.

12: Ropes of Passage

CHRISTMAS EVE, a Friday, on the subway home from work—my first full-time job—I got off on impulse at 116th Street, the Columbia-Barnard stop. There were some good bookstores in the area (none in my neighborhood, only drugstore and candy-store classics: the Reverend Doctors Norman Vincent Peale and Billy Graham; His Eminence Fulton J. Sheen; His Pre-Eminence Francis Cardinal Spellman, who had written a *nihil obstat* novel, *The Foundling,* which he'd had no trouble getting imprimatured; a lot of unreadable sex, crime, and cowboy; and Dale Carnegie's book on how to make people like you. I'd given that one a try and decided I didn't have it in me). I also wanted to walk home, which was only a mile away, though it was so different from this Columbia-Barnard area that it might as well have been another country.

At work, Vulcan Office Equipment, Inc., I sat all day in the shipping department typing address labels and form letters to Dear Sirs or Madams who wanted to know when the latest catalog on our "new line of products" was coming out, or how come that new swivel chair or filing cabinet they'd just bought was caving in. We had a form letter for every emergency, very polite letters; we didn't want to get into trouble with the Small Claims Court. The one time I defied form and wrote my own reply to an angry customer, I almost got fired for telling the truth, which the head of sales insisted wasn't the truth, "just your own wise-ass misconception of the truth, Malánguez." I didn't agree, but I needed the job (fifty a week), so from then on I stuck to form and kept the truth to myself. No more caveat emptors from Malánguez. "Because he should not be ignorant of the property that he is buying." I had a paperback dictionary of foreign phrases back in my room.

And after work, four days a week from six to ten, I sat in night-college classrooms and took notes or daydreamed, or looked out the window at five-story buildings burning down in Harlem, one a night, sometimes two.

After my last class I sat and read in the subway down to 96th and Broadway; then I sat and read in another subway, a one-stop ride up to 110th and Lenox, which was only a short walk from home, and not a dangerous one for me, because by that time I was so tired and sorry-looking that I must have resembled a mugger or desperate rapist myself. At home, in the dining room, I sat and read through one of Mami's warmed-over dinners (except for juice in the morning, and coffee all day, I fasted to keep my weight down, and not to purify my soul, as the priests of Saint Misericordia's Church recommended to their parishioners); then I sat in my room, doing homework till two or three; then I slept on my back till eight, when a new round of sitting set in. I was turning stiff, soft, and more cynical than was good for me. I blamed it all on too much sitting and almost no exercise, and the walk I intended to take across 110th Street on this cold Christmas Eve, with a fat soft-cover novel in my coat pocket, would do me good.

There was another reason, though, a more important one: I hadn't been able to buy Papi and Mami a couple of presents, and I didn't feel in a hurry to get home and tell them they'd have to wait three days, when the banks would reopen and I could cash my payroll check, which included a ten-dollar Christmas bonus for a total of sixty dollars, the most I'd made in any one week. Not that they gave a damn about presents, though they always had something for each other, and for me, but I did, even if I had a good reason, or excuse, for going home empty-handed.

Vulcan's payroll office hadn't distributed the week's checks till after the banks closed. The computer, or something else, had broken down. Dozens of workers, office and factory, had threatened insurrection over the "tragic breakdown of that goddam gizmo," as one of them had put it. Some said they were going to turn in their resignations.

The payroll manager, the personnel manager, the sales manager, the advertising manager, and their right-hand men and women, the vice-presidents to one thing or another, the vice-president to the president, and the president himself (over the phone; he was on Christmas vacation already) had teamed up and told "labor," as they called the rest of us, to go right ahead and turn in our resignations if we thought we were so unexpendable. "The labor pool in this metropolis," the president's vice-president told us, "is a dime a dozen. Inexhaustible is another way of putting it. But it adds up to the same thing. Another way of putting it," he went on, "is that there's plenty more unemployed people where you folks came from, and they wouldn't hesitate to jump at the vacancies you'll leave, due to mechanical failure."

"If you ask me," the payroll manager had added, "this is a clear-cut case of ingrate insurrection, and in my considered judgement, it will abort. Your grievance has no cornerstone to stand on, my friends." He was addicted to elegant language and snobbish misspellings. He spelled labor "labour," check "cheque," catalog "catalogue," and judgment "judgement." "Because that's the way the British spell it," he explained. "And they should know what they're talking about. It's their goddarn language, after all." Pronouncements like that, issued in an affected British accent with a heavy trace of Coney Islandese, intimidated labour; and his prophecy that the insurrection would abort was accurate.

No one resigned—at least not on the spot. And if you weren't going to resign on the spot, you might as well stay on till you were sixty-five, for all the effect it was going to have on management.

So those of us (most of us) who were counting on those Christmas checks with the Christmas-bonus "riders" to buy presents for our dear ones and others, would just have to wait till Monday, when the banks would be mobbed. That was the only reason so many of us at Vulcan were opposed to having Christmas fall on a weekend. "It's the kind of inconvenience," a woman from billing had said, "that those people up in Washington can do something about. That's why we vote for the bastards, isn't it?" No one answered her. She went on to denounce politicians, and the grievance against management was forgotten until it was time to go home, when it was too late to insurrect.

So we had an abortion instead of an uprising. Some of us said they were going to hunt down a check-cashing place on the way home, one of those ever-present usury outfits that charged 10 percent or upward of your weekly take for the privilege. That's what we got for Christmas falling on an arbitrary weekend, and for payroll gizmos breaking down. Things weren't looking up this year. There wasn't even snow in sight. The fifteen dollars I had on me wasn't enough to buy a couple of decent presents.

So while waiting for the light to change on the Columbia-Barnard corner, I began thinking of not going home at all this Eve. I had enough on me, just about enough, to sleep in an SRO for the night. The area was full of them. A lot of older people and others lived in them. They sat, weather permitting, on the benches that divided Broadway into uptown and downtown for traffic. Some of them fed pigeons, others stared, few talked.

After the Columbia-Barnard traffic light turned green, I walked up to a paperback bookstore with a Latin-looking name: The Papyrodorsal. Its display window was transparent, dust-free. I couldn't see my own reflection in it, despite the soft fluorescence highlighting its latest acquisitions: a quality-cover reissue of Bernard Berenson's *The Italian Painters of the Renaissance* ($4.95; the City College Bookstore still had it for a buck and a quarter); Lionel Trilling's life of Matthew Arnold; Ortega y Gasset's *The Dehumanization of Art* and *The Revolt of the Masses;* the Penguin *Don Quixote* with the cover by Daumier (I had this one back in my room, along with a Spanish edition, both marked up; I had read them almost simultaneously for a Spanish translation course. The antique Spanish had almost destroyed me; Chaucer had been a breeze by comparison); the *Studs Lonigan* trilogy (longer than the Bible; I'd read every word on the IRT over a two-month period); Kierkegaard, *Purity of Heart Is to Will One Thing; On the Genealogy of Morals* and *Ecce Homo* (I'd read about this ecce homo in a parochial school Vulgate: Thou art the man who's about to get it); and a bunch of others, all nicely lit up behind that smudgeless, dustless window. There were plenty more inside.

I headed for the fiction shelves, the ones that took up most store space. The entire section was labeled FICTION (hand-lettered in old script, white paint on brown Formica), and under that, in the same script, the legend: "We House the Classics in Accecsible Editions." Another misspelling. This was some language, English, "full of orthographic booby traps," as one of my Spanish teachers had put it. Just the same, a misspelled word in a bookstore that housed the classics had to be some kind of sin. I ignored it and began browsing through the fictions.

But not for as long as I'd planned. There were only three other customers in the place, plus the floorwalker, a student type, husky enough to be on the Columbia Lions football team. He was wearing a herringbone jacket, a button-down shirt, blue jeans, and striped track shoes. And he was trying to pass himself off as another customer, an innocent browser among the Penguins. His eyes kept shifting from the shelf of Penguins to the customers, and when I walked in he began looking at me as well. I tried to ignore him but couldn't. There must have been a lot of stealing going on in this place if they had to hire somebody special to spy on people.

I decided to pick out something in a hurry and leave before it started snowing. *Moby Dick* would do. "Must reading," one of my instructors had called it. We had read *Benito Cereno,* "Bartleby," *Billy Budd,* and "The Town-Ho's Story." I had written a term paper on that last one. The point of my paper had been that Steelkilt, the "inflexible mutineer," as I had called him (borrowing the phrase from my instructor), was really a "metaphor for those who will not serve the devil," who in this case was "personified by the captain of the ship." And I tried to back up my point by referring to the other Melville stories, and by throwing in a couple of casual comments the instructor had made in class, when he didn't think anyone was taking notes. I didn't give him credit for those comments, and maybe that was why he gave me a D-plus on the paper.

On the last page of my Town-Ho disaster, he had written that I didn't have the slightest idea what I was talking about, that my interpretation didn't have a lame leg to stand on, and that I must have plagiarized it from some "unlettered hack." So much for me and the Town-Ho's paper. In a P.S. he had suggested I read *Moby Dick* and find out what Melville was really all about. "And don't go see the movie," he had gone on, carried away. "Gregory Peck is no titanic Ahab for my money. Orson Welles's Father Mapple is not as disastrous as the wooden Peck, but Ishmael was dismally miscast, and on the whole the movie should have been left unmade. On the other hand . . ."

He had run out of paper there, and I'd been too humiliated by my grade to ask him about that other hand. Maybe if I read *Moby Dick,* not one of those editions abridged for the so-called modern reader, but the whole thing, from "Call me Ishmael" to the "devious-cruising Rachel, . . . Finis," cut, I'd find out what that other hand was all about.

The cashier was talking intimately to a high-I.Q.-looking young man across the counter. He was puffing on a pipe (I guessed it went well with his intelligence) while she told him something down low. Then they had to break it up when I arrived with Melville's *Redburn.* (They had no *Moby Dicks* in sight; every copy must have been picked up in the Christmas rush.) But instead of moving aside a second while I paid for it, he put his right elbow on the counter. Now he had both elbows on it, and I had no room to pay his friend. I asked him to excuse me, and he didn't seem to like that. Neither did she. I got an unkind look from both. I must have barged in at the wrong time. Then she gave him a signal with her eyes, and he moved aside a little, just enough for me to hand her the *Redburn.* He stared down at me—he was over six feet—with the pipe in his mouth, while I pulled out my wallet. I had a ten and a five in there, plus the uncashed paycheck with the Christmas-bonus rider. I handed the cashier the five, and while she was ringing up the register, she asked me if I wanted a bag with the book.

"If it doesn't cost extra," I said, meaning no offense. I was nervous. And I didn't want to spend more money than I had to.

But she was offended. "It's *free.*"

And her friend puffed a little pipe smoke down on me. It smelled of apples.

"Okay, I'll take it," I told her.

"A Christmas present," her friend said.

Then he grabbed a book that had been lying on the counter—a C. Wright Mills—and said to her, "See you later." She nodded. "Eight-thirty." And he left, puffing away.

She put the *Redburn* on top of a little green bag that looked too small for it, and put seven cents change on the counter.

"I think I gave you a five," I said.

She threw her head back. "You think?"

"No, I know I did. I gave you five dollars, and this book doesn't come to four ninety-three. It's under a dollar. You owe me four more."

"I don't remember any five," she said.

"I do. If you'll look in the register, you'll see."

The floorwalker had come up and was standing at my side, looking straight at me. I pretended not to notice him.

"This cash register's full of fives," she said, and to prove it she rang up No Sale. She pulled out a bunch of fives and held them up for me to see. Then she said, "Which one is yours?"

I was about to tell her, but the floorwalker got his word in first. "They all look the same to me, Sue. A. Lincoln. Of course, you never know when you're going to find a counterfeit in the batch."

I ignored him. I had to. I didn't want to get into something uglier than I was in already. Besides, it wasn't any of his business. "I gave you a five," I told the cashier.

She looked at the floorwalker; he looked at me as if I'd just handed her a stick-up note. He was shifting his weight from one leg to the other, like a deckhand on a rolling ship, or an experienced standee on a subway.

"I think," I told the cashier, "maybe you were distracted when I gave you the five, and you thought it was a one. Maybe you weren't looking. It happens."

"Maybe *you* weren't looking," the floorwalker said. He was out to get me. I wouldn't stand a chance. He had about four inches on me, at least fifteen pounds, he had the reach, the four-square shoulders of someone who did pushups before breakfast, and he had the much-used striped track shoes. In my corner, I had stiff joints from all that sitting, and a pair of eyes that could use a pair of strong eyeglasses (I kept putting those off). And I wasn't in the mood to fight over four dollars. If it was also a case of cold feet, I wasn't in a mood to stick around and find out. So I picked up the *Redburn*, minus the little green bag and the seven-cents change, and started to walk out.

"You forgot your change," the cashier said when I grabbed the door handle.

"It's your tip," I said, "for courteous service," and kept going. The floorwalker didn't follow.

Out on Broadway, there were many last-minute shoppers. Trees of all sizes, their branches lashed compactly with string or wrapped in netting, were selling fast on the sidewalk outside all-night vegeta-

ble vendors', Greek greengrocers whose neat displays of fruit and
vegetables brightened up the area. There weren't many students
around. Most of them, I knew, were out-of-towners, and they must
have gone home for the vacation.

The previous year, we'd had a heavy snowfall. I'd gone with
Papi and Mami to the midnight Mass—the Mass of the Roosters,
we called it—one of the few family customs we bothered keeping
up anymore. Tego had always gone with us, before he got married
and moved to the Bronx.

We three, and the others who had packed Saint Misericordia's
Church that last Eve, had walked out into something like a blizzard.
But no one had minded. The three priests and their altar boys,
Maestro Padilla and his organ, and the choir of amateurs had put
on a good spectacle and left everyone cheered up. Then the three
of us had broken our Rooster-Mass fast (I hadn't received, but I
fasted anyway, to keep up the custom), and celebrated with a big
meal—chicken, rice, spiced bean sauce, salad, caramel custard, and
rum-spiked eggnog, which we had made ourselves with coconut
cream and nutmeg. Then we had opened up the presents, thanked
each other more than was necessary, and danced for a while before
calling it a night. They were a good dancing couple, though they
kept apologizing to each other for their clumsiness, when in fact I
was the one who kept tripping all over himself and stepping on
Mami's toes, while Papi played something fast on the guitar. We
slept late Christmas Day. They went to Tío Mito's house with
presents; I went to a movie with a hangover.

But this time around I wasn't in the mood for the Rooster Mass
and for what followed. So, instead of making a left turn when I got
to 110th and Broadway, then a right turn toward Fifth Avenue,
then another left three blocks down, I walked into a delicatessen
and bought a pastrami-with-mustard-on-rye to go, a piece of cheesecake, and a bottle of Rheingold. There was an opener on a string
next to the door; I removed the bottle's cap, replaced it, and went
to look for a cheap SRO. I might as well get used to these places.
Papi and Mami dropped hints from time to time about going back
home, and I got the impression (maybe a paranoid one) that they
were just waiting for me to finish school so they could put those
hints to practice.

"Maybe I'll open up a chicken farm," I heard him tell Mami.

"With what money?" she asked.

"Household Finance, what else?" And then he laughed, but it was a serious laugh, almost grim, and left me confused. And I had begun thinking about those SROs off Broadway.

The one I picked out had a green-and-white awning. Elysian Arms SRO, it was called, a fly-by-night resting place. Transients and Semi-Permanents. Reasonable Rates. The "Reasonable Rates" won me over; I was down to $6.50. The night clerk wanted seven; we haggled; he made me promise to pay him the fifty-cent balance first thing Monday. I showed him my paycheck as collateral.

"I can fix you up with a girlie, Malánguez. Up to you."

"A what?"

"Come on, you know what I'm talking about."

"I'm broke."

"What happened, the banks closed down early or something?"

"We had a computer breakdown at work."

"Yeah, these things happen. So come see me when you cash your collateral."

I walked up to my room on the third floor. I hung up my coat on a nail on the door and my scarf on the doorknob to cover the keyhole. The room had a washstand-sink, no stove, a tiny refrigerator with an empty ice tray, a shadeless lamp on a night table decorated with cigarette burns, a single bed with a flower-print bedspread and a huge sag in the middle: a valley, a fault, a crevasse, a pit, an eyesore. The window was hidden by a pair of curtains that matched the bedspread. On one of the pink walls, a framed print of a landscape with figures. English, it looked, nineteenth-century panoramic: a hay wagon, dogs taking up the rear, a stream, trees, cliffs in the distance, a green sky, greenish clouds, wagon driver with pipe in mouth, hay on wagon, a young couple on the hay, birds between them and the clouds, no sign of snow. This was either a Constable or a Gainsborough, an early Turner, or maybe only an all-purpose Woolworth's. It was unsigned. I was reminded of an art teacher I'd once had, a fellow Puerto Rican in his forties from 111th Street between Fifth and Lenox. Now he lived down in the East Twenties, with his wife, who was shy and generous, and his three small sons, whose first names began with the letter *K;* his wife told me she'd had nothing to do with that. "He's nuts about Paul Klee," she told me. Who was this Paul Clay? She told me.

"How come you spelled it with a double *e* and pronounced it like clay?"

"Don't ask me," she said. "That's how *he* pronounces it, and he should know." There were Klee prints and posters, framed and unframed, all over their walls, as if this Klee had been a baseball star or movie hero.

Every Friday evening, after work, he gave me and a few other boys from the neighborhood free drawing lessons for two or three hours. He always came in smelling of alcohol. He told me he and a couple of friends from the "studio" liked to get together after work for a couple of drinks in a place called the Oyster Bar inside Grand Central Terminal, to unwind after a hard day's work. He worked in a place called Cartographers Unlimited, which had nothing to do with maps anymore. He was an art director there, he told me. "And I made it to the top with nobody's help," except for the man who had given him his start: a half-Irish, half-German illustrator (whose first name had begun with a *K:* Kraus-something), a practicing Catholic who came to the community center once a week to give local boys art lessons. Tito Puente had been a student of K.'s, but somehow Tito couldn't stay away from the percussion instruments and had eventually strayed into music and turned into a big-band man. "Today he could have been a well-known illustrator, old boy. Our own Paul Clay." He had picked up that "old boy" expression at work. I didn't like it; I thought he was patronizing me whenever he used it. But it was only much later that I realized he hadn't meant anything by it. He said it automatically, casually, as if he had picked it up in grammar school or on the raunchy block where he grew up, and not on Madison Avenue.

But worse than that affectation, for me, was his horrible spelling. How, I used to wonder, could a man whose important position and livelihood depended on "cleints" like Lipton's Tea ("The Great Pacific and Atlantic People, old boy") and White Owl Cigars (his illustrations for their panatelas appeared everywhere, he told me) misspell their names in the beautiful pastel sketches he did for his students—on a tiny table with matching tiny chairs (our studio was a kindergarten or day-care center between nine and three).

"Litpons Flow-True Tae Gabs" was how he sometimes spelled his client's product in those pastel sketches. Maybe the Oyster Bar was responsible for those misspellings; maybe he was putting us on, and himself as well, and his "cleint." If that was it, I missed the joke. I was serious about spelling, a snob when it came to putting the right letter in the right place. It was my only distinction. I had once won first prize in a fourth-grade spelling bee at Saint Misericordia's School. The nuns had awarded me a framed five-by-seven print of the Sacred Heart, which I had seen on sale in Woolworth's. The remarks our principal had made during the presentation ceremony implied that I was one of those students who were destined to do our parish proud. "Any boy who can spell this well," she said, "is bound to leave his handwriting on the wall, as it were." And she was right in a way she hadn't intended (I think): I left my well-spelled graffiti on many a neighborhood wall and stoop. Correct spelling in public places became my signature, my "logo," as my art teacher might have said. "Post No Bills Malánguez," my friends called me, even after I had kicked the habit.

Then my art teacher, looking for a sidekick in what I suspected must have been misery, had tried to talk Papi and Mami into signing me out of school. "That school you go to, Santos," he told me, "is nothing but a dead end. Some of their best graduates go straight to the Tombs; then they work their way up the river. Most of them never work their way out of the house of detention. They hang themselves, or they get hanged by the guards or fellow prisoners. It's called suicide any way you look at it. And nobody gives a shit. What you want is a career, old boy. Post haste. Seize the time. How's that said in Latin?"

"*Dies Irae,* I think."

"That's the idea. Let me talk to your father and mother."

"I'll get him a job where I work," he told them over coffee and cake. They were impressed and told him it was up to me. I went along with it, and almost didn't sleep that night, a hint.

The night before the signing of my doom, I chickened out and told Papi and Mami I wanted no part of this proposal. Fine, they said, whatever I wanted, but how come I'd changed my mind? This important artist (he had put on some airs for them) was willing to start me out in an important career, one of those rare opportunities, and I was turning him down. I could always get my high-school diploma at night from Washington Irving High. In fact, I'd have to get it; they wouldn't give me any choice as long as I was living in their house, which was also my house, of course, but still . . .

"Because in the first place," I said, "I haven't got that kind of talent. In fact, it's almost nothing. I can't even copy a Mickey Mouse straight. And I don't have the vocation, either. I don't want to spend the rest of my life drawing tea bags, or smiling little men smoking panatelas, and naming my three sons with the letter *K* or something. It doesn't sound right to me. Besides, he can't spell too good."

And what did spelling have to do with pictures? they asked. I didn't have a good answer to that one, so I said, "Self-respect or something."

And that was that. I stayed in school, playing hooky three afternoons a week, sometimes four, depending on the weather; and I stopped going to Friday-night art lessons. If my art teacher felt betrayed by my refusal, he never said; he never came around to ask. Maybe he found a more suitable sidekick. I hoped he did.

I put the lamp on the floor and dragged the night table in front of the bed, pulled the pastrami-to-go out of the bag, removed the cap from the Rheingold, and sat on the edge of the bed, away from the pit. I read while I ate, holding the book with my left hand and eating and drinking by turns with my right.

Chapter One: "Wellingborough, as you are going to sea, suppose you take this shooting-jacket of mine along . . ." That was Redburn's older brother speaking, "out of the goodness and simplicity of his heart." In addition to the shooting-jacket, he throws in his fowling-piece, "and sell it in New York for what you can get." "Sad disappointments in several plans which I had sketched for my future life; the necessity of doing something for myself, united to a naturally roving disposition, had now conspired within me, to send me to sea as a sailor." I fell asleep toward the end of Chapter One.

Next morning, an old woman with all-white hair and an Irish brogue woke me up with a scream—"Christ, I'm in the wrong room!"—and slammed the door shut. My back hurt; in my sleep, I'd fallen into the bed's pit. I got up, put on my coat, looped the scarf around my neck, shoved the *Redburn* back inside my coat pocket, and left in a hurry. I knew I'd be back sometime, but no need to rush it. "Underarms SRO," I told myself on the way out.

I walked back home. No snow had fallen; most streets were empty. And when I stepped inside the apartment, Mami gave me a gloomy, worried look. She and Papi had panicked, it seemed, and come close to calling the cops. Why hadn't I called? she asked. Because, I said, I'd gone to a party at one of the bosses' homes up in Riverdale, near the home of the late-great Italian conductor, Toscanini. A classy mansion this boss had, I said. Servants, pedigreed dogs and cats to spare, a musical doorbell, and a wife and kids to match. I said I'd gotten drunk on some expensive-tasting whiskey and the boss had put me up for the night in a classy guest room. Well, why hadn't I called at least? she wanted to know. For the same reason, I said, that I hadn't been able to take the subway back: I'd been out of it, as if I'd swallowed a pint of ether. She didn't pursue the matter.

And when Papi came in with a container of milk and a pound of coffee, I told him the same lie. He hadn't even asked me. He said something about everything being closed except the church, which I took as a hint. He nodded while I told him my story, and when I was finished he excused himself and went into the dining room to do some leather tooling. Somebody from work, he said, had commissioned a leather wallet from him. Five dollars. He had promised this man the wallet by Monday, so there was no time to waste. I went back inside my room.

They hadn't eaten the post-Rooster-Mass meal. They hadn't even touched the eggnog. Not only had they lost their appetite, they explained at the dinner table, but they had seen no point in eating and drinking, and the rest, by themselves.

"If you're trying to make me feel bad about it," I told them, "please don't waste your time. These things happen to people all the time." They looked at each other as if they didn't know what I was talking about.

"Maybe," Mami said, "you should go to the seven o'clock Mass tonight."

"What for?" I said.

"To make up for the Rooster one."

"It's not the same."

"A Mass is a Mass, Santos."

I looked at Papi. He was giving his plate a deadpan look.

"It's not the same for me," I said.

"Why not?"

"Because the Rooster's special."

"All roosters are special," Papi said, looking up from his meal. This was followed by silence. We chewed and swallowed for a while. We took sips of eggnog. They were waiting for me to say something. And I did, just to say something.

"I don't like those priests too much."

"What's wrong with them?" he said.

"They're all Irish."

"So?"

"I don't know."

"A priest is a priest," she said. "No matter what the nationality."

"Maybe you're right, Mami. They're all the same."

She looked at Papi, who was dabbing at the yellow rice with his fork. "It sounds as though our son is turning into a bigot," she said. He didn't answer. Then she looked at me. "Is this something one learns in college?"

"Depends," I said, offended. "It so happens I learned it before I got to high school."

"Not in this house," she said.

"And you've been keeping it a secret all these years?" Papi said. He hadn't looked up.

I put down my fork and stood up. "It wasn't hard to." And I excused myself. In my room, I read some more *Redburn* and went over notes for an exam. Finals were coming up the following week. She was in their room doing something in silence, probably reading *The Wonderland,* and he was in the dining room, working on the wallet. At fifteen to seven, I put on my coat and scarf and went to church, out of spite. I dozed through half of it. I don't think I was the only one. The priest, half-asleep himself, droned his prayers. There weren't many people in there. Only a handful went up to receive.

When I got back home, she was still in their bedroom, and he was still working on the wallet. I sat down again to study for the finals.

From a small space between the window shade and sill in my room, I could see the dining room's lighted window, its shade drawn all the way to frustrate the peeping Toms, who seemed to get a sexual kick out of anything they saw, as long as they didn't think they were being noticed. Apparently even the sight of a partly blind man working on a wallet in his dining room, with the aid of thick eyeglasses, turned them on. Maybe brick walls did too.

The shade in our dining room was so old and worn that chinks of light showed through. Like tiny stars, I thought, turning sentimental for a minute. "Continuous as the stars that shine," I went on, "And twinkle on the milky way . . ." English Lit. I, a survey course I'd taken, was paying off in unexpected ways.

From time to time I could hear him strumming his guitar, taking short breaks from his leather tooling to give his eyes and head a rest. He stayed in there some two hours, and at ten-thirty he turned out the light and went to the john for his bath. He must have soaked in the tub, relaxing (or trying to) for twenty minutes, a long time for him; he wasn't used to indulging himself in water. On his way to bed he stopped in front of my door, which was shut, for almost a minute. The floorboards creaked every time he shifted his weight. He couldn't seem to make up his mind whether to knock or to leave me alone with my books and notes and anger. Maybe he was hoping I'd make the first move, but I thought I'd already done that by going to church, spite or no spite. At one point I was tempted to come out of hiding ("And hermits are contented with their cells; / And students with their pensive citadels"), but I fought off the urge. My anger won out; I sat still until he gave up and went to bed.

Finally, when he was snoring away and Mami had stopped coughing, I came out. I tiptoed to the john for a leak, a slow one, as if my tubes had been stopped up; then to the kitchen for coffee. A little late in the day for coffee, but I was planning to stay up half the night. There was half a pot in the refrigerator. She left it there for him every night, because he always left the house in a hurry five mornings a week; he didn't like to get to work late.

I read and drank his coffee till after three A.M. Every now and then I got the feeling, a frightening one, that they were both standing outside my door, waiting for me to come out, so we could eat the post-Rooster-Mass dinner in earnest. But when I left the room to go wash up, there was no one there, just the living room, dark.

I had a nightmare, a recurring one. A "Beowulf dream," I called it. It was a pretentious nightmare, another by-product of the survey Lit. I course I'd taken the semester before. The fight between the hero and the monster, and later between the hero and the monster's mother in her underwater hideout, had stayed with me, whereas most of the other students in the class had found it boring (those who'd bothered reading it) and not nearly as gripping as *Frankenstein* or *The Wolf Man* (the movies). One of them had read Bram Stoker's *Dracula* and called it "ten times better than this Bearwolf."

"It's not Bear," I had told this student. "It's b-e-o-w. I think you mispronounced it."

And he had accused me, playfully, or maybe not, of being a show-off. "A pedant," he said. And all I could say to that was that one could do worse. "For example, what?" he'd asked.

"For example, being a show-off in reverse. Meaning ignorant." So much for that friendship, which had just started to get going.

In the dream I got the monsters mixed up; I merged them into one monster: Grendel with huge breasts, enormous steel claws, and stringy, seaweed hair ("a certain evil-doer, a fearful solitary, on dark nights commits deeds of unspeakable malice—damage and slaughter"). Whenever I had this dream, my bedroom door was closed. (I'd once installed a latch on it. "For privacy," I had explained to Papi and Mami. They said they didn't understand what I was getting at, but they said nothing more about it and eventually I stopped latching myself in. But some of the hurt I'd inflicted on them had persisted, as had some of the rotten feeling I'd felt for installing that apparatus.)

The monster, whose face I couldn't make out in the dark, would slam the door open and stand at the entrance, staring at me, something like the movie Wolf Man, before it pounced on its hysterical, fright-frozen victims. I knew I was wide awake, but I was also paralyzed, helpless. Only my eyes moved, staring at this thing that was staring back before turning and disappearing into the living room, or stalking up to me ("a horrible light, like a lurid flame, flickered in his eyes,") and settling its weight, a ton of it, on me. The only thing to do was to let it lie there along the length of my body, and make its point, whatever that was: This monster didn't go in for explanations. Then it would get off me, growling, snarling, leaving only its bad breath and underarm odor behind, and disappear. Sometimes it went out the window. I don't know how it got down to the alley; I never looked. And in the morning my bedroom door would be open; so I came around to believing that this hadn't been a dream, or not completely a dream. Maybe I had taken Lit. I too seriously, and this was the payoff.

I spent the next day, Sunday, studying for finals and drinking coffee, and in the evening went to a movie. Afterward I treated myself (on money I'd "borrowed" from Papi) to a piece of German pastry and more coffee, in a place near the movie house, and by the time I got back home they were sleeping again. We'd hardly spoken all day.

The day of my first final exam, sociology, I stayed home from work. I didn't think I had a choice. I hadn't been able to keep up with the course work, had found it agonizingly hard to concentrate on the material: the boring lectures delivered by a man who was himself bored, the deadly class discussions (whenever he let the students open their mouths), the jargon in the text (which taught me, if not much else, the meaning of the word *obscene*), which had been written by the instructor himself, assisted by others (according to his page of acknowledgments), without whose help, et cetera. It was in its eighth edition, each edition containing "new material," meaning he'd brought the jargon up to date—and the price of the book as well.

So I stayed home to study. And at five P.M., my eyes bloodshot, my hands shaking, my head short on oxygen, I was tying my shoes when the phone went off. We'd had a phone for years but almost never used it. It was there mostly for emergencies. Tío Mito called a couple of times a week, Papi called him a couple of times back, Chuito and his wife rarely called, Mami and I never called anyone, partly because we had no one to call and partly because we were afraid of the phone. (This was a problem at work: One of my bosses called me "phone-shy" and had sometimes ordered me to pick it up when it rang on his desk; I retaliated by taking down wrong messages, and now he seemed to be waiting for an excuse to get rid of me.)

The day of my sociology final, it rang about six times, stopped, and rang again in about ten seconds. This went on for about five minutes. Mami and I were both waiting for the other to pick it up, but it wasn't working out.

"Maybe it's Papi," I said from my room.

She mumbled something. The ringing drowned her out. She finally gave in and picked it up, and within seconds she was pleading with the caller in a nervous voice. Finally she said to the pest, whom she had called "señora," that she had the wrong number, and hung up.

"Who was it?" I asked, coming out of my room.

She looked frightened. "It's a woman who says we owe her money for a set of furniture."

"So if it rings again, take it off the hook. I have to go."

"You know the noise the operator makes if we take it off the hook."

"I know, Mami. But it's either her or the furniture woman."

It rang again. I picked it up.

"Malánguez?"

"No, his son. He's out on something urgent. You have the wrong number."

"Your father owes to us for a set of furniture."

"No, he don't. Our furniture's all paid up. We didn't get it from your boss, anyway."

Convinced that I was lying, she threatened us with a court summons, with the City Marshal, whoever that might be, with a dispossess, and while she was going on with these threats, I pushed down the receiver, put the nightmare apparatus down on the floor, and wiped my hands on my pants.

"Please leave it there," I told Mami. "Don't hang it up."

"When Gerán comes home," she said. "I don't want that thing in this house."

"Maybe we should cut the cord," I said.

She nodded, and I went back inside my room to put on my coat. I was late for the sociology final.

I took a cab up to school, but I was still late. On the way there, I reviewed the "material" in my head: almost total confusion, a jumble of jargon, ordinary things passed off as profundities with the

aid of "abstractionitis." ("The home then is the specific zone of
functional potency that grows about a live parenthood . . . an active
interfacial membrane or surface furthering exchange . . . a mutualiz-
ing membrane between the family and the society in which it
lives. . . .")

The classroom was packed for the first time since the opening
day of classes, and filled with smoke. Over forty students were bent
over their examination booklets, most of them looking confused by
the questions. The professor, puffing an immense pipe, was at his
desk (manufactured by Vulcan), reading Riesman on *The Lonely
Crowd,* casually, as if it were a murder mystery whose ending he
had figured out back on page one. He didn't look pleased when I
stepped up to his desk: another pair of lungs in a roomful of carbon
dioxide and cigarette smoke.

"Yes?"

I asked him for a question sheet and an examination booklet.
They were on the desk, weighted down with the eighth edition of
his anthology.

"Are you registered in this course?" he asked.

Yes, I was. He wanted to know my name. I told him. He looked
me up in his roll book. Had I been coming to class regularly? Every
time. How come I never spoke up in class? Because I sat in the back.
It was hard to be heard from back there. I might try sitting up front,
he said. I said I would. He said it was a little late for that. For a
moment I'd forgotten what day this was. *Dies irae,* according to my
paperback dictionary of foreign phrases. Do-or-die day.

There were no empty chairs, so I walked to the back of the room
and squatted in a corner, keeping my coat and scarf on.

"Answer one from Part A, one from Part B, and one from Part
C." I had no trouble understanding that much. But my mind
blanked out on the choices in Parts A, B, and C. There was something about "group membership as the source of individual morali-
ty and social health" (Durkheim? I couldn't remember). I must
have slept through that lecture, and I couldn't remember any mention of it in the eighth edition. Another one asked for something
or other on Weber's contention that "minorities in 19th-century
Europe—the Poles in Russia, the Huguenots in France, the Non-
comformists in England, and the Jews in all countries—had offset
their socio-political exclusion by engaging in economic activity,

whereas the Catholics had not." This one had to be explained in fifteen minutes. I got around it by drawing a blank.

The easiest choice in Part C asked for "a sociological autobiography, demonstrating your command of certain relevant aspects in this course, as well as the terminology of sociology."

"Terminology of sociology." That wasn't even a good rhyme. It was also asking too much for fifteen minutes. It wasn't even enough time for my nerves to calm down. Too bad. I got up and left the room. No one noticed.

I went down to the student cafeteria for a cup of coffee, and while I drank it, I read the opening chapter of Dr. A. Alonso's *El Gibaro,* a Puerto Rican classic which I'd brought with me to reread on the subway back home. "I am one of those," it went, "and this can't matter much to my readers, who are in the habit of not sleeping without first having read something"—another one, I thought, nineteenth-century version—"and this something must be of the sort that requires more than usual seclusion, order and meditation, since I think that at no time other than the night's silence can one withdraw from the real world, to elevate oneself into the imaginary; above all when the day has been spent without affliction, something that a young man achieves from time to time, before he becomes the head of a family, or while he does not have to govern, on his own, the vessel of his future."

In the examination blue book, which I hadn't bothered returning, I translated some of these long, rhythmic sentences as best I could (no dictionary on me, for one thing), just for practice, and then, when I'd finished a second cup of coffee, I shoved the Alonso and the blue book back inside my coat pocket and left for the subway.

When I got home the phone was back on the hook. Mami was waxing the kitchen floor. "I'll be through in a minute," she said.

"No hurry, Mami. I'm not hungry yet. How come the phone's back on the hook?"

"I think you better ask your father. He took care of it."

He was in the living room watching TV, the weekly wrestling matches. Tío Mito had given him his secondhand Philco when he and Agripina decided to get themselves a new one with a bigger screen. Papi had insisted on paying him for it, in installments, but

Mito had told him not to insult him with talk of money. The only "shows" he was interested in were boxing and wrestling.

Minutes earlier, he hadn't heard or seen me walk past him to go hang up my coat; and I hadn't recovered sufficiently from the sociology disaster to strike up a conversation, so I had walked past him twice without saying a word. Now I was feeling contrite about my rudeness—and curious about the phone-back-on-the-hook.

We exchanged a kiss on the cheek. He was wearing his thick glasses, and I couldn't help wondering, nervously, whether I'd be wearing a similar pair myself someday.

"What happened with the phone, Papi?"

"Nothing. I gave that crazy woman a lesson in good manners." His gaze was taking turns between me and the TV. "When I got in from work," he went on, "it was on the floor, making a horrible noise. Like a dying animal."

"That's the operator. Playing games."

"I know. Five minutes after I hung it up, this furniture woman called again to threaten us with a court summons and other things. And when I told her I was going to call the police, she said they were on her side. So was the City Marshal."

Then, seeing that reasoning with her would get him nowhere, and that keeping the phone off the hook was no solution, he hung up and went out to look for the people this woman really wanted, the fraudulent Malánguezes. "They must have taken our name from the phone book," he said.

"Did you find them?"

"It took me a long time, but I did."

He went into every building on all of three blocks looking for the fake Malánguezes. He squinted at names on mailbox doors, some nineteen names per building, until he found them. Not Malánguez, actually, but "Malanga," which was close enough. He walked up four flights of stairs, his eyes hurting from all that squinting, and demanded an explanation. They had a new set of furniture in their living room: evidence. "The first thing they told me was that they didn't know what I was talking about."

"That's what they always say."

They had mistaken him, apparently, for a con man of some kind, and it had taken some talking on his part to convince them he was on the level. Over a cup of coffee, which they had wasted no time offering him (an admission of guilt, I thought), they admitted that they hadn't paid a single installment on their new set of furniture and attributed it to a misunderstanding.

"Misunderstanding, nothing, Papi. They were just trying to save face when you caught them redburned."

"Redburned?"

"Redhanded, I mean. With the goods, the evidence, the dope. The furniture. You should have demanded an apology, those frauds. Hypocrites."

"How could I? They never admitted to stealing, Santos. If anything, they were the ones who got robbed. You should have seen that furniture. I give it six months, maybe eight."

"Must be a rococo set. They put you and Mami through a hard time, a nightmare. Your eyes are red from all that squinting."

"That's from the TV. Why don't you sit down and watch some of this wrestling with me for a while?"

"I have more homework to do."

"How was the examination?"

"Easy. I finished early."

"Good. I thought you would. But don't overdo it, Santos. Your eyes."

"Don't worry. I'll see you later."

They were asleep—at least I thought they were—when I came out of my room for a leak and a cup of coffee. I hadn't eaten. No appetite. A little unintended fasting wouldn't kill me.

Not long after I fell asleep, Grendel-and-his-mother-merged-into-one paid me another visit. They wouldn't let up. This time, in the dream, I had fallen halfway off the bed, and It—They—grabbed me from behind in a powerful grip, a full nelson. I pretended not to notice, which wasn't easy, and tried to get all of myself back into bed, but It knew I knew. I wasn't fooling Them. They were trying to rape me, and as usual I couldn't scream or fight back. So I saved myself by waking up, sweating, almost out of breath. I stayed up reading for a couple of hours.

During that time I decided to move out. The Elysian Arms escapade hadn't been just an impulse after all. But back in bed, nearly asleep, I knew I wasn't going anywhere just yet, maybe never.

13: R.I.P.

MAMI THOUGHT PAPI WAS spending too much time in the dining room after his nap, but nothing she could tell him would make any difference, so she left him alone with his hobbies. He played his guitar in there, and sang to himself. Almost the only music he liked was the old mountain type. Homesick music, I thought, nostalgic *lamentos*, regrets he'd rather keep to himself. Maybe he was ashamed of them, or didn't think they were important or interesting enough to share.

He also kept himself busy with his leather tooling. He now made wallets, key holders, billfolds, bookmarks, small purses, and so on. Some of these things were commissioned by the men where he worked. He couldn't have made much from them, after subtracting the cost of materials. The rest he gave away on any pretext. He once gave his brother Mito a fancy wallet to commemorate the anniversary of their arrival in New York. He had already given him one like it less than a year earlier to celebrate some other "important" anniversary. Mami and I were treated to similar gifts for similar reasons. For one of my birthdays he gave me six bookmarks (each with its own design) and a wallet that had taken him over a month to make. "Special, Santos," he said. It had flowers and curlicues all over its tanned, grainy hide, his own design, suggested by an illustration in his leather-tooling handbook. He had improved on the original, in my opinion, and I told him so. Maybe,

271

he said. Maybe not. But he had done what he could. "I'm learning all the time, Santos."

For himself he was making a leather book-jacket for his Spanish New Testament, an old paperback that didn't rate a fancy cover. Mami had given him a new one for his birthday, a hardback edition, but he only used it to consult the maps of the Holy Land in the back. He'd been working on the design for months, another original (birds, tropical flowers, a couple of palm trees, mountains in the background), so meticulously that he might never live to finish it. He may not have wanted to.

Mami herself, after she was done with the housework for the day, would go inside their bedroom and curl up in bed with Volume II of the *Wonderland of Wisdom*. She had read every word of Volume I and was determined to read every word of the whole set (twenty-four volumes plus annual supplements). A door-to-door con man passing himself off as a moonlighting schoolteacher had talked her into signing up for this set, to be paid for in installments. She bought it for me, she told me, but I had no use for it. I flipped through a couple of volumes and put them back on the metal cabinet that had come with them. Entries like "The armadillo can curl up into a small ball when attacked" and "The ostrich is said to stick its head into a hole in the ground when its life is in danger" held no interest for me. I was interested in a different kind of fiction. She was disappointed by my indifference, but she kept it to herself, and was now determined to justify the waste of Papi's money by reading every single volume in numerical-alphabetical order. Junk learning, as I saw it, but I kept it to myself. I had my own version of it in my bedroom, although I saw it as anything but junk.

One part of it was a history book for a course I had enrolled in on the decline of the Roman Empire and the origins of Christianity. Sounded interesting, but the man who taught it, an "amateur numismatist," as he called himself, was boring us, some forty students, with his coin-collector's version of why Rome collapsed. Apparently the coinage of Ancient Rome had become all fouled up. "Their mint was a mess," said the professor, chairman of his department.

"And we have to pay the price, Malánguez," whispered the student who sat next to me, a full-time housewife.

At the self-indulgent rate he was going, we might never make it to early Christianity, but if we did, he was bound to connect its origins with the Roman mint, a case of "Classic inflation," and with mob rule (another hobbyhorse of his). The thirty pieces of silver Judas Iscariot collected for double-crossing Christ would no doubt be given a numismatic going-over.

On the side, Professor X didn't mind telling us, he wrote "cogent, compelling" speeches for the politician who was trying to get himself nominated for the mayoralty on the Conservative ticket. As it turned out, this candidate, who was suspected of having Mafia connections, had graduated from the same parochial school I had attended. Mami and Papi had seen him in our church one Sunday, him and some grim-looking associates. They were all dressed up, said Mami, who had a sharp eye for fashion, in flashy gray suits.

"I think it's called sharkskin," I said.

"That's a good name for them," she said.

After the Mass was over, he hung around for a while, shaking hands with priests and parishioners, smiling left and right.

For Shakespeare I, which I was also taking that semester, I was assigned a research paper on "The Swedish Element in English Midsummer-Night Revels." The woman who taught it, a Barnard graduate, had once embarrassed a student in class for not knowing that Virgil's Fourth *Eclogue* had predicted the birth of Christ. This student, a postal worker by day, had promised to go straight to the library (as soon as our fifty minutes of *Midsummer* madness were up) and borrow a copy of Virgil's *Eclogues.* His own term-paper topic was connected to the Fourth. Not long after this *Eclogue* embarrassment, the postal worker told me, in a confidential voice, that our professor's husband was "the well-known conservative historian" (whatever that meant), a close friend of my numismatics professor, and that he had considered running for mayor on the Conservative ticket but had given way to the Mafia suspect for reasons the postal worker hadn't uncovered yet. "But I will, I promise," he told me, almost as if he were set on getting back at our professor for that embarrassment. He was majoring in political science. He was going to become, he said, a muckraker. I wished him luck, and went home to look up "muckraker." Then there was Economics I, a required course, which was keeping me up late with the Gross National Product, the ways of the power elite, and the theory of the leisure class. And in the meantime, Papi was entering his own version of the leisure class. "I have six symptoms," he told me and Mami. He didn't have to. We could see them, and we worried about them and hoped they would go away.

One of those symptoms was varicose veins, picked up, he told us, in Brooklyn, at the ACC factory. The veins on his legs bulged out, just under the surface of the skin, and looked as though they might explode any day and splatter his pants with blood. He had gone to a surgeon more than once and the surgeon had done some cutting, but all that did was alleviate the condition for a while. "You have to quit that job, Malánguez," he told Papi.

Papi said he would, but back home he told me and Mami, "This doctor means well. I guess most of them do, but he doesn't know what he's talking about." He had a point. No one else would hire him with all those symptoms.

Symptom two was blurry vision. He had a tiny black spot in each eye—you had to get up close to see them—but they were big enough to give everything and everyone a dim look, as if, he said, one of the light bulbs had blown out. An eye doctor prescribed new eyeglasses for him, but these weren't normal eyeglasses, and he wouldn't be caught wearing them in public. They resembled a pair of sawed-off binoculars and gave him, in my view, a science fiction look. The one time he wore them out on the street, shortly after he got them, he attracted a lot of attention. One man, a wit, told him he was on the wrong planet. Another one told him he forgot to take off his microscope when he left the lab; someone else made a reference to the Kentucky Derby and Belmont Park and asked for a tip on the next race. He never wore his glasses in public again. "This is an ancestral problem," he told me, referring to his vision. An incurable condition.

So were his "stomach gases," the third symptom. Some days he couldn't stop belching, or he might wake up in the middle of the night with a burning sensation in the pit of his stomach. "Go see a doctor," Mami told him. He went to a general practitioner. The G.P. told him ulcers weren't in his line of work and sent him to a gastrointestinal specialist. The G.I. man gave him a quart of liquid chalk to drink while he stood stripped behind a man-sized photographic screen, his shoulders hunched forward and the tip of his jaw touching the top of the screen. When the doctor turned on the current, he could look down and see his own stomach and intestines. The nauseating liquid he'd swallowed turned his insides completely white, luminous, ghostly. He had become transparent, a see-through man. The doctor analyzed the X rays and found nothing out of the ordinary. So it must have been nothing more extraordinary than commonplace gases, what he'd been telling Mami and me all along. "Stay away from raw onions and garlic, Malánguez," the doctor told him. "Avoid beans, and go easy on greasy foods." He handed Papi a mimeographed diet, bland menus guaranteed to take the pleasure out of eating. Papi followed them for a while (Mami had to prepare two separate meals a day for weeks), but he finally gave up on them when the gases wouldn't go away. He had also dropped more weight than was good for him. So he junked the G.I. man's menus and went back to eating raw onions, garlic, and from time to time a greasy meal.

The fourth ancestral symptom was a fire in his bladder. Sometimes, he said, passing water was like pissing fire, and his "instrument" was a blowtorch. Another specialist X-rayed him, this time for stones. But again nothing turned up. He didn't complain. If the ghosts of his ancestors were out to get him, what could he do? He'd get them in the next life, he said, not always kiddingly.

The fifth symptom was called the *jaquecas.* Sledgehammer migraines left him close to unconscious when they struck. They could strike anywhere: on the job, on the subway back home, on the walk from the subway to our block, up the stairs to our apartment, in the dining room, or while he was watching boxing or wrestling on Tío Mito's Philco. Aspirin didn't help, so he treated the condition with black coffee. Too much of it, I thought. He threw in a twist of lemon peel. "For good luck," he said. Exorcising his ancestors' spirits with lemon rind. It sometimes worked.

The worst of the symptoms was the sixth. I called this one "The Shakes" or "The Trembles." Like the *jaquecas,* but less frequent, they caught him by surprise anywhere, once a month, sometimes twice. It had happened twice in church. The first time, he was on his feet and had to sit out the Mass, with Mami sitting beside him. The second time, he was on his knees, and remained on his knees, with everyone in church looking on and going through the normal motions of the ceremony. They didn't know what to make of this man going into a fit of trembling all of a sudden. Maybe he was possessed. Maybe Saint Vitus was behind it. Mami did her best to hold him still until it passed. By now the Mass was over and everyone had gone home. The priest hadn't noticed.

"Maybe it *was* a demon, Lilia, you think?" he told Mami.

"It's your nerves," she said. "Don't start getting superstitious." He couldn't help it.

"Your mother's right," he told me one night after an attack of the shakes. "It's not demons, Santos. At least not the kind I had in mind."

"Those ancestors again?" I said.

"What else?"

"What Mami said, your nerves."

He shook his head. "There's nothing wrong with my nerves." He was still shaking a little. I stayed up with him until he was ready for bed. Mami was in their bedroom, not reading in bed this time but whispering to herself, or praying.

Sometimes kids taunted him from the hallway of the building across our dining room. He had a shouting match with three of them one afternoon. He had been working on a wallet or billfold for someone at the factory, and wearing his sawed-off binoculars, and the kids, when they spotted him, couldn't help making some remarks on the strange spectacles. They called him a string of dumb names—Beebee eyes, Mr. Hermit, Mr. Goggles, and other idiocies. Instead of lowering the window shade, he called them disrespectful and ignorant, and told them to go on home. But they persisted. Mami was out shopping; I was in my room. I put on my sneakers and went after them through the roof—the two buildings were connected—but when I got there they had vanished.

I had a good view of Papi from the window of that hallway. He was leather-tooling again. Malicious or not, the three kids had been right: He did resemble a hermit, a beardless one, in those fantastic glasses. I almost called out to him to lower the shade. And instead of going back to the apartment, I went for a walk in the park and spent the rest of the afternoon watching a baseball game among "normal" people, the kind who had little trouble, it seemed, enjoying a weekend.

On the walk back home, it occurred to me that I could have invited him to spend a couple of hours in the park with me. We could have gone to 86th Street for coffee and pastry afterward, maybe to a movie, my treat. He might have begged off ("I have to finish this wallet by tomorrow, Santos," I could hear him saying), but it wouldn't have cost me to ask. He was still tooling away when I got back at sunset. The window shade was drawn. Maybe the three kids had come back for another exchange. I didn't dare ask. He didn't mention it. I fixed us coffee and sat with him for a while, working off remorse, or trying to. And trying to read his mind. I drew a blank.

"I think I'll visit Mito and Agripina this week," he said for no particular reason. "They must think I'm avoiding them."

"Are you?" I said.

"No. What for?"

"You don't see them too much anymore."

"They have their own problems, and I have all these wallets and things to make for the people at work. I can use a few extra dollars."

That sounded like an excuse, but I didn't tell him. Maybe he *was* avoiding his brother. In my presence once, Mito had told him to go out more often.

"To where, Mito?" he had asked.

"To anywhere. It doesn't matter. Just get out of the house once in a while. Go see an old movie, you and Lilia. It's for your health, brother. You look anemic."

"I can't see the movie. I don't have to tell you. My eyes."

"Wear your glasses."

"They're ugly. They attract attention."

"Who cares? Let them look."

"*I* care."

Mito gave up. He went for his coat, and left without finishing his coffee.

"I swear, Gerán," he said at the door, "you're the strangest brother I ever had."

"You didn't finish your coffee, Mito. I'll put some lemon peel in it if you want. Maybe Lilia made it too strong. She's in the habit of making it strong for my *jaquecas,* and then she forgets that most people don't like it so strong."

"Save it for me, Gerán. I have to get going. I'm painting my apartment, and I have to get up early for work. Agripina worries. Call me anytime."

"I will."

He didn't. They were out of touch for weeks, unusual for them. Then regrets set in, remorse, and one day he visited Mito straight from work. The subway ride took over an hour.

At ten P.M. he called us (a prearranged, secret ring: ring once, hang up, ring twice, hang up again, ring again and keep ringing till you get an answer).

"It's me, Santos. Your father. I'm at Mito's. I'm helping him paint the apartment—otherwise he'll never finish. Tell your mother I'll be home by midnight, maybe twelve-thirty. I had dinner here. I'll eat whatever she cooked for me tomorrow at work. I'll see you later." He gave me his blessing.

We didn't see him at midnight or twelve-thirty, but at two A.M., in the hospital. He got hit up in the Bronx. Two drunken drivers collided; one sent him crashing through a rotten wooden fence. He came to a stop in the weeds of an empty lot. Hit-and-run. He was found by a pedestrian who went inside the lot for a leak. "I guess he pissed on me," Papi joked much later, when he had come to. "But I can't complain. He saved my life."

He spent a couple of weeks in the hospital, on and off the critical list. Among other things, a spinal injury and a cracked leg bone. The doctors tapped his spine and patched up his wounds and bruises. A dentist attached to the hospital pulled out three of his teeth ("Just put your Hancock right here, Malánguez, and we'll get right down to work"), including his gold cap, which he never saw again. "I guess he thought I was gone, Santos," he told me at home. "And why bury the gold with the dead?"

He had come home with about a dozen prescriptions and a walking stick. "My new leg," he joked.

Two weeks later, against everyone's advice, he was back on the American Combining Company's payroll, hobbling now, demoted by his foreman to a makeshift position: a flunky's flunky, a middle-aged errand boy. He was responsible for fetching an abundance of coffee, donuts, crullers, Danishes, sandwiches, cigarettes and cigars, Life Savers, breath fresheners, toasted corn muffins with butter or cream cheese, malteds, and aspirin. He also swept the floors. His co-workers, his former *"compatriotas,"* were now his betters, his bosses. He didn't complain. He was lucky to have a job,

he told me. The ultimate *maroma,* I thought. The supreme stunt.
Curtains. And hid in my books to keep from thinking about it.

In the fall of that same year, one of his six symptoms, the shakes,
got out of hand. He had to go back to the hospital. It turned out
to be multiple sclerosis; causes unknown, said the doctors; no cure.
He was sure *he* knew what the cause was ("It's those ancestors,
Santos. I could have told them that"), and for that reason the thing
was incurable.

I looked up this M.S. in a medical encyclopedia. According to
the entry, he was going to spend the rest of his life in bed and in
a wheelchair. Gradual attrition of muscles, breakdown of vital functions, deterioration of cognitive functions, loss of speech, infantile
regression, short-lived attention span, bedsores a problem; physical
therapy helps retard the inevitable. According to one theory ("ad-
mittedly novel," went the entry, "but no less outlandish than the
rest"), it all originated with a certain Hindustani goat. This "carrier
goat" transmitted its virus to the shepherd while he went about his
business (unspecified in the article), and he in turn passed it on
across the Hindu Kush, until it made its way into the Ancestral
Nervous System of unsuspecting types like Papi; "the terminal
hosts of this mysterious killer," continued the entry. At least one
host blamed it on his ancestors, and who could prove him wrong?
If a goat, why not a gang of ghosts?

"Maroma Sclerosis," I took to calling it.

But the book was accurate about the symptoms and effects of
M.S. Within six months he had put on ten years physically and taken
off twenty or more mentally. Mami went and talked to the pastor
of our church. One of his priests paid us a visit once a week to give
Papi the Eucharist. After a while, there was no need for Confession;
he had nothing new to confess. Except that he wanted to go back
to our village, where he said he was going to start a chicken farm,
or open up a small *bodega.* "Now I know how to run a business,
Santos," he said, recalling his and Tío Mito's attempt to start a
business for the plane tickets to a new life.

His bladder broke down for good, and the doctor cut a hole just
below the belly button and stuck a catheter in the hole. A "bypass,"
this was called. The tube drained into a plastic bag strapped to his

thigh. It was a strange way to urinate. The catheter had to be removed from the hole once or twice a week and his bladder cleaned out by suction with another plastic tube and a high-priced sterile fluid. The doctor who'd cut the hole showed Mami and me how to do it, a simple procedure, but I got squeamish and backed out. It wasn't only squeamishness; I couldn't bring myself to see him that way. Just the same, I should have overcome my "respect." Mami was squeamish herself, at first, but that didn't stop her from doing what she had to do, what he himself would have done in her place, no hesitation.

Then it was constipation. We bit our lips and did what we could. When the intestinal spasms came on him, night or day, no advance notice, we'd lift him by the arms and legs, bundle him up in a sheet and a blanket, carry him down the stairs (I used to count them: 91 steps going down, 91 back up, 182 round trip), and roll him on his classy-looking wheelchair (a gift from Tío Mito) to Mount Sinai's emergency clinic five blocks away. All weathers.

The clinic was crowded and smelly, chaotic. We'd sit and wait an hour or two, unless Papi couldn't contain the pain anymore and started moaning up high. But even then it depended on who else needed attention. There were priorities. Slashed throats and cracked skulls were at the top.

I was taking a Dickens course that fall and didn't have to worry about running out of reading while we were waiting our turn to wheel Papi behind the doctors' and nurses' green curtain. While I read ("Melancholy streets in a penitential garb of soot . . . Nothing for the spent toiler to do, but to compare the monotony of his seventh day with the monotony of his six days . . ."), Mami kept her eye on him or stared in front of her, as if out of it, but actually thinking things out (and keeping most of it to herself) and making sure no one sneaked ahead of us.

Back home, while both of them slept, or waited for sleep (he had his own bed now, a hospital one, another gift from Tío Mito), I continued reading for school. Mito visited regularly after work. Sometimes he spent the night. I told him to sleep in my room, I'd take the sofa, but he wouldn't have it. If Mami and I got too hospitable, he said, he wouldn't stay over again. "Just go about your business," he told us. "Pretend I'm not here." We couldn't. He played his guitar for Papi, sang and hummed old songs

(*"Lamento Jíbaro"* had priority), talked to him, told him jokes, though he knew Papi couldn't follow a conversation by now.

Late at night, when I got home from work and school, I'd go and sit with him for a while, unless he was asleep (his mouth twisted to one side, his face muscles collapsed and stiffened). If he was, I'd go and sit with Mami in the dining room, eating my warmed-over dinner while she summarized their day for me. Brief rundowns: Nothing much had happened, nothing new. Then I'd get up, not always finished with my meal, and go join him. Even if he was still sleeping, I'd sit there, in his favorite chair, which Mami had dragged in from the dining room, and read until he woke up. Sometimes he didn't wake up at all—he might continue sleeping straight through to morning—and after hours of sitting there fighting sleep, looking up from my book every minute or so, I'd go back inside my room and continue reading—as if everything depended on print—until my eyes and my head, and my nerves, couldn't take any more.

Next night I might come home from school and find him wide awake and "lucid"—a hopeful word I applied privately to his deceptive, short-lived recoveries.

During those brief improvements, he might want me to hear out his fabulous chicken-farm scheme, and to reassure him that any day now he'd be walking again.

"I'm feeling much better, Santos."

"Absolutely, Papi. You're looking it, too. You're looking fine. As soon as you get over this thing, I'll buy you and Mami a huge meal on Eighty-sixth Street. And a bottle of German beer. They make the best beer—I'll say that much for them."

"I don't like beer, Santos. It gives me gases."

"One pint won't harm you. It'll do you good. Vitamins. Malt and hops."

"Very well. As soon as I can walk again."

"You're looking much better."

That lie might encourage him to tell me he'd gone to the toilet that day just after I left the house. "I saved us a trip to the clinic today, Santos."

"That's a good sign, Papi."

Next night he might confuse "toilet" with "bedpan." On her own, Mami had discovered a disposable enema called Fleet, which

I couldn't help calling the Sixth Fleet; it was that potent. And it was to this Fleet that I attributed his miraculous recall of poems he'd memorized as a boy in Maestro Malconsejo's schoolhouse shack. On and off all day, as if possessed by a benign demon, he'd lie in bed reciting stanzas, sometimes long poems that went on and on, every beat and rhyme in its right place, as precisely as some of the prayers he'd been saying all his life. This Maroma Sclerosis was a strange disease, and he was a strange victim of that Hindustani goat virus, or whatever it was.

But after a while, confused and tired and caught up in my work (exams were always coming up, papers always due), falling asleep on his former chair while listening to him reciting poems in Spanish or going on about the chicken farm, I began feeling the urge to avoid him as much as possible; and I did, for a few nights. But my conscience and Mami got after me, a pair of strong opponents. I had, she said, no right to avoid him. "No matter what he sounds and looks like, Santos." She called it a moral obligation, among other things, and I couldn't disagree. So I gave up my easy evasions and went back to reading in the bedroom chair. He didn't seem to mind if I read while he talked. The important thing was that I was physically, if silently, there.

Before leaving the bedroom, I'd give him a hug, and a kiss on the forehead, and that put him at ease, or seemed to, for a while. He'd hold my hand in a tight grip, as if this was it, as if Mami was going to wake up with a scream in the middle of the night to tell me he was gone. He still had a strong grip, despite his wasting muscles. It was a frozen handclasp, a clamp, a strong hint of rigor mortis. To free myself I had to pry his fingers loose, gently, with my free hand. Then I'd back out of the room, feeling behind me for the door, so he wouldn't think I was deserting him, walking out for good, and let Mami take over again, "spelling" me, as I put it, borrowing the word from a sea story I'd recently read.

At one-thirty or two in the morning, if I was still up taking notes and underlining, he might call me in a low voice, a moan almost; but unless he needed something, I stayed put. I had to; if I didn't draw the line, I might be up all night, and then pay for it at work next day and get chewed out—and sleep through my classes that night. Mami, exhausted herself, sometimes slept through those summonses of his. But usually she'd wake up and stay up with him for hours, talking to him in a hushed voice so as not to wake me up. And I'd play along, keeping still.

One day he told Mami he wanted to "die there." This was after a nightmare in which he discovered he wasn't going to last much longer. "I don't like the cemeteries here, Lilia."

"If you talk like that," she told him, "I'll leave the room. You have a lot of years left. You're still stronger than I am."

"No, I'm not."

"Yes, you are. You have the strongest grip of anyone I know."

"Don't be misled, Lilia. It's that goat germ Santos told me about."

"Goat germ nothing. He doesn't know what he's talking about. None of you do."

She told me all this later, shaking. "What *there* was he talking about, Mami?"

"The village—where else? He forgets what that place was like. Maybe not. Maybe it's time to go back."

So, less than two years after the car accident, Tío Mito gave Mami money for two plane tickets. "What about you, Santos?" he asked me. "Do you want one, too? Just say the word. I have something sitting in the bank. You can pay it back any time and any way you like. But I'd rather you didn't. I've never given you anything worth much. Consider it a back-payment, or a gift. Whatever."

I thanked him and turned down his offer, which had tempted me for a few minutes.

"Whatever you like," he said. The Elysian Arms SRO, like it or not.

To make the leavetaking less painful, I told Mami I'd join them when I finished school, but I don't think I fooled her. "At least you'll come and see us as soon as you can. When you finish school, you'll have all the time in the world. And maybe, who knows . . ." I nodded, and we left it at that.

They left a month after Tío Mito's gift. They took the hospital bed and the wheelchair with them. Her *Wonderland of Wisdom,* their winter clothes, and his leather-tooling set, Calleja's *Manual* of the orator, and his guitar stayed. So did his old Fada radio and Tío

Mito's Philco TV. Mito took some of these "mementos," as he called them, to the Bronx, but almost everything stayed in the apartment, our super's property now. "Let him make a few dollars on the side," said Mami. "I hope he won't spend it all on that cheap wine that's killing him, though I wouldn't blame him."

I took my own things to the Elysian Arms. I got a different room this time, but it was almost a duplicate of the first one. The print on the wall was different, a botched-up Rubens, or one of his pupils' poor renditions. The overweight clouds looked as though they might collapse any minute and crush the unsuspecting picnickers on the turf below. No Central Park, this landscape. Another Woolworth's.

Papi and Mami moved in with Tego, now a croupier at the San Juan Hilton, or the Sheraton—he kept switching hotels for higher pay. His wife's uncle, a veteran of the gambling casinos, had found him his first job in the tourists' Condado, and he had no intention of coming back to New York. He had two kids, a boy and a girl, plus his wife's daughter from the repatriated Filipino, and said he was settled there for life. "Even if they open up casinos in New York," he had written me once, "I wouldn't go back there." He didn't write often. He said his grammar wasn't good enough for letters. "Specially with show-ofs like you, Santos, Im' just kidding (maybe.)."

"Grammar's got nothing to do with it," I had written back. "Besides, there's nothing wrong with your grammar. It's perfect, take my word."

He didn't answer. Maybe if I had written him an ungrammatical reply, with words misspelled on every line, he would have written back. Or maybe he would have seen through my dirty trick and felt insulted. But I had double-checked grammar, spelling, and punctuation before mailing my letter, and that must have inhibited him.

He built Papi and Mami their own apartment on top of his one-story house in a neat cement suburb of San Juan. Planes, from Piper Cubs and aquaplanes to Jumbos, flew back and forth overhead all the time, he had told me in that letter. "Right over the roof, Santos." And most of his neighbors, for some strange reason, preferred to keep plastic plants in the windows and on the porches, instead of growing their own on an island that was overcrowded with natural ones. "I guess its' the thing to do, Santos. They must think its classy. Dont look at me."

He paid for everything Papi and Mami needed, and some things they didn't: furniture, electrical appliances, a fourteen-inch TV that dubbed soap operas and situation comedies from the North, a radio that was both portable and plug-in, prints of birds from Sears, a plaster bull (black) with gold-tipped horns, and a porcelain matador doing a fancy *verónica* in front of the bull. All of this on the installment plan. He was making decent wages plus tips, and could carry the expense. "And I'm a high school drop out, Santos."

"Don't rub it in," I wrote back.

In his letter he told me he had pebbles on his lawn. "Its cheaper than keeping up grass, Santos. I don't have time for grass. I work nights and sleep days." And his wife was "too busy with the housework to bother with the turf." There were a couple of natural shrubs in front of the house. "I planted them myself," he had written. "So Im not all useless around the house. One of thems already six feet high and growing with a vengeance. Theres nothing like natural things. Its what makes the world go around. Come and see it when you get a chance. Well put you up for free. Nothings' too good for my brother."

His son and both girls were enrolled in a parochial school. He had big ambitions for his boy, "either a baseball player"—third base or the mound, depending on his arm—"or a professional soldier, an officer." He was going to enroll the kid in a military academy, "when he finishes the parochial. They have good sports and dicsipline. Thats what I needed more of myself, dicsipline, instead of playing cards all the time with the guys."

"You didn't do too badly, Tego," I wrote back. "So let's not start sounding like those people who swear their life went all wrong." And I cut myself off there; he hated sermons. I couldn't blame him. Just the same, he didn't answer.

Papi was close to completely out of it by now, and Mami was indifferent to most "things." In one of her letters to me, she said he had stopped speaking altogether. He was reduced to slobbering and grunting, moaning. Snapshots she sent me showed him in his wheelchair, in pajamas and slippers, his crewcut hair gone totally gray, grinning and squinting at the Instamatic. But even the grins were misleading: face muscles twisted into smiles by Maroma Sclerosis.

One day I received a telegram from Tego. The Elysian Arms night clerk handed it to me when I got in from school. "It's been here all day, Malánguez." He didn't know where I worked.

"Come quick," it read. "Papi real sick. Maybe for good. Stop." A couple of hours later I took a cheap middle-of-the-night flight to San Juan and spent the time reading for finals. They were coming up again, the last of them. My overnight bag was loaded with books and underwear.

The hospital had a pink stucco façade and was surrounded by an assortment of tropical plants, including palm trees with coconuts. I hadn't seen anything like this, except in movies and travel ads, since early childhood.

I got there too late to catch Papi's last convulsions and whatever else he had gone through before his lights went out. They had already sent him down to the morgue, and I began to lose my temper; he should have waited until I'd finished with my finals. I had planned on making a photocopy of my diploma and sending it to them as proof of something. Not that it would have made any difference to him, no more than that chicken farm he had talked about when the disease overwhelmed him; but it would have made a difference to me, and I was feeling selfish just then. No particular reason.

The mourners included Tío Mito, Mami's sisters (most of them), and tiny Calpurnia Cardona, looking tinier than ever. Octavio had died years back of diabetes. Her arms were loaded with wedding-anniversary bangles, more like rings of widowhood now, weighing her down with whatever gold and silver they contained. Chuito had telegraphed to say he'd be arriving late, minus his wife, who'd have to stay home with the kids. Through Calpurnia, who kept up connections, Tío Mito had tracked down the elder brother, Elias. He was shy, formal, tall, and sickly-looking; he leaned on a walking stick. And his daughter was with him—he was a widower— fifteen years old and slightly retarded; she'd never get married. She stayed close to her father, looking frightened, disoriented.

They were having a lunch of some kind on folded chairs: plastic-wrapped sandwiches and brownies from a coin-op machine in the back of the funeral home, which faced a busy highway, and which could use a new paint job; and bottles of Coke from another machine in the lobby. Mami was up front with Papi, anything but hungry; she had lost weight and her black dress was loose-fitting. His hands were crossed in the prescribed casket style; someone had hooked a rosary to his fingers; his cheeks were stuffed with cotton; he was wearing his best suit, a gray one, slightly baggy; a white carnation had been pinned to the lapel of his jacket. The tie he wore had a V-knot and was striped black and white. His face was powdered, his cheeks and lips rouged for authenticity, vitality. The funeral makeup man hadn't missed a thing, and I began to feel dizzy from the sight of Papi like that—from not enough sleep, from loss of appetite, from the heat (poor ventilation in that showroom), and from I-didn't-know-what-else and didn't want to know just then. And was distracted, without wanting to be distracted, by some lines I had underscored a long time ago in the copy of *Redburn* back in the SRO. I had reread them various times, on impulse. With an antique guidebook his father had left him, Redburn tries to retrace his dead father's footsteps through the streets of Liverpool:

"So vivid was now the impression of his having been there," the son remarks, "so narrow the passage from which he had emerged, that I felt like running on, and overtaking him. . . . But I soon checked myself, when remembering that he had gone whither no son's search could find him in this world. And then I thought of all that must have happened to him since he paced through that arch. What trials and troubles he had encountered; how he had been shaken by many storms of adversity, and at last died a bankrupt. I looked at my own sorry garb, and had much ado to keep from tears. But I rallied. . . ."

After the condolences (hushed by politeness) and other funeral-parlor courtesies, the guests assembled for prayers. I'd forgotten most of my Spanish prayers long ago and was anyway in no mood to join in, or to sit silently through them. Neither was Tego; he had stopped going to church himself, though he insisted that his children attend services and receive the sacraments, as if he were willing to risk his own soul but not theirs.

"Let's go for a walk, Santos. We'll get back in time."

We were in short-sleeved shirts, mine a loan from him, a little baggy on me; he was anything but skinny now. It was a hot, sunlit day; typical tropical weather, he told me. I'd forgotten.

"Tourists save up all year for sun like this, Santos. They pay through the nose for this mild stuff. They could spend their money worst."

"You mean *worse*, Tego."

"What's the difference?"

I told him, just to change our mood a little. "Bad, worse, worst, Tego. You should remember that from Saint Misericordia's."

He shrugged. "Who the hell remembers that far back?"

"I do."

"Yeah, I know. That's a problem you still got. You're still some kind of show-off, too. Remember when you were a stoopball showboat?"

"Sure. Delia and El Judge. The Conquistadores. You lost the last play-off game. Norma got to you."

"Forget that shit, Santos. Let the dead bury the—" Here he caught himself and shut up.

We didn't talk much after that. I asked him a few questions about Mami, about Papi's last days, about himself, his job, his plans. He gave me short, gloomy answers; telltale omissions, I thought, trying to fill in his blanks.

"Tomorrow we'll talk up a storm, Santos," he finally said, tired of my questions. "I'll drive you around after my nap (unless I can't sleep). I'll throw in a free driving lesson. You should learn to drive. The whole world is going to the highways, and you still can't drive."

"Next time," I said. "I have to get back tomorrow."

"For what? What's the hurry?"

"Finals."

"What, tomorrow?"

"Next week."

"So wait a day or two. You got all your books here, don't you?"

"Only some. About half. I couldn't pack them all."

"You got about a hundred of them in that basketball bag you brought. I took a look. You forgot to pack your toothbrush. I'll loan vou one."

"Next time I'll get a bigger bag. And I'll stay a month or two, or for as long as you can stand me."

"Read the ones you got here, Santos. Let the others wait a while."

"It's my job too," I said. "They expect me back tomorrow."

"So let it wait. From what you wrote me, it's a lousy job anyway."

"It pays my rent, buys my books."

"I'll loan you for a month's rent. And you don't need more books. You know how much money tourists pay to spend a week or two here?"

"I can imagine, but I didn't come here as a tourist."

"I don't like the look of them bags under your eyes. It looks like you packed some books in there too."

"We better get back before they bury him."

So we walked back to the funeral place without talking, and before our small procession got back to the cemetery—some in private cars, others in limousines paid for by Tego—it was drizzling, a light spray, not enough for umbrellas. When we got to the cemetery, three gravediggers, impassive-looking good-conduct convicts from the state prison nearby, were waiting with shovels. All three were tall and muscular, handpicked types, looking anything but handicapped. Maybe this job cut down their sentences. They'd dug the grave long before we arrived, it seemed; the mud on their shoes and shovels was caked hard, despite the drizzle, and their faces and gestures showed no signs of impatience. They had all the time in the world. During the lowering of the coffin and the filling-in of the grave, I tried to follow their stolid example, but I didn't do nearly as well (I was shaking, for one thing, and I couldn't keep from biting my lip). They had experience with the dead; this was just another stranger's corpse to them. When they got done tamping the mound, they stood by at attention, shovels at their sides, and squinted critically at the rest of us to see how we liked their skill. Mami, always polite, walked up and thanked them; they nodded, pleased. Then Tego, who knew a thing or two about tipping, slipped them something and whispered his own thanks. In a little while, a prison guard came by to escort them back "home."

When we got back to Tego's house, the mourners, grown-ups and children (the children were given no choice), went to pray in the upstairs apartment. I stayed downstairs, drinking coffee and staring out at Tego's pebbled lawn and healthy plants. The pebbles were white and green; the plants looked exotic; I'd seen a few like them in the Bronx Botanical Garden one Sunday as a kid, when Papi took us there just to get away from Central Park for a change.

After about fifteen minutes, Tego came down from the group prayers. His eyes were swollen. "I couldn't take any more, Santos. I was choking up in there. And they were just getting going, too. I guess I'm out of practice."

"Sounds to me like you're turning into a pagan, Tego."

"I guess I am. I've been one, I mean. What about you?"

"Same thing. The only Mass I go to anymore's the Rooster one. And I even missed that one last time around. I slept through it. Why don't we fix us a drink? I'll give you a hand."

"Better yet," he said, "just stay in your seat and talk to me while I fix them."

I watched while he mixed a blenderful of piña colada. "A little too sweet for serious drinkers like us, Santos, but I don't think we should get into the heavy stuff just now."

We drank the tourist drinks and talked, but not about Papi. Neither of us was in the mood.

"What about Mami?" I asked. "What's she want to do now?"

"The upstairs apartment's hers, Santos, but she says she doesn't want to stay there. I don't blame her. I know how it is. She was watching him pass away up there all them months. She didn't get much sleep, believe me. I used to come home from work at seven, eight in the morning and she was still up. I could hear her from down here, and I could tell she hadn't been sleeping. Most times, if I wasn't dying of sleep myself, I used to go upstairs and scold her back to bed. I used to sit in front of his bed until she fell asleep. That's what I mean, though. I don't blame her for moving out."

"To go live where?"

"I'll just have to find her a place somewheres. Near here, if that's what she wants. There's plenty vacancies in the area. The rents don't come to much."

"She's never lived by herself, Tego. It's no fun, let me tell you."

"I'm wise. I've never done it myself, I mean, but I can just imagine. Let her try it, anyway. I'll keep an eye on her, don't worry. Why don't you come live down here when you're finished up with

school? At least give it a try. You're still unattached, no? Then you
can get married. You don't even have to get a legal license. This
place is becoming more American all the time. It's not that hard
once you start looking around. My personal problem was who to
pick from all them women I wanted. And I'm not even showing off.
It's just the way things are."

"Thanks for the offer," I said. "I'm sure you could get me fixed
up in no time. Just the same, I think you're tanked up already. These
coladas don't taste so weak to me."

"It's a standard mix. Strong enough to keep the customers
happy. What I had in mind, Santos, was you could get a job down
here. You could go work for the government. You could teach if
that's your kick. You know two languages—that's a big trump
card."

"It's down to one and a half, if that much."

"In six months, Santos, guaranteed, you'll pick up the missing
half. I did, and I was a high-school dropout. At least look around
before you decide. What's that place you live at like, anyway? A lot
of women?"

"Fix me another piña, and I'll tell you."

While we sipped coladas, I told him a couple of facts and more
than a couple of half-facts about the SRO and whatever else I was
up to, or wasn't up to. He said it all sounded so boring to him—
despite my attempts to make most of it sound interesting—that as
far as he was concerned, it wasn't even a choice between staying in
the city and coming down to the island, or at least trying it out as
an experiment. It sounded to him, he said, like the case of someone
who's been locked up in the Tombs so long that he forgets what
it's like outside. I was telling him that the Tombs was only a house
of detention, not a permanent residence, when the others came
down and cut me short, which was just as well. The drinks were
making me preachy, and him sleepy.

Before going back to New York, I decided to take a trip to our
old village. Tía Celita, a schoolteacher now, was driving back home
that afternoon and invited me to spend the night at her house. She
and one of the other aunts, both unmarried, shared a place on the
main street of the village. Tego agreed to pick me up the following
afternoon, then drive me back to his house for dinner and good-

byes, then to the airport, "for a decent seat on a decent airplane," as he said, and insisted. Mami turned down her sister's offer to go with us to the village and to stay there for as long as she liked. She wouldn't even discuss it.

"I don't know why *you* want to go there," she told me.

"For a last look, Mami. It's just one day. Less, even. I want to take a look at the improvements. Maybe they've got condominiums coming up in the hills. I wouldn't put it past SROs."

"I wouldn't be surprised," she said, "but it doesn't interest me. Don't get lost."

"I don't see how, with Celita for a guide."

"Well, you never know," she said, worried.

In the village, not far from Tía Celita's house, we came across Luisa Lugones, my first-grade teacher. She recognized me right away, which cheered me up some. She had been a redhead; now most of that red had turned white and her slimness had plumped, but she hadn't been cursed by *tristeza*, the sad surrender, from the looks of her.

"Are you sure it's him?" Celita asked her.

"*Pues,* of course I am," she said. "It's that same Santos Malánguez who got into a terrible fight with Antonio Carretas. For God's sake, Santos, come out and give me a hug."

I was embarrassed for a few seconds, but got ahold of myself and stepped out of the car to give her the hug and to chat for a while. She remembered a lot more about me than I did. As for Antonio Carretas, who had bloodied my nose, the last she'd heard from him he was living with a wife and six or eight kids somewhere in the South Bronx and working as some kind of "cutter" in some kind of *"factoría"* in a place called El Garment District. Had I ever heard of it?

Yes. I had a job there once, I said. Doing what? I was an assistant packer while taking classes at night. Had I seen Antonio Carretas there? No, unless I had and didn't recognize him. Had I been to El South Bronx lately? Not since a girl friend of mine, Delia something or other, whose only flaw had been a chipped tooth, got involved with Louie something or other and had a child by him.

"She had a child unmarried, Santos?"

"No, no, Mees Lugones. She married him, all right." Not quite true; misleading, anyway. Delia had been pregnant a couple of months before they got married, but what of it? I just didn't want to get into gossip just then. Besides, I wasn't sure Mees Lugones would understand. In some ways, I could see now, she was like an old-fashioned nun, though not the kind that went in for child abuse, and I didn't want to upset her sense of how certain customs should be upheld. I also knew, even while standing there chatting with her, that all my good intentions of writing her a long letter in the language of my first dreams would come to nothing. Maybe I'd send her a Christmas card and hope she'd send one back. But I didn't want to commit myself to anything just then. No promises. I couldn't bring myself to pick up where I'd left off that long ago.

When we got to Celita's house (the other aunt, Milagros, was out visiting the parents of students, Celita told me), she fixed us what she called·"a Bautabarro *lonche,*" an oversized snack consisting of boiled green bananas cut up in chunks, slivers of desalted codfish, onion rings, olives and capers, sliced hard-boiled eggs, wedges of a root called *malanga* and another one called *yautía*—all of it in olive oil, and more than enough, I thought, to destroy the stomach of anyone not used to this diet, which I wasn't anymore. A less heartburning version of this *lonche* had been Papi's favorite snack. Sundays he had called it lunch; evenings, as a snack, he had called it a *serenata;* I couldn't remember why.

Celita and I took this Bautabarro special out to the porch (I also took a glass of milk; she poured herself a glass of *tamarindo* drink), and sat on white metal chairs in front of a matching table. She and Milagros must have spent a lot of time in those chairs, eating their lunch and talking things over, correcting their students' homework. There was a glass vase on the table, with sweet-smelling fresh flowers in it. "They grow wild all over the area," she told me. She had taken a wreath of those same flowers, and others, to the funeral parlor. Now, along with the other wreaths, it was lying on top of Papi's grave. . . . The porch was paved with Moorish-looking geometric tiles. I almost asked her if Papagante had left a lot of money behind, but checked myself. It was none of my business; wrong time for it anyway.

While we ate, taking our time, she greeted whoever passed by—she must have known everyone in the entire village personally —and introduced me to most of them. The only ones she left out were those she didn't like for one reason or another, "the ones I'm holding a grudge against, Santos." At least eight by my count, six of them men.

"This is my nephew Santos," she'd tell them, and instead of leaving it at that, she added, every time: "He's in college in Nueva York. Right, Santos?"

"Do you have to tell them that, Tía?" I asked her after about the twelfth time.

"Of course," she said. "I might as well show off while we're sitting here."

"I don't think that's anything to show off about."

"What do you know about these things?"

". . . in college in Nueva York."

"You don't say so, Celita?" one of her acquaintances said from the other side of the gate. He looked at me as if I were some kind of hybrid.

"Watch your tongue, Juan Ángel. He graduates next week. Is that right, Santos? Next week?"

"I think so, Tía. It's nothing. Everybody's doing it now. It's a big fad in the States."

"Maybe so, but they're not all in my family."

"That's what I say, Celita," Juan Ángel said. "I have to go on home now. Your lunch is making me hungry."

"Go ahead, then. Who told you to talk so much?"

She brought me up to date on Bautabarro. "For one thing," she said, "it's not really a village anymore. It has a charter that says, 'This is a town.' *I'm* not impressed. But that was bound to happen, no? One of these days those politicians will call it a city and ruin it. 'This is a city.' Why don't you come and live here after you graduate?" Here we went again. "We can use another schoolteacher. My classes are overcrowded. There's too many babies being born in this *town* in my opinion."

"I'm grateful for your offer," I told her, "but Tego already made me one just like it this morning. Very tempting, but . . ."

"Tego? What does he know? He's a gambler. What is it they call themselves these days? Croupers? Cruppers? Something French. Help me out."

"Croupiers, I think."

"Anyway, it's a vice. They're corrupting our island with it. I keep up with events. I read two newspapers every morning with the breakfast. And we have a radio."

"What else do you have time for, Tía?"

"Don't get fresh." She went on to denounce the tourist hotels, the racketeers, domestic and northern, the plague of tourists who were jacking up the price of staples "beyond the means of our people, Santos. We can't afford our own food anymore. Most of it is sold to the North, and then they sell it back to us for twice the price. Our beaches are not ours anymore, most of them. They have these guards in front of the hotels, *compatriotas* without shame. The kind that sell their own self-respect for a few dollars a week."

"They have to make a living too, Tía."

"Not that way. Let them better starve is what I say. I would. And then these traitors, if you try to get inside our own beaches, they ask you to show them the key to your hotel room. They did that to me and Milagros once. I won't repeat to you what I told that son of a pimp. He'll never forget me."

"He's not the only one," I said. "Come on, Tía, tell me what you told that son of a procurer."

"If you move back down here I'll tell you. Otherwise I'll take my secret to the grave." She crossed herself twice quickly and kissed her crossed thumb and index; then she gave me a guilty side-glance to see if I was offended. I pretended not to notice and swallowed some milk to give my stomach a break.

After we washed up, I asked her to take me to see our old shack.

"It doesn't exist anymore, Santos. Didn't you know?"

"Nobody told us."

"Sure. A hurricane flew off with it. Years ago. I forget which saint that one was named after. A male one, anyhow. Isn't it always? He took Malconsejo's shack, too. Nobody missed that one."

But I insisted on going ("I think you owe it to me, Tía"), and she gave in. "I don't think you're going to be too impressed, though. I also think you've caught your father's nostalgia."

Our destination wasn't that far from her house. Fifteen minutes or less on foot. We had to walk, because no car could make it there, over the hills and ditches, cowpaths and bushes, and the hairpin turns of the "road" that Papi had taken with the mule Mafofa to Jayuya's market. Along the way Celita talked nonstop about the topography and points of interest. She could have made a living as a guide and chronicler of those hills—if anyone other than a rare visitor like myself had been interested. It wasn't the kind of land that was ever likely to attract tourists or development, though who could tell? The Amazon itself, of all primitive places, was being carved up, "civilized" by bulldozers. Brasilia was built in the middle of nowhere. The heights of Machu Picchu had been discovered and exploited. A fragment of Pablo Neruda's poem came to mind: ". . . and not only death, but many deaths came to each one . . . dust, worms, a light flicked off in the mud. . . ."

"There," Celita said, pointing to a ravine, "is where Papá's one-horned cow, La Manca, met her maker. They dragged her corpse back up with ropes and mules. She was covered with mud, poor thing. We ate her. Papá butchered her, and then he divided her among the men who helped him. And there was still enough of her left over to make us sick of beef for weeks." She didn't stop once; I didn't interrupt.

And when we passed the level spot where Papagante's house had stood (long since torn down and the lumber sold for whatever her brother Hortensio could get), she said, "Remember the time I caught you looking up my dress from the floor? You were imitating an animal. I was ironing, pretending not to notice. I punished you. You're not sorry I did, I hope."

"Of course not, Tía. I had it coming to me." What else could I say?

"That Chuito was ruining your morals."

"I survived it, Tía. And I apologize."

"After all this time . . ."

At one place she stopped abruptly and pointed to a tree in the middle of what looked like elephant grass. (I'd seen it in Tarzan movies.)

"That's the sweet-lime tree your father planted when your brother was born. And the one next to it is the one he planted when you came along."

"He should have given them more distance," I said. "They're choking each other up, it looks like."

"Or holding each other up," she said. "Depends on how you see it. They've lasted a long time that way."

I was looking at the mountains now. No condominiums or

housing projects in sight. Papá Xavier must have been buried around here somewhere. His bones, or what was left of them. Calcinated dust. I asked her if she knew.

"Why do you want to look *him* up?" she said. "Of all people. I didn't even know you knew about him."

"Papi dropped his name a couple of times."

"I don't see why, after what Xavier did to himself. To them. Three orphans."

"Papi didn't like to hold grudges. I think he forgave him, if that's the right word. So did Mito. I don't know about Elias. We didn't get a chance to talk."

"I'm not sure where he's buried. That's not the kind of thing we keep track of around here. I'm not even sure I know where Mamá was put, rest her soul. It's a disgrace. She's somewhere around here. Sometimes I walk around here by myself, or with Milagros, and we can feel their ghosts walking alongside us. Don't get me wrong, though—I'm not one of your superstitious types. It's just a feeling we get. Someday me too. The two of us. No markers, nothing."

"So whereabouts is he, Tía?"

"If my big nose is still good, you're almost standing on him."

She grabbed me by the elbow and steered me forward a few feet, close to the two lime trees. She stepped on the approximate spot, a small mound buried in "elephant grass." A tiny tumulus, I thought, pulling out another Lit. I word. "He should be here under us somewhere, Santos. It might as well be where we're standing. Now what? You don't plan to dig him up, do you?"

"No, I wouldn't disturb whatever's left of him." I pictured myself on the plane back home, an urn containing his ashes on my lap. Morbid. "Necrophagia," as my old vanished neighbor of the poetry anthology had called it before he took the Jumbo out of our life.

"All I know of him, Santos," Celita was going on, "is that he was a very strange private type. The kind that spend their lives locked up in rooms with books and other manias, as if they were doing penance for something. You can see where it got him, too. Don't take after him, whatever you do." I said I wouldn't. "Not," she continued, "that anyone else in his time got any better than he did. Just the same . . ."

"He overdid it?"

"At least some of us think so. 'Heartbreak!' What kind of excuse is that, for Godsake? I don't know anything about this heartbreak business, and I don't want to know." I didn't believe her, but didn't push it.

She looked sad all of a sudden, stepped off Papá Xavier's mound, which may have only been his grave in my head, and walked off a short distance to stare down at the village. We were on a mountain and we had a good view of the area—of areas; it seemed to me we could see the entire island from up here—the Cordillera, the island's spinal column, its Rockies. Cows and goats on hillsides, humans going about their business: moving dots. Tiny huts, shacks, lean-tos, sheds, but also quite a number of newer buildings. Signs of slow progress. Papi would have been surprised; maybe not.

And his father, who was buried somewhere beneath me, maybe not, his bones, or the dust that was left of them, crumbled calcium probably, underground ashes on which many a worm had made love and other things: Papi's father, the butt of Mami's father's scorn, had left a confusing example behind him, which so far thank God none of his three sons and neither of his two grandsons had tried to follow . . . but he'd also been some kind of poet, the plus side of him; and a "Mariolater" (a frustrated troubadour?); and a teacher, doing his best to spread the literacy around a little, anti-ignorance . . . couldn't hold *that* against him . . . one could do worse than follow that example, though the cult of Mary wasn't in my line. . . . "Thus when I am laid to rest—" I couldn't remember the rest of the line, or who'd said it.

I pulled up some weeds from the spot Celita had indicated. They'd grow back as soon as I turned my back, but that didn't matter. And if Celita, who wasn't the sentimental type—at least not in the open—if she hadn't walked back to where I was busy weeding and said it was time to get back and that enough hanging around the dead was enough, I might have worked up a sweat till sunset. "You can visit again," she said. "As many times as you want." I nodded, straightening up, but I didn't mean it. I had other things to do back home.

We walked back in a hurry, to beat the end of the day. She did all the talking again; she brought me up to date on what had happened and what hadn't in all these years, and when we were almost there she asked me what I wanted to eat for dinner, and what to drink.

"I'll give you a hand, Tía," I told her. "I can't cook too good, but I can help."

"Not in my house, you don't," she said, almost offended. I didn't argue back; I was afraid to.

". . . turned to bones, I should wish to be laid to rest." Was that it? Somebody's "Brown Burial"? "Earned Burial"? Maybe "Bourne Aerial." Whatever, something silly, count on it. I'd brood about it on the flight back home.

About the Author

EDWARD RIVERA was born in Orocovis, Puerto Rico, and grew up in New York City. He attended parochial and public schools in Spanish Harlem, the Art Students League during his senior year in high school, and the Pratt Institute for one semester. Following his high school graduation, he worked at a succession of odd jobs in offices and factories, and at the Central Branch of the New York Public Library, "drying photostats in the basement division." At the age of nineteen, he enrolled in the Evening Division of the City College of New York, and two years later was inducted into the army. He spent six months of his army "hitch" in Heidelberg, where he did duty as a Pfc. typist stenographer at the headquarters of the United States Army.

Following his discharge, Mr. Rivera worked for one year as a filing clerk and form-letter typist at a savings bank, and resumed his night studies at the City College. After receiving an associates degree, he transferred to the Day Division and received a B.A. in English in 1967. For five months after he received his college degree, Mr. Rivera worked as a "neighborhood organizer" in the Morrisania district of the East Bronx, "persuading—sometimes successfully—grass roots denizens to participate in and eventually take charge of a free clinic to be named in honor of Dr. Martin Luther King, Jr."

Mr. Rivera holds an M.F.A. from Columbia University and is currently teaching English at the City College of New York.